French Fortifications,
1715–1815

ALSO BY JEAN-DENIS G.G. LEPAGE
AND FROM McFARLAND

*Vauban and the French Military Under Louis XIV:
An Illustrated History of Fortifications and Strategies* (2010)

Aircraft of the Luftwaffe, 1935–1945: An Illustrated Guide (2009)

Hitler Youth, 1922–1945: An Illustrated History (2009)

The French Foreign Legion: An Illustrated History (2008)

*German Military Vehicles of World War II:
An Illustrated Guide to Cars, Trucks, Half-Tracks,
Motorcycles, Amphibious Vehicles and Others* (2007)

The Fortifications of Paris: An Illustrated History (2006)

*Medieval Armies and Weapons in Western Europe:
An Illustrated History* (2005)

*Castles and Fortified Cities of Medieval Europe:
An Illustrated History* (2002)

French Fortifications, 1715–1815

An Illustrated History

JEAN-DENIS G.G. LEPAGE

McFarland & Company, Inc., Publishers
Jefferson, North Carolina, and London

LIBRARY OF CONGRESS CATALOGUING-IN-PUBLICATION DATA

Lepage, Jean-Denis G. G., 1952–
French fortifications, 1715–1815 : an illustrated history / Jean-Denis G.G. Lepage.
    p.   cm.
Includes bibliographical references and index.

ISBN 978-0-7864-4477-9
softcover : 50# alkaline paper ∞

1. Fortification — France — History — 18th century.
2. Fortification — France — History — 19th century.
3. Fortification — France — Pictorial works.
4. France — History, Military — 1715–1789.
5. France — History, Military — 1789–1815.
6. Military art and science — France — History — 18th century.
7. Military art and science — France — History — 19th century.
8. France — Colonies — History — 18th century.
9. France — Colonies — History — 19th century.
   I. Title.
UG429.F7L47   2010
623'.19440903 — dc22   2009046691

British Library cataloguing data are available

©2010 Jean-Denis G.G. Lepage. All rights reserved

*No part of this book may be reproduced or transmitted in any form
or by any means, electronic or mechanical, including photocopying
or recording, or by any information storage and retrieval system,
without permission in writing from the publisher.*

Cover images ©2010 Shutterstock

Manufactured in the United States of America

*McFarland & Company, Inc., Publishers
Box 611, Jefferson, North Carolina 28640
www.mcfarlandpub.com*

Acknowledgments

The author wishes to thank Jeannette à Stuling, Anne Chauvel, Eltjo Jakobus De Lang and Ben Marcato, Nicole and Robert Fresse, Jacques Jouy, Jan van Groningen à Stuling, Wim Wiese, Michèle Clermont, Véronique Janty, Jean-Pierre Rorive and Herman Treu for their friendly and helpful collaboration.

Jean-Denis G.G. Lepage

L'organisation des forteresses repose sur le même principe que la disposition des troupes: elles doivent servir aux opérations.
(The organization of fortresses rests on the same principles as deployment of troops: they must serve operations.)

Napoléon in 1806

Contents

Introduction 1

1. **HISTORICAL BACKGROUND** 5
   Louis XV 5
   Louis XVI 6
   The French Revolution 8
   The Consulate 21
   The Napoleonic Empire 24

2. **FORTIFICATIONS OF THE ANCIEN RÉGIME** 46
   Bastioned Fortifications 46
   Louis XIV and Vauban 50
   Fortifications in the 18th Century 54
   Montalembert 61
   Siege Warfare 82
   Projects Under Louis XV and Louis XVI 84
   French Fortifications in Overseas Colonies 97

3. **IMPERIAL FORTIFICATIONS** 114
   Napoleonic Style 114
   Artillery 117
   Military Engineering Corps 135
   Napoleonic Génie Leadership 141
   Siege Warfare 158
   Coastal Defense 163
   Cartography and Relief-Maps 171
   Futuristic Weapons 172

4. **NAPOLEONIC FORTIFICATION PROJECTS** 176
   Dismantlement of Obsolete Places 176
   Napoleonic Arsenals 176
   France 183

The Netherlands 223
　　　Germany 241
　　　Italy 246
　　　Illyrian Provinces 252
　　　Corfu 253
　　　Malta 256
　　　Military Roads and Canals 258
　　　The Heritage of the Empire 262

Appendix
　　　French Republican Calendar 267
Bibliography 269
Index 271

Introduction

The fascinating personality of Napoléon I, Emperor of the French people, has been the inspiration for numerous books by biographers and historians of the Consulate and Empire, but has also inspired novelists, poets and playwrights from Lord Byron to André Malraux, musicians from Beethoven to Prokofiev, painters in the 19th century and filmmakers in the 20th. The Napoleonic Empire, which was the product of the French Revolution, left an indelible print on France and Europe.

What was Napoléon? Genius? Opportunist? Tyrant? He has been all things to all men, and is therefore one of the most colorful and controversial figures of history. Theories have arisen from the controversy, and these theories have bred too much dry prose about one of the most interesting men who ever lived. It is often said that more books have been written on Napoleonic France and Europe than days have elapsed since the Emperor's death in 1821. This is probably true, as the shelves of libraries are weighed down by biographies, monographs, descriptions of battles, and detailed analyses of policy.

On the whole, historians and biographers tend to divide between admirers and detractors, and attitudes were—and still are—often colored by the political affiliations of the writer, particularly but not exclusively in France. As is the case with great historical men, it is evident that each writer, and indeed each reader, constructs his own Napoléon from the mass of evidence available. Admirers emphasize his role as a genuine people's Emperor standing firm against obscurantism and monarchist reaction, a dynamic and glorious conqueror, a military genius, a key figure in the development of the modern state, the first in a line of "providential saviors" like Cavaignac, his nephew Louis Napoléon III, Thiers, Clémenceau, Pétain and de Gaulle, men of destiny who were seen as solving a major crisis. Many focus on his constructive achievements, especially religious toleration, and the programs of legal, administrative and financial reforms. They extol the warrior who preserved the achievements of the 1789 Revolution, the guardian of liberty who reconciled authority and democracy, maintained public order and security of property, and affirmed the principles of equality, as well as careers open to talent and merit.

On the other hand, Napoléon's detractors denounce the "Corsican Ogre," riposte by highlighting the darker aspects of his regime and the cynical and calculating side of his personality, portraying him as an unprincipled adventurer, a tyrant with an insatiable lust for glory and conquest, a despot who distorted the legacy of the French Revolution, the man who reintroduced slavery in the colonies, the forerunner of 20th century totalitarian dictators like Stalin, Hitler and their subsequent imitators, a ruthless man of blood responsible for pointless wars, deaths, disablement, and loss of all meaningful political liberty.

Napoléon's military career, government and administration, personality, sex life, even his very anatomy, have been subjected to minute scrutiny. Books continue to pour from the presses dealing with his career, his impact on laws and institutions in France and Europe, and all other aspects of his rule. Volumes have been written on the subjects of his imprisonment at Saint-Helena, the treatment he received, and the causes of his death. The public is still deluged with operational accounts of battles and campaigns, tactics and strategy, the colorful uniforms of his soldiers and all other aspects of Napoleonic warfare. It might therefore appear reasonable to suppose that there is nothing left to write about the Napoleonic era. Closer examination of the abundant mass of Napoleonic military literature, however, reveals that there has yet been little effort to analyze Napoleonic fortifications, and the present book is intended to be the record of that somewhat neglected aspect.

The existence, structure, role and location of Napoleonic fortifications are only quickly mentioned in the relations of campaigns and battles. Napoleonic fortifications are also hidden behind the fact that Napoleonic wars marked a clear break in warfare, which raised the amplitude of armed conflicts to new heights. Napoleonic warfare provided the substitution of wars of people for the traditional dynastic wars of monarchs. "People war," based on the concept of the "nation in arms," concerned not only professional soldiers but almost each and every French family. The 17th and 18th centuries had been characterized by static siege warfare, in which fortification and artillery played a central role, the final objective being not the extermination of the enemy but his surrender. Strategy was dominated by carefulness and most risks were calculated in advance. Eighteenth-century rulers and their strategies often preferred the controllable and codified siege warfare rather than the hazardous chances of a bloody and uncertain battle in open field. Great battles of this period were seldom decisive, in the sense that they brought the wars to an immediate end. They were often irrelevant unless they helped to determine the outcome of a siege. The era of Napoléon, on the contrary, was marked by large movement warfare punctuated by highly decisive and bloody pitched battles mainly fought by infantry, cavalry and artillery. Napoleonic strategy also aimed to obliterate not only enemy forces, but actually enemy states themselves, with the goal of changing their regimes. Therefore, historians have generally overlooked the place held by Napoleonic fortifications.

French Napoleonic military architecture represents an interesting transitional development in the history of fortification. It was based on the bastioned system, which had originally been developed by Italian engineers in the 16th century, and which had been greatly improved by countless European engineers in the 17th and 18th centuries, notably by Louis XIV's main engineer, Vauban. It also featured important innovations designed by farsighted engineers whose work paved the way for modern 19th-century fortification. The main events that occurred during this highly complicated period of European and French history are described in part one. To have a good understanding of Napoleonic fortification, it is absolutely necessary to know what the Ancien Régime's bastioned system was, and what these innovations were. That is dealt with in the second part of this book. In a third part we shall describe Napoléon's artillery (which directly influenced and determined the evolution of military architecture) and engineering corps; and in the fourth part the general imperial strategy, as well as planned and completed projects of the short period of the Consulate and Empire. The focus is on Napoleonic fortifications, but this book also covers the 18th century, or, more precisely, the period from the death of Louis XIV in 1715 to the fall of Napoléon in 1815.

Because this volume is not a specialized full-length academic work, and does not pretend to scholarship, I have not interrupted the text or burdened the pages with footnotes. But because every reader is entitled if he wishes to know what evidence is being called, I have set out my authorities in a bibliography at the end of the book.

Intended for the general reader, the reader with an interest but little specific knowledge in the subject of French 18th-century and Napoleonic fortifications, this book is an attempt partially to correct the existing situation, to stimulate interest, and to point up new areas for research.

1

Historical Background

Louis XV

Louis XV (b. February 1710) was King of France from 1715 to 1774. He was the great-grandson of Louis XIV and the third son of Louis, Duke of Burgundy, and Marie Adelaide, Princess of Savoy. Louis XV was only five years old when Louis XIV died in 1715, and Duke Philippe of Orléans (Louis XIV's nephew) was declared regent with full powers. The regent replaced the middle-class bourgeois ministers with councils of leading aristocrats, substituted the austerity of the previous reign with a frivolous and lighthearted lifestyle, and pursued peace in place of warfare as a foreign policy. The regent also encouraged the experiments implemented by a Scotsman named John Law, issuing paper money and commercial investment shares which, at first and for a short while, met with resounding success. In 1723, Louis XV (aged thirteen) was declared to have attained his legal majority, shortly before the death of the Duke of Orléans. His cousin, the Duke of Bourbon, was minister for a short while. In 1726 the Duke of Bourbon was replaced by the king's tutor, the aged Cardinal Fleury, who exercised almost absolute power, for the young king manifested little interest in affairs of state. Fleury encouraged Louis XV's marriage to Maria Leszczinska, the daughter of Stanislaw, the King of Poland, who had lost his throne but who was Duke of Lorraine. After Stanislaw's death in 1735, the province became French. Up to this point Louis XV's reign and Fleury's administration had been prosperous, and the king gained the nickname of *Louis le Bien Aimé* (the Well-Beloved). But from this time on, France's national strength declined. In 1740 the War of Austrian Succession broke out and France, in spite of her victories at Fontenoy and Raucoux, gained little, all benefits going to her ally, King Frederick II of Prussia. On Fleury's death in 1743 no one took his place, and the king decided to follow the example of Louis XIV and to rule by personal autocracy. But he was not strong enough in will or intellect to give unity to the administration. The king was handsome, elegant, intelligent, not without ambition and devoted to the ideal of peace, but often timid, skeptical, hesitant, giving the impression of being only periodically interested in serious matters, and without sufficient tenacity of purpose to come near to realizing what he had resolved. Although he seemed enthusiastic about European affairs and diplomacy, he was quickly bored, his health was frail, and he gradually turned to a frivolous and dissolute life with many mistresses. One of them, Jeanne-Antoinette Le Normant d'Étiolles (1721–1764), born in Poisson from bourgeois roots, was eventually made Marquise of Pompadour, and acquired a measure of influence over the weak king.

In addition to tension within Europe, there was an ongoing confrontation between France and England in North America and India. Louis XV repudiated the alliance of Frederick the Great and allied with France's old enemy, Austria. It was the cause of immense disasters for France, for after a promising beginning, both by land and sea, France suffered serious reverses. After the Seven Years' War (1756–1763), France lost India and Canada to England, and was deprived of the leading position she had so long held in Europe. The king was blamed for the diplomatic failure, and his prestige was ruined by military failure and colonial losses. To the last Louis XV maintained the pretense of personal rule, but his reign was marked by ministerial instability (e.g., Choiseul and Maupéou) and parliamentary unrest. The machinery of government fell out of gear, and the disorder of the finances was paramount and never solved.

The French artistic and cultural prestige, however, was at its peak in the 18th century, but the Capetian-Bourbon monarchy flourished on a basis of injustice that ultimately led to its dramatic collapse. It was brilliant, elegant and refined, but being based on archaic feudal rules and medieval customs, it was obsolete and wasteful of the life and substance of its common people. The clergy and nobility were protected from taxation by a system of exemption that threw the whole burden of the state upon the middle and lower classes. The peasants were ground down by taxation, and the wealthy upper bourgeois and middle classes were dominated and humiliated by the nobility. For these reasons, there arose during Louis XV's reign a strong reaction against ancient prejudice, old-fashioned tradition, religious fanaticism, the obsolete monarchy and its unfair methods. Known as the Age of Enlightenment, the period saw the appearance of philosophers, intellectuals, Freemasons, writers, journalists, encyclopedists and reformers (e.g., Montesquieu, Voltaire, Diderot, Rousseau and others), who challenged and criticized the archaic existing society by spreading knowledge, advanced ideas, new principles, and projects for audacious reforms. When Louis XV died in 1774 of smallpox, he left a country that was exsanguinated and a greatly weakened and much criticized monarchy. Both his sons had died young, so Louis XV was succeeded by his grandson.

Louis XVI

Louis XVI (born in August 1754) was King of France from 1774 to 1791. He was the son of Louis, dauphin of France, who was the son of Louis XV, and of Maria Josepha of Saxony. He was just twenty years old when the death of his grandfather, Louis XV, placed him on the throne in May 1774. Although he had inherited a catastrophic financial situation and a badly impaired image of the monarchy, Louis XVI's reign started under good auspices. Filled with the very best of intentions and a will to do his utmost for the French people, the king was a generous, conscientious, hard-working, cultured, educated man who was originally open to the new ideas of the Age of Enlightenment. Although he realized that there was a need for reforms, he was unfortunately not the right man for the job. Louis XVI was pious, weak and irresolute in character, and mentally dull. He lacked authority, was easily influenced, and chose unfortunate advisers. The greater part of his time was spent hunting. He also amused himself making locks, and a little at masonry. Awkward and uncourtly, at heart shy, he was but a poor figurehead for the stately court of France. His diary shows how little he understood or cared for the business of a king. Days on which he had not shot anything at the hunt were blank days for him. The entry on July 14, 1789 (when the people of Paris took the Bastille prison, marking the start of the French Revolution), was: "Nothing." His policy in the face of the crisis was both feeble and false, and he was singularly unfortunate even when he gave in to the demands of the revolutionaries, reluctantly delaying his agreement until it had the air of a pitiful surrender. His wife, the Austrian Marie Antoinette Johanna von Habsburg-Lothringen (1755–1793), whom he had married in 1770, obtained an ascendancy over him that was partly responsible for the extravagance of the ministry of Calonne, and brought on the Revolution by the resulting financial crisis. Marie Antoinette, by her bad influence, frivolousness, taste for luxury, legendary excesses and thoughtless conduct, discredited him, and it was largely she who encouraged him in underhanded opposition to the Revolution while he pretended to accept it. It has often been said that Louis XVI was the victim of the faults of his predecessors and the bad company around him, but this is only partly true. He was also the victim of his own irresolution, weakness, lack of vision, stubborn intransigence, contradictions and inconsistencies.

The first part of his reign was characterized by well-intentioned but aborted reforms. In August 1774, Louis appointed a liberal controller general, the economist Anne Robert Jacques Turgot, baron de L'Aulne (1727–1781), who instituted a policy of strict economy in government expenditures. Within two years, however, most of the reforms had been withdrawn and his dismissal forced by reactionary members of the nobility and clergy, supported by Queen Marie Antoinette. Turgot's successor, the financier and statesman Jacques Necker (1732–1804), similarly accomplished little before his downfall in 1781, also because of opposition from the reactionaries. Nevertheless, Necker won popular acclaim by publishing an accounting of the royal finances, which revealed the heavy cost of privileges and favoritism. During the next few years the financial crisis only steadily worsened.

In foreign affairs, Louis XVI supported the American War of Independence (1775–1783), which greatly helped the establishment of the United States of America, but which led to a further worsening of the financial situation because of the use of loans. Louis XVI's reign was also marked by intense technological researches which were eventually developed in the 19th century in the Industrial Revolution. The last part of his reign was marked by the continuation of the financial crisis, public unrest, general hostility and opposition. The advocates of fiscal, social, and governmental reform expressing ideas derived from the Enlightenment became increasingly vocal, and in August 1788 the Parliament of Paris demanded a meeting of the States-General, an assembly made up of representatives of the clergy, the nobility, and the commoners.

As general public discontent played an increasing role in politics, the meeting of the assembly that started in May 1789 announced that a large part of the French population expected and demanded important reforms. If American colonists in Boston and Philadelphia enjoyed a free society based on the principles of Enlightenment, why should such a society be impossible in old Europe? The meeting of the States-General quickly turned to a deadlock on procedure of vote, but finally, on June 17, the insurgent commoners' State, led by Emmanuel Joseph Sieyès (1748–1836) and Honoré Gabriel Riqueti, Count of Mirabeau (1749–1791), proclaimed itself the National Assembly. In swift retaliation, Louis XVI deprived them of a meeting hall. The National Assembly responded, on June 20, by gathering in a tennis court and swearing, in what is known in history as the *Serment du Jeu de Paume* (Tennis Court Oath), that it would not dissolve until it had drafted a constitution for France.

At this point, serious conflicts divided the ranks of the upper two privileged estates, and a number of liberal representatives of the lower clergy and of advanced-minded aristocrats joined the National Assembly. Continued defiance of royal decrees and the mutinous mood of the royal army forced the king to capitulate. On June 27 he ordered the refractory nobility and clergy to join the then designated National Constituent Assembly. Yielding to pressure from the queen and the Count of Artois (later to become king Charles X between 1824 and 1830), the wavering Louis XVI planned to use violence, and gave orders for the deployment of several loyal foreign regiments in Paris and Versailles.

The French Revolution

THE NATIONAL CONSTITUENT ASSEMBLY

The people of Paris responded to Louis XVI's provocations with open revolt. Insurrection and rioting started on July 12, and on July 14 the infamous Bastille, a medieval castle that was used as the royal prison for political prisoners and symbolized the despotism of the monarchy, was attacked and captured. Even before the Parisian insurrection, sporadic local disturbances and violence, as well as peasant uprisings against oppressive nobles, took place in many parts of France, alarming the wealthy bourgeoisie, rich landowners and noble castle-dwellers. In the countryside peasants took arms, attacked castles and destroyed archives and documents setting up ancient feudal rights. Panic-stricken over these threatening happenings, the Count of Artois, the Count of Provence, leading princes, high-ranking courtiers, and other prominent reactionaries, the first of the so-called *émigrés* (exiled), fled abroad. The Parisian bourgeoisie, afraid that the lower commoners of the capital of France would take further advantage of the collapse of the old administrative machine and resort again to violent action, hastily formed a provisional local government and created a militia known as the *Garde Nationale* (National Guard). A red, white, and blue tricolor replaced the white banner of the Bourbon monarchy as the national flag.

Provisional local governments and militia units were soon established throughout France. The National Guard was placed under the leadership of the marquis de Lafayette, the well-known hero of the American Revolution. Unable to stem the rising tide of revolt, Louis XVI again yielded. He ordered the withdrawal of his loyal troops, recalled the popular minister Necker, and formally legalized the measures that had been taken by the provisional authorities. Provincial unrest and disorder, known as the *Grande Peur* (Great Fear), stimulated the National Constituent Assembly to make a great sweep of the chief injustices of the absolutist regime. Indeed, the remains of the feudal system had come to an end. During the night session of August 4, 1789, the clergy and nobles renounced their privileges; henceforth all Frenchmen, noble or commoner, rich or poor, were equal *citoyens* (citizens). A few days later the assembly passed a law abolishing feudal and manorial prerogatives, but guaranteeing compensation in certain cases. Torture, arbitrary imprisonment, and persecutions for heresy were abolished. Parallel legislation included interdiction of the sale of public offices, of exemption from taxation, and of the right of the Catholic Church to levy tithes. The absolute monarchy had collapsed. The assembly then proceeded to grapple with its primary task, the drafting of a constitution. In the constitutional preamble, known in history as the Declaration of the Rights of Man and of the Citizen, the delegates formulated the revolutionary ideals later summarized as *Liberté, Égalité, Fraternité* ("Liberty, Equality, Fraternity"). Article I proclaimed, "All men are born free and remain free and equal before the Law." Article II defined the citizen's rights: "liberty, property, security and resistance to oppression."

In the meantime, a hungry and discontented Parisian mob, mostly women, marched on Versailles and laid siege to the royal palace (October 6, 1789). On demand of the crowd, the king and his family were obliged to sojourn henceforth at the Tuileries Palace in Paris, almost as prisoners. This episode showed that both the royal court and the assembly had become increasingly subject to pressures from the Parisian citizens.

The first constitution, particularly favorable to the middle and upper classes, was acknowledged by the king and adopted on July 14, 1790. It contained further important reforms: the ancient provinces of France were abolished, and the country was divided into *départements*, each provided with a local elective administration; hereditary titles were outlawed; trial by jury in criminal cases was ordained; and fundamental modification of French law was projected, notably the freedom of the press, which allowed for numerous newspapers and the development of revolutionary clubs, parties and factions whose members soon fought each other for power. The constitution vested legislative authority in a Legislative Assembly, composed of 745 members elected by an indirect system of voting. Strict limitations were imposed on the king's powers, and severe restrictions on the power of the Catholic Church: dissolution of most monastic orders and confiscation of all ecclesiastical estates, the so-called *biens nationaux*, which were "placed at the disposal of the nation" and sold to rich bourgeois in order to reabsorb the national deficit; and election of priests and bishops by the voters.

Things could have ended there and France would have become a parliamentary monarchy like England, but Louis XVI and the conservatives accepted these changes only with reluctance. In fact the king felt himself a prisoner in the Tuileries Palace. In 1791 the experiment of constitutional monarchy in France was brought to an abrupt end by the action of Louis XVI. In the night of June 21, the royal family, working in concert with aristocratic and monarchist friends, left Paris in secret, the king's aim being not to join the *émigrés* in Germany and to direct the counterrevolution from abroad, but to go to the fortress of Montmédy in Lorraine, where the royalist governor held some 6,000 soldiers ready for the king. With the backing of this small force Louis XVI wanted to renegotiate in strength a new constitution and hoped to regain some of the rights he had been deprived of. The king and his family rode on a coach under a false name and with a forged passport, but at the village of Varennes (near Metz in eastern France) were recognized, caught, and brought back to Paris under strong escort.

A mood of suspicion and discontent followed. The king had lost all his credit and prestige, he was accused of being a traitor ready to sell the Revolution to foreign powers, and the French revolutionary movement turned toward radicalism and flamed up into a passion of patriotic republicanism. On July 17, 1791, the Republicans of Paris demonstrated, demanding the deposition of Louis XVI. The National Guard opened fire on the demonstrators and dispersed them, but the bloodshed only immeasurably widened the cleavage between the republican radicals and bourgeois sections of the population. After

suspending Louis for a brief period, the moderate majority of the Constituent Assembly, fearful of the growing disorder, reinstated the king in the hope of stemming the mounting radicalism, and of preventing foreign intervention. Louis XVI took the oath to support the revised constitution on September 14. Two weeks later, with the election of the new legislature authorized by the constitution, the Constituent Assembly was dissolved and replaced by the Legislative Assembly. Meanwhile, the French Revolution and the ideas it defended and wanted to spread began to worry European monarchs. Tension grew between the French revolutionaries and Leopold II of Austria (Queen Marie-Antoinette's nephew) and Frederick William II, King of Prussia, who both openly supported the activities of the anti-revolutionary royalist *émigrés*. The idea of a war began to gather momentum. The revolutionaries, divided into several opposing groups, declared war on Austria on April 20, 1792. The series of conflicts known as the French Revolutionary Wars started.

*Member of the National Guard, 1790
The National Guard was an armed militia — an auxiliary police force intended to protect goods, property and persons in period of turmoil. In wartime it could be engaged with the regular army. It was composed of unpaid civilian volunteers from the middle and upper-middle classes. It existed in Paris and in all important French cities from 1789 until 1871. In 1790, the hat was black with a tricolor cockade and red plume. The tunic was blue with red cuffs and red collar. The waistcoat, breeches and gaiters were white. The weapon was the model 1777 flintlock musket with bayonet.*

The First Republic

The war began with defeats for the revolutionary armies, which were ill organized, poorly armed, and badly commanded, as many senior noble officers refused to serve or had chosen exile. The subsequent invasion of France produced major repercussions in Paris. In July 1792, after Sardinia and Prussia joined the war against France, the Legislative Assembly, now dominated by the Montagnards' faction, under the leadership of the lawyer Georges Jacques Danton (1759–1794), declared a national emergency. Reserve troops were dispatched to the hard-pressed armies, and volunteers were summoned to Paris from all parts of the country. On September 20, at Valmy (near Saint-Menehould in eastern France), a hastily raised army of enthusiastic volunteers, commanded by General Charles François Dumouriez (1739–1823), defeated the Prussian army that was marching on Paris. The Battle of Valmy, an artillery duel that demonstrated that the artillery corps had retained its discipline and cohesion, was a modest victory, but it showed the scope of French determination and enthusiasm. Dumouriez, his deputy Kellermann, and the French artillery corps had saved both Paris and the Revolution.

After the victory at Valmy, the newly elected National Convention convened in Paris, and took radical measures. The delegates abolished the monarchy, deposed Louis XVI, and proclaimed the establishment of the First Republic on September 21, 1792 (also known as Year I of the Republic). Now the revolutionaries decided to free all oppressed peoples of Europe from the monarchic yoke. According to them, not only France but the whole of Europe had to become republican. The French armies assumed the offensive, won the Battle of Jemmapes (November 6, 1792), conquered the Austrian Netherlands (present-day Belgium), and successively captured Mainz, Frankfurt am Main (Germany), Nice, Savoie (Italy), and other areas by the fall of 1792.

The National Convention, which had made France a republic, proceeded to the next major affair: the fate of the king. In January 1793, Louis XVI (now no longer addressed to as Your Majesty but as "citizen Louis Capet") was brought to trial for treason. On January 15, 1793, by an almost unanimous vote, the convention found the monarch guilty as charged. But by a vote of only 387 to 334, the delegates approved the death penalty. Louis XVI was guillotined on January 21, 1793, at Paris — on the former Louis XV Square, then renamed Place de la Révolution (present-day Place de la Concorde). Maximilien Robespierre (1758–1794), a lawyer elected to the States General and re-elected to the Convention, declared: "You have not passed a sentence against a man, you have taken a measure to ensure public safety." The execution of the king further divided the various factions, notably the conservative Girondists, the moderate Plaine, and the radical Montagnards.

There was now no turning back: the members of the Convention were regicides, and they constituted a challenge and a threat for European monarchs who formed an anti–French coalition including Great Britain, the United Netherlands, Spain, and several smaller states. The coalition represented a great danger for the Republic, and it was decided in early March 1793 to raise an army of 300,000 drafted men. Special commissioners were dispatched to the various departments for the purpose of organizing the levy. This unpopular measure was exploited by Royalists and clerical foes of the Revolution who stirred the anticonscription feelings of peasants in the Vendée into open rebellion. Civil war quickly spread to the neighboring western departments of France.

On March 18, the Austrians defeated the army of general Dumouriez at the Battle

of Neerwinden, and Dumouriez deserted to the enemy. The defection of the major leader of the army, mounting civil war in the western departments, and the advance of enemy forces across the French eastern and northern frontiers inevitably forced a crisis in the Convention between the Girondists and the Montagnards, with the more radical elements stressing the necessity for immediate bold action in defense of the Revolution. The Montagnards then had the Convention adopt a series of emergency measures in April 1793, including shorter delays before suspects were brought to court, confiscation of *émigrés'* property, forcibly borrowing funds from the wealthy, and the dispatch of representatives on missions in the departments to supervise local execution of the laws and to requisition men, supplies and ammunition.

THE COMMITTEE OF PUBLIC SAFETY

An executive organ of the Republic, known as the Committee of Public Safety, was set up on April 6 in order to apply Assembly decisions immediately and without mercy. The Girondist delegates, worried by these encroachments on individual freedom, private property and civil rights, tried to resist. On June 2, 1793, they were arrested, and the radical Montagnard faction took control of the government of Paris. However, the leadership of the Committee of Public Safety passed, on July 10, to the Jacobin party, who completely

Guillotine
Designed with the best of intentions by Dr. Joseph Ignace Guillotin (1738–1814) in order to shorten the suffering of criminals and political opponents condemned to death by decapitation at one stroke, the device was intended to be an egalitarian, painless and humane alternative to the medieval barbarities of the wheel, the stake, hanging and decapitation with an axe or a sword. Introduced in April 1792, the guillotine was composed of a standing wooden frame including two strong upright poles joined by a crossbar, whose internal edges were grooved and greased with tallow, allowing a heavy and sharp blade to fall by its own weight. The blade was raised and locked via a rope and pulley, and released by the headsman. The whole construction was mounted on a high platform for public execution. The machine was nicknamed la Louisette (probably because of Louis XVI) and eventually la Veuve (widow-[maker]). It remained officially in use until October 9, 1981, when President François Mitterand abolished the death penalty in France.

1. Historical Background

Sans culotte

Sans-culotte (French for "without knee-breeches") was a term created around 1790 to 1792 by the French aristocracy to describe the poorer commoners (members of the Third Estate), according to the dominant theory, because they usually wore pantaloons (full-length trousers or pants) instead of the silk culottes (knee-breeches) then in fashion. The term came to refer to the ill-clad and ill-equipped volunteers of the Revolutionary army during the early years of the Revolutionary Wars, but above all, to the working class radicals of the Revolution. Traditionally a typical sans-culotte would wear a red Phrygian cap (a symbol of freedom, dating to the time of the ancient Phrygian Greeks), a gray or black felt hat with tricolor band and cockade, a short blue carmagnole jacket, striped tricolor pantaloons and a red sash.

reorganized it. Three days later the radical politician Jean Paul Marat (1743–1793), long identified with the Jacobins, was assassinated by the aristocrat Charlotte Corday, a Girondist sympathizer. Public indignation over this crime considerably broadened the Jacobin sphere of influence. On July 27 the Jacobin leader Maximilien Robespierre was added to the Committee of Public Safety and soon became its dominant member, thereafter playing a decisive role in the conduct of the Revolution. Aided by Louis Saint-Just, Lazare Carnot, Georges Couthon, and other prominent Jacobins, the fanatical Robespierre instituted extreme measures to stamp out any possibility of counterrevolution. The powers of the committee were renewed monthly by the National Convention from April 1793 to July 1794, a period known in history as the *Terreur* (Reign of Terror). This was supposed to work quickly and effectively, protecting the Republic from enemies and quickly solving problems with the necessary brutal force.

Militarily the situation of the Republic was extremely precarious. The enemy coalition had resumed the offensive on all fronts. Mainz in Germany had been retaken by the Prussians, Condé-Sur-l'Escaut and Valenciennes (two important fortresses on the way to Paris) had been captured, and the port of Toulon in the Mediterranean had been seized by the British. Royalist Catholic insurgents (known as

Chouans or Whites) controlled large parts of the Vendée and Brittany provinces. Caen, Lyon, Marseille, Bordeaux, and other important localities were in open rebellion in the hands of the Girondists. By a new conscription decree, issued on August 23, the Committee ordered the raising of fourteen new armies, numbering about 750,000 men, who were hastily formed, trained, armed, equipped, and quickly deployed to the fronts, owing to Lazare Carnot's efforts. Along with these military actions, the Committee of Public Safety, now a true dictatorship run by Robespierre, struck violently at internal opposition. The revolutionary Tribunal was set up and went to work, and a steady slaughter began. The Committee demanded the arrest and execution of anyone who "either by their conduct, their contacts, their words or their writings, showed themselves to be supporters of tyranny, of federalism, or to be enemies of liberty." The reign of Robespierre lived, it seemed, on blood, and needed more and more executions.

On October 16, 1793, the deposed Queen Marie Antoinette was tried, found guilty of treason, and beheaded. Her son Louis XVII, the titular king of France, then a child aged 8, was given into the keeping of a cobbler, Antoine Simon, who had been named his guardian by the Committee of General Security. The boy eventually died under unspecified, controversial and mysterious circumstances in June 1795. Together with the ex-queen, twenty-one prominent Girondists were executed on October 31, 1793. Beginning with these reprisals, thousands of Royalists, nonjuring Catholic priests, Girondists, and other elements charged with counterrevolutionary activities or sympathies were hastily tried, convicted, and guillotined. In Paris alone the number of executions amounted to 2,639. All over France hard treatment was meted out to traitors, real and suspect. The number of victims of Robespierre's Reign of Terror has been estimated at approximately 40,000.

As a part of its revolutionary program, the Committee of Public Safety, spurred by Robespierre, tried to reshape the fundamental basis of France according to their own extreme concepts of civic ethic, puritan patriotism, radical devotion to the public good, social idealism and fanatical humanitarianism. It seemed like the French Revolution had gone mad; the goal was now the creation of a "Republic of Virtue." Anticlerical hatred found expression in the abolition, in October 1793, of the Julian calendar, which was replaced by a Republican calendar (see Appendix); the closing of all churches in Paris; and the sponsoring of a new, extravagant, patriotic and revolutionary religion (known as the Cult of Reason) worshiping the "Supreme Being."

Meanwhile at the front, mass mobilization and reorganization of the French armies began to bear fruit, and gradually the tide of battle turned in favor of revolutionary France. General Jean-Baptiste Jourdan (1762–1833) defeated the Austrian army at Wattignies in October 1793. This was the first of a series of victories achieved by young generals such as Lazare Hoche (1768–1797). By the end of 1793, the eastern borders of France had been cleared of invading foreign troops. Eventually Jourdan won another decisive victory at Fleurus (June 10, 1794), which opened the way for the reconquest of Belgium. Elsewhere towns that had passed to the enemy were recaptured, and Toulon had been liberated owing to a young artillery officer by the name of Napoléon Bonaparte. Of equal significance, the Committee of Public Safety had largely crushed with extreme savagery the insurrections of the Royalist Chouans in the western provinces.

These successes, however, had not put an end to political constraint. The dictatorship, the Reign of Terror, and the bloody purges became unbearable, and Robespierre lost the backing of many leading Jacobins. On July 27, 1794 (9th Thermidor, Year II, by the Republican calendar), representatives who feared for their own lives fomented a conspiracy, and finally succeeded in overthrowing the dictator and his followers, who were immediately guillotined. The Ninth Thermidor is generally regarded as marking the end of the "Republic of Virtue" and the Reign of Terror, and the beginning of a period of relief and appeasement led by a conservative faction known as Thermidoreans. The revolutionary tribunals were abolished, the extravagant Republic of Virtue's aims were abandoned, freedom of worship was reinstated, major work was done in the educational sector, notably by the foundation of central schools and high leading colleges, including the Ecole Normale Supérieure and Ecole Polytechnique.

The morale of the French armies was undamaged by these events on the home front, and military successes continued. Peace was restored to the frontiers, and in the winter 1794–95, Belgium was occupied, eventually annexed, and the Netherlands turned into the Batavian Republic, a satellite of France.

Republican General
As many French army noble senior officers refused to serve the newly created Republic, and had chosen to emigrate, there were plenty of opportunities for young officers to make a career and rapidly climb the steps of the ladder. François Kellermann became general in 1791, aged 56; Jean-Baptiste Kleber was promoted to the rank of general of brigade in 1793, aged 40. Joachim Murat became general in 1796, aged 29; Michel Ney became general of brigade in 1796, aged 27; and Napoléon Bonaparte at the age of 26. The depicted young general wears a black bicorne hat decorated with tricolor cockade, blue-white-red pompons, a dark blue jacket with golden buttons and golden oak-leaf patterned lapels, a tricolor sash, white gloves, white tight-fitting trousers and black boots with golden facing. Red épaulettes (shoulder straps) were discarded at the time of the Revolution as being too "monarchic," and were reintroduced in 1803.

The victories made it possible to make peace with some members of the coalition, until only England and Austria remained at war with France. For nearly a year, however, a stalemate prevailed between France and these powers. Thermidorean conservatism was transformed into sharp reaction. Indeed, with the Thermidoreans the Revolution had lost its popular character and shifted henceforth under the leadership of the bourgeois middle and upper classes. During the spring of 1795, bread riots and protest demonstrations spread from Paris to many sections of France. The uprisings were bloodily repressed.

THE DIRECTOIRE

The National Convention then completed the draft of a new constitution. Formally approved on August 22, 1795, the new basic law vested executive authority in a *Directoire* (Directory), composed of five members called Directeurs. Legislative power was delegated to a bicameral legislature, consisting of the Council of Ancients, with 250 members, and the Council of the Five Hundred, elected by a restricted property-owning franchise. Parisian Royalists, reacting violently to this decree, organized, on October 5, 1795, an insurrection against the government. The uprising was promptly quelled by troops under the command of the young Napoléon Bonaparte, who became very popular as the savior of the Republic. Bonaparte was indeed too popular, and soon received the command of an army that was send to Italy to fight the Austrians.

The Directoire, dominated by Barras, Talleyrand and Fouché, formed a curious interlude in the history of the French Revolution. Designed to serve the interests of property owners who had profited from the Revolution, and working under crippling financial burdens, exacerbated by economic stagnation, the Directoire never operated satisfactorily, and proved a source of constant conflict and instability. The Directeurs were confronted with serious problems, notably an acute financial crisis, the spirit of Jacobinism which still flourished among the lower classes, Royalist agitation, and wealthy bourgeois political groupings determined to preserve their hard-won status as those who had most benefitted from the Revolution. The financial difficulties led to an ethical and social crisis, for rapid and scandalous fortunes were made owing to the black market, illegal dealings and speculation. As a reaction there appeared the so-called Equals' Conspiracy. François (alias Gracchus) Babeuf advocated equal distribution of land and income and proposed an egalitarian, communist society under the motto: "No more private property. The Earth belongs to no one; its fruits are the property of all." The conspirators were denounced and arrested, brought before the Court of Justice, found guilty and guillotined in May 1797. This egalitarian ideology, known as Babouvism, was a foretaste of the later collectivist Marxist system.

As the war continued, the Directoire regime became increasingly and dangerously dependent upon its generals, both abroad and at home. Finding it difficult to attract mass loyalty at home, the Directors looked abroad to increase their popularity and reputation by allowing the army to carry out an aggressive and expansionary foreign policy. The propagandist zeal of the revolution carried the French armies into Holland, Belgium, Switzerland, south Germany and north Italy. Everywhere monarchs were expelled and sister republics set up. But the republican zeal did not prevent the looting of the "liberated" peoples to relieve the catastrophic financial embarrassment of France. The wars of the French became less and less holy wars of freedom, and more and more aggressive wars for plunder.

At home the army had intervened on several occasions to re-establish law and order and support the government. The army played a key role, but Bonaparte, for the time being a cumbersome hero as a result of his successes in Italy, was again sent away on another campaign, this time to conquer Egypt, with the mission of cutting England's trade route. By 1799, the French people were weary of ten years of violence, purges, political uncertainty, corruption, and general disorganization within the country. They no longer trusted the Directoire, which had taken things as they came, had discredited itself, and had become very unpopular. The leaders of the Directory were rechristened the "Five Monkeys." In the opinion of Lucien Bonaparte, Napoléon's brother and president of the Council of the Five Hundred; of Joseph Fouché, minister of police; of Sieyès, then a member of the Directory; of the versatile diplomat and politician Charles-Maurice de Talleyrand-Périgord and other political leaders, the crisis could be overcome only by drastic action, and the then highly popular General Napoléon Bonaparte was seen as a solution.

Napoléon Bonaparte

The Bonapartes, a Corsican family of Italian Lombard origin, stepped onto the historical stage of France thanks to their most illustrious member, Napoléon. Nabulione di Buonaparte (in Corsican), who later adopted the more French-sounding Napoléon Bonaparte, was born in Ajaccio (Corsica) on August 15, 1769, the second son of a lawyer of humble noble ancestry. By the time of Napoléon's birth the island had only just passed from the hands of the Genoese to those of the French. Napoléon was only narrowly born a French subject of King Louis XV. His father, Carlo Bonaparte, managed to obtain for him a scholarship to the prestigious military school at Brienne near Troyes in the province of Champagne. The young Nabulione first had to learn French before he entered the school, and it seems that he spoke the *langue de Molière* with a marked Italian accent and never learned to spell properly. During these school years he was somewhat an oddity to his schoolfellows, who often teased him for his funny accent. The young Nabulione buried himself in study, and was very good in mathematics and history. He was of a romantic, melancholy and self-willed temperament, somewhat solitary but capable of acquiring a few close friends.

In 1784, aged 15, the adolescent Napoléon moved on to the École Militaire (military academy) in Paris. He must have looked set for a fairly undistinguished career as an obscure officer. The great military genius graduated on October 28, 1785, ranking only 42 in a class of 58, and obtained a commission of Second Lieutenant in the Régiment de la Fère artillery. By then his sense of responsibility was increased by the death of his father in 1785, leaving him, as a much stronger character than his elder brother Joseph, the effective head of the Bonaparte family. Napoléon served on garrison duty in Valence and Auxonne until after the outbreak of the Revolution in 1789, when he took nearly two years of leave in Corsica and Paris, during which he started to engage himself in politics. Whereas the officers of French navy and the line regiments emigrated en masse, particularly after 1791, in a sort of general strike against the Revolution, the artillery officers, better educated and drawn mainly from the minor, poor nobility, were more inclined to stay in their posts.

Like many of his fellow young officers from the lesser nobility, Bonaparte approved of the Revolution in principle, while strongly disliking the increasingly frequent disorder, mob riots, and the populace's "anarchy." He was profoundly influenced by Enlightenment writers like Montesquieu and Rousseau, but also by 17th century authors like Corneille, whose classic heroes were devoted to their duty and destiny. He therefore welcomed the Revolution, not only because of the opportunity it provided for putting Enlightenment principles into practice, but also for the possibilities it opened up for talented and ambitious young men like himself. Yet his enthusiasm was always selective. He cared nothing for the basic principle of popular sovereignty; for him, hierarchy and authority were perfectly acceptable provided they were founded on rational principles. He was by nature and by his military education authoritarian, never a democrat nor a humanitarian. His Revolution was that of the philosophers, not that of the *sans culottes*. From the start the only consistency in his actions stemmed from his own individual view of freedom: maximum personal freedom was to be achieved only by means of maximum personal power.

French was a second language to him, and it is even doubtful whether Bonaparte ever really considered himself a true Frenchman. Corsican society, with its strong emotional ties of family, corruption, clientelism, and fierce vendettas against enemies, was actually closer to the clan relationships of the Scottish Highlands than to the culture of France. His keen sense of clan and his loyalty to family, clients and friends were a result of his Italo-Corsican background. His Italian, Lombard and Genoese origins enabled him to view France with a certain detachment and objectivity, which frequently verged on contempt and cynicism.

Bonaparte was a short man, 1.69 m (5 ft 2 in), just under average height for a Frenchman at the time. He was a dark-haired Mediterranean type and looked unimpressive in civilian clothing. Therefore, some psychologists have suggested that he suffered from a subconscious inferiority complex, which would inevitably have driven him to overcompensate, the result being his spectacular achievements, megalomania and extreme schizotypal behavior.

Napoléon's personality was always complex and many-sided. He was high-strung of temperament, and his mood was often changing. He was capable of being coldly efficient, exudingly charming, genuinely affective and loyal, but also cruel, vindictive, and ruthless. He could be taciturn or talkative, on occasion even eloquent when haranguing his soldiers, whose fighting ardor was often aroused by his inflammatory proclamations. For example, in 1815, just before Waterloo, he declared to his troops: "Soldiers, we have forced marches to make, battles to fight, dangers to encounter, but with constancy the victory will be ours; the rights, the honor of our country will be reconquered. For every Frenchman who has courage the moment has come to conquer or die!"

Napoléon had an extraordinary and impressive intelligence, a prodigious memory, and an indefatigable working capacity. He was indeed a hard-working man with a perfectly ordered mind who could quickly understand complex problems, find adequate solutions and make rapid decisions. A product of the Enlightenment and the Revolution, he was entirely emancipated not only from customary principles and traditional ideas but from moral scruples as well. Openly Napoléon claimed to be a devout Catholic but in private his beliefs were realistic and atheist. In fact he had less admiration for the weak, peaceful and hypothetical Jesus Christ than for the Islamic prophet Mohammed, whose existence was incontestable and who had been a conqueror and a sovereign during his lifetime. Bonaparte was a skilled politician, a brilliant publicist, and, having served a rigorous apprenticeship in the intricacies of Corsican politics and the factional struggles of the French Revolution, a cunning opportunist who picked up the pieces and put them together to his own advantage. He did not like music, but possessed serious scientific and literary interests. These were broad, with a preference for history, law, military science, and public administration. The range of his reading, even when on campaign, was impressive. He was incredibly ambitious, thirsty for power, as well as a tenacious and a remarkable organizer. His manners were coarse and direct, and he often lost his temper. He was megalomaniac, cynical, and stubborn. He had excellent leadership qualities, and an exalted belief in his destiny as a latter-day Prometheus, Hannibal, Caesar, Alexander the Great or Charlemagne. He followed his "star," was full of himself, and was only concerned with his own glory. His complex personality was unique, while his military genius has never been surpassed. He was not significantly troubled when faced with the prospect of war and death for thousands, but at the same time always showed great physical courage: most of the time he commanded at the front, often within enemy weapons' range. Nothing escaped his solicitude, no triviality seemed too humble to receive his attention, he occupied himself with the most minute details, and he wanted everything to bear the imprint of his genius. He institutionalized plunder of conquered territories. Napoleonic soldiers were often pillagers, and French museums still contain artworks stolen by his forces from across Europe. In the end the habit of marching ever forward to victory cost him dearly.

It would be a mistake, however, to think of Napoléon simply as an inhumane intellect, a cold-blooded manipulator and a bloody tyrant. To some extent this aspect of his personality was a mask deliberately assumed in the interest of his political image. By origin and temperament a Latin man from southern Europe, he was capable of warmth, violent passions, lasting comradeship, affection and consideration, vivid imagination, gaiety and keen humor, great charm, and generosity. If enemies and those who challenged him were rarely forgiven and often punished with all the zeal of a Corsican vendetta, yet Napoléon would always show loyalty to old friends, gratitude to companions of his youth, overindulgence to loyal subordinates, and attachment to family members, even to the detriment of his policy. He was a multi-sided, ambivalent and fascinating man, typical of an era of transition, who embodied the 18th century, the Age of Enlightenment and the Revolution, and the 19th century, the Age of Nationalism and the Industrial Revolution. His stature was, however, too great for France, but too small for Europe.

The paradoxes in Bonaparte's character can be indefinitely multiplied, but by 1799, he was, or seemed to be, just what France needed and looked for after the upheaval of the Revolution: a "providential savior" who would guarantee the bourgeois order and at the same time be the continuator of the Revolution.

Napoléon Bonaparte first distinguished himself at Toulon in December 1793. With the support of a fellow Corsican, the revolutionist politician and diplomat Antoine Christophe Saliceti (1757–1809), he was appointed artillery commander of the French forces at the siege. The port had risen in revolt against the republican government and was occupied by British troops. His command of the artillery was skillful and decisive. Napoléon spotted a well-placed hill that allowed French siege guns to dominate the city's harbor and force the British ships to evacuate. The assault on the position, during which Bonaparte was wounded, led to the recapture of the city and his promotion to Brigadier General. These actions also brought him to the attention of Paul Barras (1755–1829), who soon became an important figure of the Revolution.

Following the fall of Robespierre in the Thermidorian Reaction, Napoléon narrowly missed serious troubles (perhaps even the guillotine) because he was dangerously implicated in political quarrels and denounced as a Jacobin associate. Owing again to his fellow Corsican and political patron Saliceti, he was saved and, instead of being put to death, he was imprisoned in the fortress of Antibes in August 1794. Although he was released after only ten days, he remained out of favor, adopted a low profile, and carefully and patiently cultivated contacts with leading politicians.

His next chance to come to public attention was during the Vendémiaire Royalist uprising. This insurrection on October 5, 1795 (Vendémiaire 13 in the Republican calendar), was a battle in the streets of Paris — more particularly in the Rue Saint Honoré— between the French Revolutionary troops and Royalist forces, who threatened to overthrow the Convention. Napoléon Bonaparte, who by chance was available, seemed the logical man to quell the revolt. His troops opened fire on the insurgents, who were rapidly dispersed. The clash was largely responsible for his rapid advancement, earning him overnight fame and the patronage of the Directory. Vendémiaire allowed the ambitious Bonaparte to put his feet firmly on the ladder to power. He was appointed second-in-command to Barras and leader of the Army of the Interior.

By that time, now a personage of importance, Bonaparte passionately fell in love with Barras's former mistress, Joséphine de Beauharnais (born Marie Josèphe Rose de Tascher de la Pagerie, 1763–1814), the young and ravishingly pretty widow of Viscount General Alexandre de Beauharnais. Bonaparte married her on March 9, 1796. Joséphine was not only an extremely pretty woman, she also enabled the rising Bonaparte to have access to the best social and political circles. The honeymoon was brief. All his life Napoléon was a man in a great hurry. No true Frenchman ate such hurried meals or drank watered-down Chambertain. Two days later the bridegroom rapidly left Paris to take command of the French army in Italy, where his resounding victories led to his outstanding and lightning-paced career.

Bonaparte's Italian campaigns of 1796–97 were indeed tremendous. Waging a sort of swift and brutal *Blitzkrieg*, he won a dozen victories in as many months, drove the Austrians from north Italy, became a self-supporting and independent statesman as he himself negotiated the conditions of peace (Treaty of Campo Formio on October 18, 1797), and established a Cisalpine republic, modeled on the French system, in the Po Valley. In fact, Bonaparte made the incurably incompetent, corrupt, irresolute and divided Directory government in Paris dependent on him.

Throughout the five years of the Directoire, Bonaparte, basking in the glory of his victories in Italy and his less fortunate Egyptian adventure, had been scheming and working for self-advancement. The French campaign in Egypt, Palestine and Syria in 1798, however, ended in a failure. Intended to protect French trade interests and undermine Britain's access to India, it started with several important victories, but eventually Napoléon and his army were forced to withdraw owing to disease, local hostility, overwhelming British naval power, and politics in Paris. The campaign received much better publicity at home than it actually deserved.

After his return from Egypt, Bonaparte, in spite of the Egyptian failure, was currently not only a popular officer but also a central political figure whose steadily rising star could no longer be ignored by politicians. By now, in the hard school of revolutionary politics, he had learnt how to judge men, handle situations, and turn events to his advantage. He was a true product of the revolutionary age—a time when the crust of social custom had been broken, and nothing seemed impossible to men with clear minds and strong wills. Bonaparte's early realist romanticism was now overlaid by a colossal egoism and a devouring ambition. Cunningly positioning himself between the Republican Jacobins and the Royalists, General Bonaparte felt the time was ripe to seize power. The idea of maintaining the Republic as a free or constitutional government was given up. Lucien and Napoléon Bonaparte joined the Director Emmanuel Sieyès in preparing a *coup d'état*.

The Consulate

Brumaire

The aim of the conspirators who supported Bonaparte's coup was the achievement of constitutional revision by using as an instrument the prestige and popularity of Bonaparte. The essence of what happened was that the instrument took charge. On November 9–10, 1799 (18–19 Brumaire), under the pretext that a (false and forged) conspiracy was threatening the Republic, the legislative chambers had been transferred to Saint Cloud, a quiet suburb near Paris. Napoléon Bonaparte, in his rank of commander of the troops in the Paris region, was put in charge of the protection of the delegates. In fact, the whole affair was a planned trap, but the plot almost miscarried. The delegates included many staunch Republicans and Jacobins, and when Bonaparte appeared before them an uproar broke out and the Corsican general's outlawry was demanded. Napoléon's brother Lucien, then President of the Council of the Hundreds, easily convinced a company of loyal Bonapartist grenadiers conveniently waiting outside the hall to intervene. The soldiers, who harbored little respect for politicians, rushed into the meeting chamber where several Jacobin deputies were seizing Napoléon Bonaparte by the collar and shaking him violently. Almost fainting, Napoléon was rescued by Murat's soldiers who, with fixed bayonets, firmly but without bloodshed, intimidated and forced the parliamentarians to leave, many of them climbing out of the windows in the confusion. Although vaguely conceived, ill prepared, and poorly executed, the weak and confused Saint Cloud coup had somehow succeeded.

Brumaire 18 marked the actual end of the French Revolutionary Republic. France did not protest. In Paris and all over the country, there was no resistance and very little opposition, because of the Directoire's unpopularity and the overwhelming majority of public opinion in favor of Napoléon. Government bonds rose rapidly on the stock exchange when the news of the coup spread. At Bonaparte's request, a semblance of legality was preserved by inducing a docile rump of deputies to validate the coup. They set up a new executive government, resulting in the Constitution of 22 Frimaire of the Year VIII (December 13, 1799), which was solemnly ratified by a plebiscite overwhelmingly in Napoléon's favor. A new regime was instituted, the Consulate, based on a system prevalent in antiquity. Originally the new regime was considered only a temporary form of emergency government, which was to hold service for ten years. In fact it became a despotic republic led by Bonaparte, which only lasted until 1804.

Bonaparte, aged 31 and in his prime in 1799, appointed himself First Consul, and for the sake of appearances selected two other subordinate Consuls who merely had an advisory role. In ancient Roman fashion, a Senate of sixty men and a Tribunate of 100 members were nominated by Bonaparte; they could discuss legislation but not vote on it. Legislation itself was to be proposed by the Council of State, whose chairman was none other than Bonaparte himself. He quickly removed Sieyès, who as a compensation received the Presidency of the Senate. He imposed a new constitution — the so-called Year VIII Constitution, which vested him with dictatorial power allowing him to appoint and dismiss ministers, and to draft laws, for example. The First Consul rapidly shaped the revolutionary zeal and idealism of France to his own ends. It was the fulfillment of Robespierre's prophecy that the Revolution would be concluded by a Messiah in army boots. The mention *République Française* headed official documents until 1804 and remained on coins until 1808, but the Consulate amounted to a dictatorial monarchy in fact if not in name. From the outset, power rested securely in the hands of the First Consul, who soon showed his determination to reconcile the old and the revolutionary France, and to deliver the goods desired by the mass of the war-weary French people: a victorious peace; public tranquility; internal social stability; and economic prosperity.

Marengo to Amiens

Although Bonaparte attracted much public support in 1799 as a man of peace, the regime depended from the start on military success beyond the borders of France, and on redressing the military situation. The First Consul was willing to make peace, provided France should retain substantial foreign conquests, especially in Italy. When Austria, which had reconquered Italy during his absence in Egypt, rejected Napoléon's offer, he launched the second Italian campaign. With his troops he crossed the Alps, captured Milan, and defeated the Austrians at the Battles of Montebello and Marengo (June 14, 1800), which resulted in an armistice. Napoléon's brother Joseph led the peace negotiations in Luneville. Joseph reported that Austria, emboldened by British backing, would not recognize France's newly gained territory. As negotiations bogged down, Bonaparte ordered General Moreau to strike Austria once more. Moreau led France to victory in Germany, won the Battle of Hohenlinden (December 3, 1800), and pushed the Austrians beyond the Danube. As a result, the Treaty of Luneville was signed in February 1801, by which Austria was forced to recognize French possession of Northern Italy, Belgium, the Netherlands and Luxembourg. The treaty also marked the end of the Second Coalition, as the Czar of Russia withdrew his forces from Western Europe.

A little later, the British signed the Treaty of Amiens in March 1802. Britain was weary of constant warfare, as her economy began to feel the effects of the conflict. The peace between France and Britain was, however, uneasy and short-lived. Each side remained wary of the other. Napoléon had no intention of restraining his expansionist ambitions. Britain and the monarchies of Europe were still reluctant to accept French hegemony, and to recognize a regicidal and dictatorial republic, as they feared the ideas of the revolution might be exported to them.

Napoléon had gained an enormous prestige from the peace, which gave him the opportunity to silence all opposition, and enabled him to increase his power by being proclaimed Consul for life.

France had finally realized her age-long dream of stretching her boundaries to the

Rhine. In her orbit there was now a constellation of sister republics, all of them molded on the same pattern. It was, unhappily, often an uncongenial one, forced upon them by Napoleonic oversimplification coupled with French rationalization.

Reforms

As so often happens when a dictatorship is set up, the first reforms instituted were desperately needed and seemed providential to a war-weary and disillusioned public. The period July 1800–May 1803, when Napoleon was able to give his attention to the internal reorganization of the country, is one of the most important in the whole of French history. For good or ill, the institutions—financial, legal, administrative and ecclesiastical—which were taken over, were to be the framework of 19th century France. The reforms of the Consulate, considered as a whole, were both a continuation of the Revolution and a surreptitious return to the institutions of the Ancien Régime. These important achievements cannot, of course, be ascribed solely to Napoléon. The myth of his omniscience and omnicompetence has been a gross exaggeration; in fact, the reforms were a collective work with numerous and talented collaborators.

The religious policy of the Revolution had turned out to be a conspicuous failure, and had led to civil war in Vendée. Napoléon shared the Voltairian skepticism of his contemporaries, educated in the anticlericalism of the Enlightenment, but he realized the importance of religion as a means to increase obedience and his control over the French people. Of an acute but cynical realism, he therefore sought to reconcile the mostly Catholic population to his regime by negotiating, after protracted bargaining, the Concordat of July 1801 with Pope Pius VII (Count Barnaba Niccolo Chiaramonti, born in 1740, pope from 1800 to his death in 1823). The Concordat, which regulated public worship in France, and the relations between the French state and the papacy, was a dramatic gesture of reconciliation and appeasement, which satisfied the French clergy and gained Napoléon a large popular support. Protestant and Jewish worship was tolerated and protected by the state. Friendly relations with the Pope were, however, not to last long.

The First Consul damped down political conflict and dissent not merely by repression, but by drawing into the service of the state men of talent from all factions and parties. Further national reconciliation was boosted by negotiations with rebels and pardon for the Royalists, a number of political amnesties allowing the return of many *émigrés* (at least those willing to serve the new regime), the returning of confiscated estates that had not yet been sold, and the granting of top functions, jobs and honors to former revolutionaries of all factions. He also pacified with harsh methods the last sparks of the royalist Chouans' armed uprising in Vendée. By using the stick and the carrot, the First Consul for life succeeded in isolating both the radical Republicans and the radical Royalists, who became insignificant minorities.

Bonaparte, in order to complete the work begun during the Revolution, instituted fundamental administrative and monetary reforms. This huge, long-lasting and important work included an increased centralized administration of the *départements*; higher education (notably the creation of *Lycées*, or militarized grammar schools) and the Imperial University, a kind of centralized Ministry of Education; control over expenditure; a tax code in the interest of property owners; national and regional roads and urban sewer systems; the stabilization of the currency (the *Franc Germinal* from April 1803, which held its value until

1914); the creation of the *Banque de France*, the country's central bank, which had the right to issue bank notes; and a set of civil unifying laws, the Code Civil, now known as the Napoleonic code, which is important to this day in many lands in Europe, Latin America and the U.S.A. The Code Civil, based on principles of reason rather than on the customary prejudices and special interests of the past, acknowledged the gains of the Revolution, such as equality of all before the law, the rights and duties of individuals, liberties, property, interpersonal and intra-family relations, for example. *Liberté* and *Egalité* were, however, only for the white people: slavery, which had been abolished by the Revolution in the French overseas colonies, was re-established. The Code Civil was prepared by committees of legal experts under the supervision of Jean Jacques Régis de Cambacérès (1753–1824), who held the hollow office of Second Consul from 1799 to 1804. Eventually, in 1808, a Code of Criminal Instruction was published, which enacted rules of due process.

The First Consul also created in May 1802 a distinction, the prestigious *Légion d'Honneur*, divided into five ranks: *Chevalier* (Knight), *Officier* (Officer), *Commandeur* (Commander), *Grand Officier* (Grand Officer) and *Grand-Croix* (Grand Cross). The prestigious honorific distinction was intended to bring together the socially meritous elites, including soldiers, administrators, scientists, artists, and all professional men whose talent was recognized and rewarded, but also safely placed under government control. According to some sources Napoléon declared about it: "We call these children's toys, I know, it's been said already. Well, I replied that it's with such toys that one leads men." The *Légion d'Honneur* still exists today, and continues to be a prestigious symbol of talent, courage and dedication to the nation. Its motto is *Honneur et Patrie* (Honor and Fatherland), and its seat is the *Palais de la Légion d'Honneur* (also known as Hotel de Salm) in Paris.

In 1803 Bonaparte recognized that French possessions on the mainland of North America would be indefensible and sold them to the United States. The so-called *Vente de la Louisiane* (Louisiana Purchase) encompassed portions of 15 current U.S. states and 2 Canadian provinces: all of present-day Arkansas, Missouri, Iowa, Oklahoma, Kansas, Nebraska, parts of Minnesota that were south of the Mississippi River, most of North Dakota, nearly all of South Dakota, northeastern New Mexico, northern Texas, the portions of Montana, Wyoming, and Colorado east of the Continental Divide, and Louisiana west of the Mississippi River, including the city of New Orleans. In addition, the Purchase contained portions of territories that would eventually become part of the Canadian provinces of Alberta and Saskatchewan. The land included in the purchase comprised a territory of 2,147,000 square km (828,800 square miles), around 23 percent of the territory of the present-day United States. The total cost was about $15,000,000. Napoléon Bonaparte, upon completion of the purchase, stated: "This cession of territory affirms forever the power of the United States, and I have given England a maritime rival who sooner or later will humble her pride."

The Napoleonic Empire

THE CORONATION OF THE EMPEROR

By 1802, the dictatorship of the Consul for life was permanently and firmly established. War started again with Britain, which could not accept the overwhelming French predominance on the continent. The Royalists showed signs of restlessness within the country, and one of them, the Chouan Georges Cadoudal, came to Paris to attempt to assassinate the Consul. He was arrested and guillotined. In January 1804, Bonaparte's police uncovered another assassination plot against him, ostensibly sponsored by the former royal rulers of France, the Bourbons. The unfortunate immediate effect of the failed plot was to give the Consul Bonaparte an excuse for harsh measures of reprisals and repression. In retaliation, Bonaparte ordered the arrest of Louis-Antoine-Henri de Bourbon-Condé (1772–1804), the Duke of Enghien, a young *émigré* Bourbon prince who sojourned in Germany. In violation of Bavarian neutral sovereignty, the Duke was kidnapped and brought back to France by French secret agents. After a mock *in camera* trial, without a scrap of solid evidence being found, the Duke of Enghien was condemned and executed by firing squad in March 1804. This affair was above all a political act, and a clear message: Bonaparte showed that he would never accept and allow the return of the Capetian Bourbon dynasty.

His dictatorship required a stable foundation and an assurance of law and order. A new hereditary monarchy in France, with him as hereditary Emperor, seemed to be the best solution. Napoléon then believed a Bourbon restoration would be impossible once the Bonapartist succession was entrenched in the constitution. Hereby Napoléon not only greatly consolidated his own power, he also reassured all those who had benefited from the Revolution: the regicide politicians, the bourgeoisie, the rich landowners, the buyers of *Biens Nationaux* (properties confiscated from *émigrés* and from the Church sold to wealthy individuals) — in short, all those who had put him into power, and who did not feel safe so long as the survival of the regime depended solely on Napoléon's life. Should he be assassinated or killed in battle, for example, they were threatened with a return to Jacobin radical republicanism or a royal Bourbon restoration.

The Consul for life was proclaimed Emperor of the French by the Grace of God and the Constitutions of the Republic by the docile Senate, under the name Napoléon I. The sumptuous coronation, immortalized by a huge painting by David, took place in great pomp on December 2, 1804, at Notre Dame Cathedral in Paris. Pope Pius VII had agreed to attend and bless the ceremony in an attempt to confer upon the newborn Empire the recognition which would put it in the ranks of the ancient monarchies by divine right, but it was Napoléon himself who placed the crown on his own head before crowning his wife Joséphine. Eventually, at Milan Cathedral on May 26, 1805, Napoléon was crowned King of Italy with the Iron Crown of Lombardy. The establishment of an authoritarian hereditary Empire meant the revival of some disconcerting features of the *Ancien Régime*. The French people ceased to be *citoyens* (citizens) and returned to the status of *sujets* (subjects), for example.

The constructive period of the Consulate was over, to be followed by the somber, sterile and tragic magnificence of the Empire.

From Boulogne to Tilsit

The Consulate and the newly proclaimed Empire rested on a strong army inherited from the Revolution. The new Emperor needed victories over the European coalitions, and this dragged France into a never-ending spiral of bloody wars.

In 1805 Britain convinced Austria and Russia to join a Third Coalition against France. Napoléon now considered a landing in England. A fleet and a large army were gathered in Boulogne, ready to cross the Channel. But because Austria and Russia had prepared an invasion of France, Napoléon had to change his plans and turn his attention to the continent. The newly formed *Grande Armée* marched to Germany in a turning movement. Napoléon's army defeated the Austrian forces at Ulm on October 20, 1805. The next day, however, the French fleet was defeated at the naval Battle of Trafalgar near the Strait of Gibraltar, a terrible setback which left England's Royal Navy in control of the seas, thereby rendering the conquest of England not feasible.

While the French were being humbled at sea, they were triumphant on land. Napoléon continued to advance towards Austria, entered Vienna, and defeated Austria and Russia at the Battle of Austerlitz on December 2, 1805, the first anniversary of his coronation. The Battle of the Three Emperors, as it became known, was a strategic and tactical masterpiece; it had unfolded precisely as Napoléon had foreseen. The victory was received ecstatically in France and inflated Napoléon's popularity at home. It brought an end to the Third Coalition and forced Austria to make peace. The brilliant ice-cold winter sun of Austerlitz became for a time the symbol of Napoléon's bright fortune. The following Treaty of Pressburg abolished the German Empire and led to the creation of the German Confederation of the Rhine with Napoléon named as its Protector.

It did not take long for French pillage and exactions to create an embryonic German nationalism that led Prussia to enter the war (Fourth Coalition). The French victories at Jena and Auerstadt (October 14, 1806) enabled Napoléon to enter Berlin and put Prussia out of commission. After the difficult and inconclusive butchery of Eylau, fought in a snowstorm against the Russians (February 8, 1807), and the decisive Battle of Friedland (June 14, 1807), the Czar agreed to negotiate. Napoléon and Alexander I of Russia met in Tilsit on a pavilioned raft in the middle of the Niemen River in July 1807. The Treaty of Tilsit, which appeared to set a seal on the Napoleonic Empire of the West, divided the European continent between the two powers. Napoléon, now at the zenith of his career, placed puppet rulers on the thrones of the German states, including his brother Jerome as king of the new Kingdom of Westphalia. In the French-controlled part of Poland, he established the Duchy of Warsaw.

Napoléon felt himself carried along by his successes and he wanted to dominate Europe. However, English hostility never faltered, and the British refused to accept the French domination. With his Berlin (1806) and Milan (1807) decrees, Napoléon attempted to enforce a Europe-wide commercial boycott of Britain called the Continental System. This act of economic warfare was intended to force Britain to its knees and make her sign a sustainable peace by starving the British people and ruining English trade and industry. The System was also a permanent protectionist policy designed to divert the axis of European trade from Britain to France. The blockade, an instrument of French economic domination of European markets, exerted considerable pressure on England in 1807 and 1808, but it could only be decisive if it were applied thoroughly and over a long period. In fact the embargo did not succeed in the end. Napoléon had seriously underestimated the resilience of both Britain's economy and her political system. The boycott only encouraged British merchants to smuggle goods into continental Europe and Napoléon's exclusively land-based customs enforcers could not stop them. The blockade required coastal surveillance and a struggle against smuggling, which proved impossible but led to new conquests in Spain and in the Roman Papal States. The Continental System, which failed to bring Britain to her knees, was more or less abandoned in 1813.

Corvette

The 18th century and the Napoleonic era marked the great time of the sailing warship. The ship-of-the-line, with its classical simplicity, net elegance, and powerful armament, represented a limit in human achievement. It was both the peak and end of centuries of development. The Battle of Trafalgar, fought off Cadiz in Spain, saw the British decisively defeat a combined French and Spanish fleet on 21 October 1805 in the most decisive and important naval battle of the Napoleonic Wars. Following the battle, the Royal Navy was never again seriously challenged by the French fleet in a large-scale sea engagement. Napoléon had already abandoned his plans of invasion of Britain before the battle and they were never revived. The illustration shows the French corvette *Aurore*, built in 1767. The light and fast, one-decked, three-mast corvette (the British sloop) was a class of warship under the frigate serving for patrolling, reconnaissance, and attacking, as well as escorting and protecting commerce and cargo vessels. It carried 18 to 20 guns, and was operated by a relatively small crew.

The Arc de Triomphe at Étoile Square

The Arc de Triomphe, the most prestigious symbol of Napoléon's grandeur, stands in the center of the Place Charles de Gaulle, also known as the Place de l'Étoile in Paris, at the western end of the Champs-Élysées. It was designed in 1806 by architect Jean Chalgrin, to commemorate the victory of Austerlitz (December 2, 1805) and Napoléon's Grande Armée. Completed only in 1836, the gigantic and impressive monument, inspired by ancient art (the Roman Arch of Titus), is 50 m (162 ft) in height, 45 m (148 ft) in width and 22 m (72 ft) in depth, and is decorated by numerous statues and sculptures by Rude, Etex and Cortot.

The Spanish Adventure

Portugal refused to subscribe to the Continental System, remaining loyal to the long-standing alliance with Britain. Accordingly, in 1807, Napoléon decided to invade it. Under the pretext of a reinforcement of the Franco–Spanish army occupying Portugal, Napoléon invaded Spain as well, replaced King Charles IV with his own brother Joseph, and placed

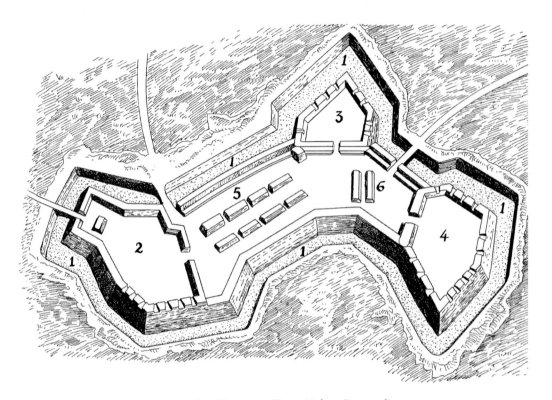

Fort San Vicente at Torres Vedras (Portugal)
Worthy of mention among the fortifications of the Napoleonic Era are the lines of Torres Vedras built by Wellington's army in the period 1809–1811. Designed by Colonel Fletcher and constructed under the leadership of Captain John T. Jones, the lines were composed of many field works, forts and redoubts made of earth, sited with care to take full advantage of the hilly landscape in order to guard the passes leading to the capital of Portugal, Lisbon, which lay some 20 km to the rear. There were two major lines stretching across the province of Estramadura from the Atlantic coast to the Tagus River: the northern position followed a line on the hills dominating the cities of Cortada, Torres Vedras, Sobral, Aruda and Alhandra; the southern line went along St. Lorenza, Mafra, Cabeça de Montachique, Bucellas and Alverca. Each had a length of about 25 km (9.5 miles); they were armed with 232 field guns and manned by 17,500 soldiers, both British and Portuguese. In fact they were not lines in the continuous sense but a series of detached fortified points joined by natural obstacles. In addition, British gunboats were deployed on the Tagus to prevent any outflanking move up the river. From these entrenched positions, Wellington turned withdrawal into victory. Indeed, Masséna, with over 100,000 men, forbore to attack them, knowing full well that the line was too formidable an obstacle even for him to overcome. The depicted Fort San Vicente, one of the largest works in the Lines of Torres Vedras, had a total garrison of 1,720 men. 1: Ditch; 2: Fort 20 (armed with eight guns); 3: Fort 21 (nine guns); 4: Fort 22 (nine guns); 5: Bombproof traverse protecting against enemy shelling; 6: Magazines

his brother-in-law Joachim Murat in Joseph's stead at Naples. Napoléon possessed only a superficial knowledge of the Iberian Peninsula. Although there existed modernizers who embraced French ideas and schemes of reform, the majority of the Spanish people remained loyal to their former monarch. This led to spontaneous and fierce resistance from the Spanish army and civilians in the *Dos de Mayo* uprising (May 2, 1808), followed by terrible French reprisals led by Murat and immortalized by Goya's painting. The Spaniards' resistance led to the capitulation of General Dupont in Baylen, ending for the first time a myth: the invincibility of Napoléon's armies.

The English took advantage of this new front to land troops in Portugal under the leadership of Arthur Wellesley, the future Lord Wellington (1769–1852). The French army found itself confronting an enemy as implacable as it was elusive, inflamed with fanatical patriotism and religious ardor, fighting its own war of liberation which it also looked upon as a anti–French crusade. The organizers of popular resistance were the lower clergy

Redoubts at Torres Vedras
The redoubts, posts, fortlets, batteries, artificial embankments and infantry emplacements in the Lines of Torres Vedras varied in size and shape according to their position of importance and the ground upon which they were sited. They displayed a remarkable adaptability on the part of the British engineers, and clearly showed that the French did not have a monopoly on the subject of good fortification. The British defenses of Lisbon exploded the myth of French invincibility, and also demonstrated that in certain circumstances defense, after decades of reverse, could once more prove successful. They illustrated the value of the irregular arrangement of fortifications closely suited to ground conditions. They announced the later concept of creating a belt of forts supported by a field army to oppose to an enemy offensive. They were an embryonic system of barrier-fortresses, a theory that was to find its fullest expression in the 19th century forts.

and the monks, enraged by the prospect of the secularization of church property. Following a French retreat from much of the country, Napoléon himself took command and defeated the Spanish army, recaptured Madrid and then outmaneuvered a British army sent to support the Spanish, driving it to the coast. Before the Spanish population had been fully subdued, Austria again threatened war and Napoléon returned to France.

Meanwhile, to improve the continental blockade, and counting on the weakness of the Pope, Napoléon ordered the invasion of the Papal States because of the Church's refusal to support the Continental System. Pope Pius VII excommunicated him but was arrested and imprisoned. The Holy Father remained confined for five years, and did not return to Rome until May 1814. This conflict led many French and European Catholics to turn their backs on the French imperial regime.

The costly and extremely brutal Peninsular War in Spain continued, taking the form of a terribly costly guerilla campaign. The whole affair was a grave mistake, a crippling move that eroded French morale and prestige, and, in Napoléon's own words, an ulcer that drained the lifeblood from the French army. Napoléon was obliged to leave 300,000 of his finest troops to contain Spanish guerrillas as well as British and Portuguese forces commanded by Wellington. The rising of the Spanish people was hailed in Europe as the turn of the tide and the first example of national resistance to Napoleonic domination. French control over the Iberian Peninsula deteriorated and collapsed in 1813. The war went on through allied victories and concluded after Napoléon's abdication in 1814.

WAR OF THE FIFTH COALITION

Four years had passed since the sun had risen on Austerlitz, and from victory to victory, condemned forever to the pursuit of his own glory, Napoléon continued to chase after an elusive peace. In

Spanish guerillero
The guerillas' elusive hit-and-run fighting methods and fanatical behavior rendered life and operations most difficult for French occupying troops. Guerilleros fought a war "to the death," and neither gave, asked nor expected quarter. The depicted Spanish raider wears a regional civilian dress including sunhat, shirt, short sleeveless vest, trousers and espadrilles (rope-soled sandals). He is armed with an escopeta (carbine) and carries a ventral cartridge pouch.

April 1809, Austria, who had made herself the champion of the German people, took advantage of France's difficulties in Spain to take up arms again. They abruptly broke the alliance with France, and Napoléon assumed command of forces on the Danube and German fronts. The Emperor defeated the Austrians once more at the battle of Wagram (July 6, 1809), and forced them to submission by the Treaty of Schönbrunn.

By that time, Joséphine had not yet produced an heir, an impossibility due to the stresses of her imprisonment during Robespierre's Terror, or because she may have had an abortion in her twenties. Napoléon was obsessed with creating a legitimate and permanent dynasty. Despite their repeated and numerous infidelities, Napoleon and Josephine had a profound and passionate relationship, but reason of state was stronger than true love. Napoléon ultimately decided to sacrifice and divorce her so he could remarry in search of an heir. Napoléon tried to marry the Grand Duchess Anna of the House of Romanov, younger sister of Tsar Alexander I of Russia, but his proposal was refused. The alternative bride on the list was the 18-year-old Maria Luisa von Österreich (known in French as Marie Louise), Archduchess of Austria and Duchess of Parma (1791–1847), the Austrian Emperor Francis II's daughter. After a marriage by proxy, the subsequent wedding took place at Paris on April 1, 1810, in one of the greatest and most solemn ceremonies staged by the Empire. The bride's father intended the marriage to strengthen links between the Austrian Empire and the French Empire. As for Napoléon, he sought the validation and legitimation of his Empire by marrying a member of the House of Habsburg, one of the oldest and most prestigious ruling families of Europe. And most importantly, he hoped to cement his position by fathering a legitimate heir.

There was a feeling of superstitious unease in France, however, over the importing of an Austrian princess. The last one, Queen Marie Antoinette, married to Louis XVI, had been decidedly unlucky for France, and the brand-new Empress was a double grandniece of Marie Antoinette. Many staunch Republicans found the marriage repugnant. Napoléon's divorce strained the Emperor's relations with the Church, and thirteen cardinals were imprisoned for non-attendance at the marriage ceremony.

Napoléon's greatest love was Marie Walewska, whom he met at Warsaw in 1807. She bore him a son, Count Walewska, and she was one of the few who consoled him in exile at Elba. Napoléon and Marie Louise remained married until his death, though she did not join him in exile. The couple had one child named Napoléon Francis Joseph Charles (1811–1832), known from birth as the King of Rome. Hereby the future of the Bonaparte dynasty seemed assured and Napoléon's satisfaction was immense. The King of Rome later became Napoléon II, or *l'Aiglon* (Eaglet), although he never reigned. After his father's fall, he was educated in Austria, was awarded the title of Duke of Reichstadt in 1818, and died of tuberculosis in 1832, aged 21, with no children.

Napoléon's Apogee

By 1809–1811, the Napoleonic Empire had reached the zenith of its territorial and political expansion. It stretched from the Tagus to the Niemen, from the Baltic to the Adriatic Sea. The family-minded Corsican Napoléon, now at the peak of his power, had given Europe a new face and showered wealth and position on his brothers, sisters and close friends, despite their grumblings, constant intrigues, incompetence, sulkings and indiscretions. The Kingdom of Holland had been entrusted to his brother Louis, as Spain had been to Joseph. The Kingdom of Westphalia had been created and attributed to yet another brother, Jérome. Napoléon himself was king of Italy, including Milan and Venice, with his stepson, Eugène de Beauharnais, appointed viceroy. In Naples, Joseph had been replaced by Joachim Murat, the husband of his sister Caroline Bonaparte. Another sister, Elisa, was made Queen of Etruria (Tuscany), but sister Pauline only received 1,490,000 francs and the castle of Neuilly.

Poland enjoyed a revival, having been turned into a French-controlled hereditary Grand Duchy headed by Marshal Lefèbvre, an old friend and veteran of plebeian origin married to a former washerwoman. The old Holy Roman Empire, created in A.D. 962 by Otto I the Great, had been abolished and replaced by the Confederation of the Rhine, with states, duchies, bishoprics, principalities and small kingdoms "protected" and controlled by France. Napoléon's policy was a continuation of the policy of Richelieu and Louis XIV: to keep the Germans divided by encouraging the particularism of the client kingdoms and principalities in the Confederation. The satellite states were primarily intended to serve the interests of France, namely to provide the Empire with troops, supplies, and above all money, by means of taxes and forced requisitions. Napoleonic rule was, however, fragile, as it rested on military force. There was no way that the European peoples would have accepted French hegemony of their own free will. Once Napoléon was beaten in Russia, then French rule was rapidly shuffled off.

The *parvenu*, self-made Napoléon tried to give his dictatorship the trappings of a real monarchy, by creating imperial nobility, setting up his own court where etiquette was rigid and boring, and instituting high-ranking positions such as Imperial Field Marshal, Arch Chancellor, Grand Chamberlain, Arch Treasurer, and other sonorous and empty titles. The megalomaniac Emperor turned state occasions into instruments of propaganda, great public shows and sumptuous trappings of royalty. The image he wanted to project was an inspiring and impressive one, compounded of grandeur, patriotism, honor, and glory. He used every available means of propaganda: press, art, war bulletins, pageantry of nobility, and artful creation of his own legend. Despite the displayed splendor of the Imperial court, after 1804, Napoléon himself led a rather abstemious life in private, eating and dressing simply. Private reality differed greatly from the romantic, heroic, and superhuman portraits of him presented to the public by artists like David, Ingres and Gros.

Napoléon drew support from dignitaries and notables from the middle and upper classes — all those who had risen to social rank owing to the Revolution or thanks to their commercial or financial talents. The never-ending war brought changes to the imperial regime, which became even more despotic. Napoléon ruled by senatus-consult or by decree. Civil liberties were restricted and the press put under surveillance of Fouché, whose police played an increasingly important role. Arbitrary detention was reintroduced, censorship reappeared, and even art, theatre and literature were monitored for "the defense of the country and the throne."

The Emperor was also careful to woo the masses, and for a long time succeeded in retaining their enthusiasm and loyalty. Whether or not people were happy under Napoléon is an open question, but in spite of censorship that became increasingly petty and intrusive, of the police that became gradually brutal and arbitrary, and of the heavy burden of the wars, hardly anyone, except the die-hards, regretted the *Ancien Régime* wiped out by the Revolution and from whose ruins had sprung the new Napoleonic rule. Once order had been established, the common people were able to enjoy the fruits of the imperial regime. The increase in the consumption of wine and meat was a clear indication of the improved standard of living. Most tenant farmers and laborers were able to live off the land, the cost of living was rather low, grain harvests were abundant until 1810, and cattle breeding was enjoying a period of steady growth and improvement. The imperial administration worked to introduce new crops (e.g., sugar beet, chicory and potatoes), facilitated industrial innovations, spurred the development of metal industry, gave impetus to textile production (e.g., the loom in the silk industry), and improved networks of communication. The creation through Napoleonic conquests and territorial annexations of a large market for goods encouraged inland trade, facilitated industrial development, and spurred the manufacture of new products. In spite of the Continental blockade and the permanent state of war, the imperial age was a period of economic growth. Fairs, exhibitions and generous state subsidies helped all forms of industry. Napoléon, a great believer in centralized control, was deeply interested in every phase of the nation's growth, and

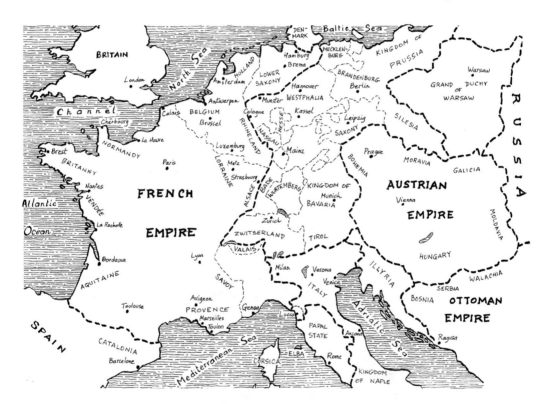

Napoleonic Western Europe 1811
The map shows the maximum expansion of the French Empire in 1811 including the Low Countries, Luxemburg, northern Germany and the Italian Piedmont. Italy itself was divided into four main parts (Italy, Naples, Sardinia and the Papal States). The Venetian Empire had been conquered and France occupied both Venice and its possessions on the Adriatic coasts. The German states formed a conglomerate of vassals known as the Confederation of the Rhine. The Grand Duchy of Warsaw (Poland) was a satellite. Switzerland, although neutral, had to yield the canton of Valais to France. Denmark, Sweden and Norway were made harmless by French diplomacy. By that time Prussia and the Austro-Hungarian Empire had been neutralized.

kept himself informed of every new development. He distributed prizes right and left, encouraged, ordered, visited, criticized. The Emperor's popularity remained intact, or almost so, among the common people, who were not prepared to renounce glory even though they paid for it so dearly.

All this, of course, had a price and required a great deal of money. The *Cour des Comptes* (Court of Account) kept a watchful eye on the spending of public funds while the newly created Bank of France stabilized the currency. The greatest expenses incurred were obviously for wars. These were met in part by what today would be called "reparations," in fact plunder, which became a key aspect of government policy as long as the French armies were victorious. Plunder helped finance war, fed and paid troops, and also assisted the regime to become more firmly established. The demands of war obviously increased the scale of the iron and steel industries, but a widespread industrial revolution and take-off into sustained growth on the British model had to wait until the reign of Napoléon's nephew after 1851. In the long run it was the wars that ruined the Empire.

The Army

The army was the pillar of the regime. The key to the success of Napoléon's *Grande Armée* was his organizational innovation of making army corps under his command self-sufficient armies. On average, they numbered 20,000 to 30,000 men, usually commanded by a marshal or senior general, and were capable of fighting independently. Each was composed of two or more infantry divisions of about 12,000 men, a brigade of cavalry (about 2,500 men), and six to eight companies of artillery (each about 100 to 120 men). In addition, each corps had a company of engineers, plus a headquarters staff, medical and service units, and supply train for baggage and ammunition. Napoléon commanded that each army corps never be more than a day's march, about 20 miles, away from any other so they could support each other on the battlefield. The elite of the army was the Imperial Guard, another of Napoléon's creations — a body of handpicked, seasoned troops, a kind of personal army at the heart of the imperial forces.

The never-ending Napoleonic wars had an impact on many French homes. Military service was mandatory for all able-bodied Frenchmen between the ages of 20 to 25, but rich people could be exempted by paying for a replacement. A reasonable estimate of the number of Frenchmen conscripted between 1800 and 1814 would be about two million out of a population of 28 million. Judged by the standards of 20th-century wars, this was not an excessive proportion. In theory soldiers were eligible for discharge after five years, but after 1804, most discharges were only for serious medical reasons. The veterans were responsible for training new recruits, thereby combining experience and young talent. Promotion was always based on personal merit and valor in combat. Over time, needs changed these basic rules.

The weight of the Napoleonic wars was also a burden on allied and dependent European countries, which were required to supply military contingents. At times Napoléon's army included soldiers from Italy, Denmark, Poland, Belgium and the Netherlands. In 1804, Switzerland provided 16,000 soldiers. The states of the German Confederation were heavily drawn on for contributions. In 1805 Bavaria provided 30,000 men, Cleve-Berg 5,000 in 1806, Westphalia 25,000 in 1807, Saxony 20,000 in 1812. The Grand Elector of Württemberg, having been a loyal ally of France during the war of 1805, was rewarded by the title of king, but the new realm was obliged to supply a contingent of 12,000 soldiers in 1806. Other smaller states, like Waldeck, Anhalt, Hessen-Darmstadt, Mecklemburg, Lippe, Nassau, Baden and Prussia, had to provide contingents too. When Napoléon decided to invade Russia in 1812, his *Grande Armée* included soldiers of twenty different European nations. These foreign troops, raised from regular national draftees or volunteers, did not always remain loyal, though. Napoleonic armies also included some foreign mercenary units, notably Irish exiles, deserters and mercenaries ("Wild Geese"). In August 1803 an Irish battalion was formed, growing to regiment size in 1809; it was known as the "Third Foreign Regiment" in 1811, and was disbanded in 1815.

As supplies were frequently lacking, the Napoleonic soldier was often a villainous looter, a pitiless brigand

Infantryman
An infantry soldier's life revolved around his section, consisting of six to twelve men, with whom he would eat, sleep, march and fight during battle. Each soldier was armed with a model 1777 smoothbore 0.69 caliber flintlock musket. A cartridge containing a ball weighing 4/5 of an ounce and gunpowder was rammed down into the muzzle of the weapon. A well-trained soldier could fire up to three shots a minute and could hit a target at a hundred yards. Small units, such as a battalion (840 men) or demi-brigade, could fight independently or as part of a larger force as necessary. A battalion was generally composed of four companies of fusiliers (light, fast-moving infantry), one company of grenadiers (shock troops selected of the tallest, bravest men) and one company of voltigeurs or tirailleurs (skirmishers) that would precede the battalion in attack.

forced to live off the countries he passed through, friend or foe. Yet a military career remained an enviable possibility and high-ranking officers, generals and marshals could build up huge fortunes. Eighteen marshals of France were created in 1804 as Grand Officers of the Empire, receiving army command but also large fiefs and revenues. Napoléon believed, a bit simple-mindedly, that devotion could be bought with money and honors. Besides the large emoluments that went with certain offices, there were also considerable fringe benefits. Marshal Berthier, for example, was the happy recipient of an annual sum of 1,300,000 francs. The Empire believed devoutly in the glories of military life and in

Imperial Guard
Left: The Imperial Guard was the elite fighting force of Napoléon's armies, made up of tall, brave, and experienced troops. Guards needed to have been soldiers for 10 years, have served in at least two campaigns and be of good character. The Imperial Guard was formed from the Consular Guard in 1804 with one regiment of grenadiers (two battalions of eight companies each) and a similar formation of Chasseurs à Pied. It also included two companies (16 guns) of artillery and two of train troops. The bond with the Emperor was strengthened by special uniforms, excellent equipment, and better pay than regular troops. The Imperial Guard, originally intended to be a small unit of personal bodyguards, was continuously expanded. In 1800 it counted 3,000 men, and 26,000 in 1814. They became Napoléon's last-resort weapon and were gradually committed in battle.

romantic if hazardous feats of arms, so Napoléon exploited to the utmost his soldiers' burning desire to distinguish themselves on the battlefield. He developed to a fine art the cult of personality, and most French soldiers of the ranks worshipped the Emperor. His familiar manner, simple uniform (grey frock, typical bicorne or uniform of a colonel of the guard), and demagogic bonhomie aroused great enthusiasm. Old hands, young ones, and *grognards* (grumblers) of the Imperial Guard had an almost fanatic reverence and admiration

Cavalryman
Right: Napoléon's cavalry was divided into heavy and light units. The heavy units, cuirassiers and carabiniers à cheval, consisted of brawny men on massive horses. They wore metal breast and back armor and metal helmets, both useful for fending off blows as they attacked lines of enemy infantry. Each man carried a pistol and a straight, heavy saber used for thrusting.
The light cavalrymen, used mostly for flanking maneuvers, reconnaissance and pursuit, wore no armor, and were armed with curved swords for slashing. Other units of light horsemen included dragoons, hussars, and chasseurs à cheval. A cavalry regiment usually consisted of 1,200 to 1,800 men and horses. The depicted man is a Corporal of the Grenadiers on Horse of the Imperial Guard.

for the *Petit Caporal* (Little Corporal), as they affectionately nicknamed Napoléon. Many soldiers, rejoicing and basking in the reflected glory of the Emperor, never complained about their efforts and sacrifices, since fame, honors and booty were their rewards. New recruits and veterans, at least those who returned home safe and sound between campaigns, could show off their glittering medals and handsome uniforms. War was inconvenient but for some men it was also glamorous. The deep attachment that existed between Napoléon and his soldiers was not a gratuitous invention, nor a posthumous legend; it was a reality, which continued as long as his victories lasted and in many cases lived on after his fall, exile and death.

In the field of military organization, as we shall further see in Chapter 3, Napoléon largely borrowed from previous theorists and the reforms of preceding French governments, and only developed much of what was already in place. He continued, for example, the Revolution's policy of promotion based primarily on merit. Artillery was integrated into reserve batteries, the staff system became more fluid, and cavalry once again became an important formation in French military doctrine. Uniforms, although flamboyant and colorful for parade, were often ill-fitting, uncomfortable, inappropriate and inadequate for men in the field. Boots rarely lasted more than a few weeks. Weapons and technology remained largely static through the Revolutionary and Napoleonic eras, but operational mobility underwent massive restructuring. Napoléon's biggest influence was in the conduct of warfare on the move, and was regarded by the influential military theorist Carl von Clausewitz as a genius in the operational art of war. A new emphasis towards the destruction, not just outmaneuvering, of enemy armies emerged. Since armies could not live off the land indefinitely, Napoleon always sought a quick end to any conflict by a decisive pitched battle. Invasions of enemy territory occurred over broader fronts, which made wars costlier and more decisive—a phenomenon that came to be known as Napoleonic Warfare.

THE CAMPAIGN OF RUSSIA

By 1811 the bright sunlight of Austerlitz was beginning to fade. Tensions were building up between France and Russia, as both countries remained rivals on the continent. Both Napoléon and Alexander were megalomaniacs, both possessed distinct and antagonist ambitions, each saw himself as the greatest man on Earth, under the protection of a special "destiny." In order to perpetuate a Napoleonic Europe, it was essential to reduce Russia's power, and the entente agreed at Tilsit and Erfurt in 1808 was only a temporary truce concluded to win time and consolidate positions. Czar Alexander was under strong pressure from the Russian nobility and military staff to break off the alliance. The first clear sign the alliance was deteriorating was the relaxation of the Continental System in Russia, which angered the French Emperor. By 1812, advisers to Alexander suggested the possibility of the recapture of Poland and an invasion of the French Empire. For this purpose, Russia deployed large numbers of troops on the Polish borders. On receipt of intelligence reports on Russia's war preparations, Napoléon expanded his *Grande Armée*, and ignoring repeated advice against an invasion of the vast Russian heartland, prepared for an offensive campaign. Despite the Spanish drain on the French army, Napoléon managed to concentrate some 600,000 soldiers by calling on the vassal and allied states.

On June 23, 1812, the invasion of Russia was launched. It was a considerably dangerous gamble, which turned out to a major blunder and a determining factor in the fall of Napoléon, as it had not occurred to him that in addition to the Russian army, the French force would have to fight the Russian people and the Russian climate and immensity. In an attempt to gain increased support from Polish nationalists and patriots, Napoléon termed the operation the "Second Polish War"—the first Polish war was the Bar Confederation uprising by Polish nobles against Russia. Napoléon's objective was a decisive engagement, but the Russians had by now learned valuable lessons about Napoleonic warfare. Instead of fighting a pitched battle, they retreated ever deeper into Russia, implementing a scorched-earth policy, leaving little or nothing behind them for the invaders to live on. In the vast empty Russian spaces in the pre-railway age, the lumbering French army soon outstripped its supply trains. It was not long before the route into Russia became a *via dolorosa*. Pillaging, indiscipline and desertion soon became rife on an unprecedented scale, while diseases, exhaustion, exposure, hunger and constant harassments by partisans and Cossacks inflicted the first casualties.

A brief attempt at resistance was made at Smolensk in the middle of August. The Russians were eventually defeated in a series of battles (notably at Borodino outside Moscow on September 7, 1812), but this was less of a defeat and more of a stalemate, for the Russian army withdrew in good order and retreated past Moscow. Napoléon resumed his advance and entered the city on September 14. He then assumed its fall would end the war and force Alexander to negotiate peace. Still the Czar refused to come to terms. Instead, on orders of the city's military governor and commander-in-chief, Fyodor Rostopchin, rather than capitulating, Moscow was abandoned, deserted by its civil population, and burned in order to deny the French markets, magazines, stores and winter quarters.

By then, a general with republican ideas, the extravagant and deranged Claude-François de Malet, was attempting a coup in Paris. Malet, a conspirator imprisoned in 1806 and later moved to a mental hospital, spread rumors that the tyrannical Napoléon had been killed. With the help of accomplices he escaped the mental asylum, and announced that he had been entrusted with a provisional government. He tried to seize power and proclaimed the restoration of a republic and civic freedom. The lack of information quickly prompted rumors and speculations, but the ill-prepared conspiracy made no real headway, and only enjoyed a few hours of wavering success. Malet's plot was rapidly unmasked by the Imperial commander of the Paris garrison, the putschist was arrested, summarily tried and duly executed. The episode was short-lived but it was very disquieting. The Napoleonic dynasty had become demonstrably fragile, nearly overthrown by a madman, and the cement of victory had begun to crack. Extremely perturbed, Napoléon hastily and secretly left Moscow—a city, now ravaged by a gigantic fire, that the French were forced to abandon.

With the coming of the harsh winter, and the Russian army's scorched-earth tactics, the French army, finding it increasingly difficult to forage food for themselves and their horses, was beginning to disintegrate. Already suffering hunger and cold, the exhausted French army was obliged to withdraw. The retreat was a total disaster, and the crossing of the River Beresina in November 1812 was the most dramatic episode of all. From the Beresina to Vilna the retreat reached the climax of disaster and horror. The experiences of the *Grande Armée* in its retreat from Moscow have become a byword for suffering. The strategy employed by the Russians had worn down the invaders; the French had been decimated by the freezing cold and constantly harassed by Cossack raiders and Russian marauders. Marshal Murat, left in charge of the remnants of the army, lost his nerve and all control of the army, and the last vestiges of discipline vanished. In the course of the ruinous retreat, the heroic episodes, the sacrifices of the war-weary rear guard, the desperate last-ditch stands, were all in vain. Murat said his famous words: "*On est foutus!*" (We're doomed!) Of the 600,000 men who entered Russia, fewer than 100,000 returned to their bases in Germany.

GERMAN AND FRENCH CAMPAIGNS

There was a lull in fighting over the winter of 1812–13 while both the Russians and the French recovered from their massive losses. A small Russian army harassed the French in Poland and French troops withdrew to the German states to rejoin the expanding force there. The French force continued to grow until Napoléon was able to field 350,000 troops — at least on paper, because massive desertion, evasion and delays in mobilization meant that he had fewer men immediately available for a campaign.

Heartened by Napoléon's losses in Russia, most sovereigns, although still under Napoleonic domination, began to regain their confidence. Under pressure of vociferous patriot groups, Prussia joined in the war as part of the Sixth Coalition, which now included Russia, Britain, Spain, and Portugal. Napoléon assumed command in Germany and inflicted a series of defeats on the Allies. The French victory of Bautzen, near Dresden (May 20–21, 1813), was marred by the inability to conduct an effective pursuit because of a lack of cavalry. Despite these initial successes, the numbers continued to mount against Napoléon as Sweden joined the Coalition. The French Emperor had put too much reliance on the marriage-tie with the Habsburgs, and even his own father-in-law turned against him. Breaking the dynastical link, Austria joined the coalition as well, and Napoléon's chances of dividing the Allies by diplomatic concessions had vanished. Eventually the French army was defeated by a force twice its size at the Battle of Leipzig (the "Battle of the Nations") on October 16–19, 1813. Some German states switched sides in the midst of the battle to fight against France. This was by far the largest battle of the Napoleonic Wars, involving some 500,000 troops and costing more than 90,000 casualties in total. Napoléon recrossed the Rhine with barely 60,000 men, while many thousands more were isolated and trapped in the fortresses of northern Germany. Leipzig announced a total collapse, and the Napoleonic occupation troops, everywhere facing general revolt, pulled out of Germany, Spain and Italy. France herself was now open to invasion.

Napoléon withdrew back into France, tried to gain time and attempted to put a brake on the centrifugal force that was already making his Empire disintegrate. His force was reduced to 70,000 men still in formed units and 40,000 stragglers, against more than three times as many allied troops. The armies of the Coalition entered France, and the French forces were surrounded and vastly outnumbered. British armies pressed from the south, and other Coalition forces positioned to attack from the German states. Napoléon then recovered his talents as a strategist, moved his forces of *Marie Louises* (young recruits) in lightning thrusts, and won a series of victories in the Six Days Campaign (e.g., Champaubert, Montmirail and Montereau). Historians agree unanimously that the Emperor's campaign of France in February 1814 was one of the masterpieces of his strategy, a last brilliant flicker of his military genius. Napoléon seemed to recover all his old nervous energy, powers of concentration and quick thinking, but these were only hollow, Pyrrhic, last-ditch victories.

Napoléon, the eternal warmonger, was then more than ever the captive of his victories and of himself. Now the game was too big, the enemies too numerous and too determined, even for him. A few delaying victories were not significant enough to change the overall strategic situation. All of Europe, not only the Europe of monarchs, was rebelling against the man who had wanted to unite it at all costs, to make the old Continent more ordered, against the man who had tried in vain to make Europe, in a word, more European. For most of the enemies of France, the campaign from 1813 was a war of liberation, a crusade of traditional conservatism against those who tried to impose reform on large numbers of people who had no real wish for it, especially when it came in French garb. Moreover, Napoléon's strategy was ruined by the political and moral breakdown of his own regime. The French upper classes had lost confidence, and the soul of the nation was weary. This failure of the national will was the nemesis of the Napoleonic autocracy. Now the Corsican Emperor was doomed.

Marie Louise
A "Marie Louise" was a young recruit without experience raised in the last year of the Napoleonic era. The nickname had overtones of affection rather than scorn, as courage and devotion were not lacking.

The allied generals then decided cautiously to avoid doing battle and instead to advance for a final and decisive push on Paris, which, empty of defenders, capitulated on March 31, 1814. When Napoléon proposed the army march on the capital, his few remaining marshals urged him to abandon this hopeless struggle against overwhelming odds. On 4 April, led by Marshal Michel Ney (1769–1815), they rebelled, and told him that the army would no longer follow him.

Abdication and Hundred Days

On April 6, 1814, Napoléon I abdicated in favor of his young son, Napoléon II. This unacceptable solution was refused and the Coalition demanded unconditional surrender. Napoléon abdicated unconditionally five days later. The great adventure, immortalized by the famous painting by Horace Vernet *The Farewell of Fontainebleau*, was over. Napoléon, now a depressed and humiliated man, attempted to commit suicide. Great changes had taken place within a decade. Compared to the healthy, slim, taut and dynamic First Consul, the destituted Emperor had thinning hair, girth and a peptic ulcer, which eventually became cancerous. Already by the time of the retreat from Moscow he was corpulent, lethargic and suffering from various ailments. After 1812 he showed a brutal contempt for human nature, was less flexible and incisive, less able to distinguish between the possible and impossible, more prone to negative fatalism and irrational obstinacy, all of which made him, corrupted by absolute power, a shadow of his former self. This rapid and premature aging was undoubtedly due to the burden of ruling on his own, enormous overwork, nervous exhaustion, frustration, stress, tensions, pressures, excitation, and a vanished glory built upon the sands of military victories. His tendency to live on his nerves and attempt to repress his powerful emotions beneath a veneer of cool resolve had led to several nervous crises akin to epileptic fits. Spasms of rage or hysteria had long been breaking through his pose of calm and icy efficiency. By then Napoléon had lot his health, charm and teasing sense of humor.

By the Treaty of Fontainebleau the allied victors left him his title of Emperor, as though it were a medal or a decoration, and granted him a tiny patch of ground over which to rule: the insignificant island of Elba (12,000 inhabitants) in the Mediterranean Sea, 20 km off the coast of Tuscany, Italy. The island was halfway between a prison and a derisory independent state. It was also decided by the Allies that the French government should pay the exiled "statesman" an annual income of two million francs — a compromise between a bribe and a pension. His wife Marie Louise and his son were brought back to Vienna, Austria, never to see him again. After a few months of exile in Elba, Napoléon's lust for life seemed to recover, and he issued decrees modernizing agricultural methods, developed the iron mines, and created a small navy and army.

As a result of the first Treaty of Paris, France lost nearly all the territories that she had conquered since 1792. The turncoat Talleyrand, who had long directed Napoléon's diplomacy, persuaded the Allies to restore the Bourbon monarchy in the person of the Count of Provence. The Count had become the heir to the House of Bourbon after the death, in 1795, of his young nephew Louis XVII. The new king, known as Louis XVIII (1755–1824), was indeed the grandson of Louis XV and the younger brother of the beheaded Louis XVI. He had emigrated in 1791, had always been a radical antirevolutionist and anti–Bonapartist, and knew very little of the new France that had been born in the past twenty-five years. Louis XVIII and the returned *émigrés* were thirsty for impossible revenge; they had learned nothing, forgotten nothing, and understood nothing of what had happened.

Now back in power, the king wanted the abolition of everything that the Revolution and the Empire had brought about, and the re-establishment, exactly as it had been in 1789, of the *Ancien Régime*. Louis XVIII maintained conscription, organized constant processions, military parades and ostentatious religious ceremonies, replaced the Revolutionary three-colored flag by the royal white banner, dismissed the army veterans, purged the administration of Napoleonic supporters, victimized Bonapartists, and left the vengeful Royalists to strike fear into the hearts of the holders of *biens nationaux*— properties and lands confiscated from the Church and the *émigrés* during the Revolution. More than this was patently unfeasible, since national sentiment had altered too much for complete retrogression. The reluctant king was obliged to promulgate a charter instituting a constitutional monarchy and confirmed the main political and social advances of the Revolution. The 59-year-old king was quite unpopular, being seen by many as coming back in the wake of foreign enemy bayonets.

Napoléon spent only nine months and 21 days in uneasy retirement on Elba, watching events in France and Europe with great interest through informants, spies and agents. Soon aware of Louis XVIII's lack of popularity and of the bitterness at the terms of the Treaty of Paris, Napoléon had at the back of his mind the idea that his political career was not finished. Discontent in France and disputes among the Allies at Vienna were welcome news to Napoléon. Given what appeared to be a favorable combination of circumstances, he resolved on one last bold gamble to restore his power, as he correctly reasoned the news of his return would cause a popular uprising. He managed to escape from his island, and on February 28, 1815, landed near Antibes on the Riviera on the French mainland with a handful of loyal followers — about 1,000 faithful soldiers, a remnant of his élite Imperial Guard.

A popular anecdote illustrates either Napoleon's charisma and popularity or, if untrue, the propaganda that operated in his lifetime and has done so ever since. At Grenoble, his small force was confronted by troops sent by the king to arrest him; the men on each side formed into combat lines and prepared to fire. Before fighting began, Napoléon reportedly walked between the two forces, faced the king's soldiers, ripped open his familiar grey overcoat and said: "If any of you will shoot your Emperor, shoot him now!" The royal soldiers, of course, all joined his cause, and the march toward Paris continued. All along the way he was given an enthusiastic welcome. The adventurer was now a reinstated reigning prince. One of his key commanders, Marshal Michel Ney, one of the original 18 Marshals of France created by Napoléon, who had turned coat in 1814 and said that Napoléon ought to be brought back to Paris in an iron cage, joined him with 6,000 men on 14 March. Ney was eventually arrested, tried for treason, condemned and executed in December 1815.

And so began the ultimate Napoleonic flare, the last act of the play, or rather the epilogue of an amazing tragedy, known as the *Cent Jours* (Hundred Days — actually 111 days from March 20 to July 8, 1815). The ridiculed Louis XVIII fled again quickly into forced exile in Belgium when Napoléon arrived in Paris, where his supporters gave him a rousing triumphant reception. However, he had the wholehearted support of only a part of the army, and it is far from sure whether the whole nation stood behind him. The enthusiasm which had greeted his comeback turned out to be little more than a spark. His return nonetheless infuriated the allied European powers, and was unanimously rejected. On March 13, the Allies, who were negotiating and redefining with great difficulty the map of Europe at the Congress of Vienna, ignored his pacific assurances and declared him an outlaw. Four days later, putting aside for a while their very different views and conflicting goals, the United Kingdom, the Netherlands, Russia, Austria and Prussia bound themselves into the Seventh Coalition and resumed war. Once the Allies had refused to recognize him as ruler of France, Napoléon's only option was a quick military victory that would unite the country behind him. In a hurry, both the Coalition nations and Napoléon mobilized for a decisive clash.

By the start of June 1815 Napoléon decided to use surprise and launched a sudden offensive in an attempt to drive off the oncoming British and Prussian armies. On June 18, 1815, at the desperate Battle of Waterloo in Belgium, he was defeated by Wellington and Blücher. The French army left the battlefield in disorder, which enabled the Allies to enter France and occupy Paris.

Napoléon's brother Joseph immigrated to the United States, where he lived from 1815 to 1841. He then returned to Europe to take up residence in Florence, where he died in 1844. After considering a nebulous plan for an escape to the United States to join Joseph, Napoléon made his formal surrender to the Allies and abdicated for the second and last time.

After the Emperor's deposition, the European powers worked to rebuild a Europe that had been totally upset and changed by the French Revolution, the Consulate and the Empire. To that end, they signed the so-called Second Treaty of Paris.

Exile and Death

For the second time the Allies restored the pitiful Louis XVIII to the French throne, and the king ruled until his death in 1824.

As for the former Emperor ("Boney"), he was deported with a small personal entourage plus a large British guard to the windy island of Saint Helena in the Atlantic Ocean, off the coast of Africa, 2,000 km from any major land mass. At Saint Helena, where he had the bitter privilege of becoming his own historian, the prisoner-of-war Napoléon conducted a feud with the severe British governor, Hudson Lowe, exchanged the sword for the pen and started to dictate his memoirs, which were first published in 1823. They are a disappointing work, mostly accounts of his earlier victorious campaigns, written in a dull and impersonal style, in which he also tries to make himself into a martyr, boasts of his administrative reforms, and presents himself as the champion of equality and freedom, liberalism and nationalism.

In 1818 his health began to break down. Napoléon I, the ex-Emperor of the French People by the Grace of God and the Constitutions of the Republic, died after four months of painful illness, most probably stomach cancer, on May 5, 1821, aged 51. Napoléon had his posthumous victory in the creation of his legend.

In 1840 the French government was allowed by the British to bring back Napoléon's body from Saint Helena. He was interred with great pomp in the Invalides Church in Paris. The Emperor's body rests now beneath the imposing golden dome of the Church of Saint Louis, a major tourist attraction to the present day. Commissioned from the sculptor Visconti, Napoléon's tomb was completed in 1861. It consists of five successive coffins, one of tin, one of mahogany, two of lead, and one of ebony, which are arranged within a majestic sarcophagus of red porphyr from Finland.

After Louis XVIII's death in 1824, the crown of France then passed to his brother Charles X (1757–1836), who reigned until 1830. Forced to abdicate, Charles X was followed by king Louis-Philippe of Orléans (1773–1850), who ruled the so-called Monarchy of July until the Revolution of 1848. Then France became a republic until Charles-Louis-Napoléon Bonaparte (1808–1873), Napoléon I's nephew, took power by force in 1852, proclaimed himself Emperor of the French with the title of Napoléon III (Napoléon II was the late King of Rome and Duke of Reichstadt who died in 1832), and established the Second French Empire that lasted until 1870.

2

Fortifications of the Ancien Régime

Bastioned Fortifications

The development of siege artillery in the 15th century necessitated a complete revision of fortification since medieval high stone walls, towers and gatehouses crumbled under the repeated impact of cannonballs. In 1494 Charles VIII of France conducted a lightning campaign in Italy, easily taking fortresses and cities owing to his modern, powerful, and mobile artillery. A new system of fortification was designed in Italy in the early 1500s as a reaction to the new weapons. This new system, soon known as *tracé italien* or *bastioned fortification*, was based on mathematic and geometric principles for maximal flanking. Its basic element, the *bastion*, was a protruding terraced platform generally as high as the main wall. It was distinguishable from any previous artillery tower owing to two essential characteristics: a low ramparted profile and a pentagonal arrowheaded ground plan. The bastion profile was ramparted, which means that it consisted of a *rampart*, two relatively thin masonry walls (called revetments) retaining a thick mass of earth absorbing the smashing impact of cannonballs; the bastion was rather low above the ground in order not to be an easy target, while the depth of the interior ditch prevented scaling. Bastions and curtains (straight sections of wall between two bastions) included a thick breastwork with embrasures protecting gun emplacements; a banket (or fire-sep) for infantrymen armed with muskets; and a wide wall-walk, broad enough to be suitable for supplying, loading and firing artillery. The bastion's pentagonal outline was formed by two faces turned outwards to the enemy; both faces joined at the jutting-out *salient*. They were connected to the curtain by two portions of wall called *flanks*; the meeting point of face and flank was called a *shoulder*. The *gorge* was the back space turned to the inside of the city or fort. The surface enclosed by those five lines was called *terre-plein*. To increase the defenders' safety, bastions were often fitted with an *orillon* (or *ear*) which was composed of a recess and a protruding screen built on the shoulder, protecting the defenders in the flank from oblique enemy bombardments, but allowing them to enfilade the ditch. This protective element was round or square, shapes which gave bastions their characteristic arrowhead or ace-of-spades form. The bastion could also be fitted with a *cavalier* (also called a *cat*), a raised structure slightly higher than the rampart, whose layout was similar to that of the bastion. The purpose of this inner work was to gain observation possibility, to give additional fire-power and increased height to the bastion so as to command the surroundings. The cavalier also acted as a kind of shield preventing enfilading fire and protecting buildings in the town or fort.

At first bastions were used as replacements for medieval and Renaissance artillery towers, but soon the *bastioned front* was developed. The bastioned front was composed of a *curtain* (a straight section of wall) and two projecting half-bastions allowing a good flanking: each bastion flank protected not only the curtain but also each face of the neighboring bastion. The new bastioned system thus eliminated all blind spots (which are zones below and beyond which the ground cannot be seen and fired at), every part of the fortress being always covered by fire coming from neighboring parts. In other words, the bastioned layout restored the balance of arms in favor of the defenders as rapidly as cannons had reversed it at the end of the 15th century: it permitted a maximum defense with a relatively small garrison. The system was further improved by the creation of an important outer work called *ravelin* (also named *demi-lune*, meaning half-moon), a triangular independent unit placed in front of the curtain. Another essential feature was the *covered way*, a continuous broad lane placed on top of the counterscarp all around the fortress. It formed an observation place, and also a first line of combat defending the *glacis*, a flat and bare zone neither planted with vegetation nor constructed with buildings, surrounding the fortress and denying any cover to the attacker. In the angles formed by the covered way, re-entering *places of arms* were arranged. Placed on each side of a demi-lune, they consisted of two protruding faces and could be possibly strengthened into some kind of fortlets called *lunettes*.

Eventually additional outworks were developed in order to multiply the number of

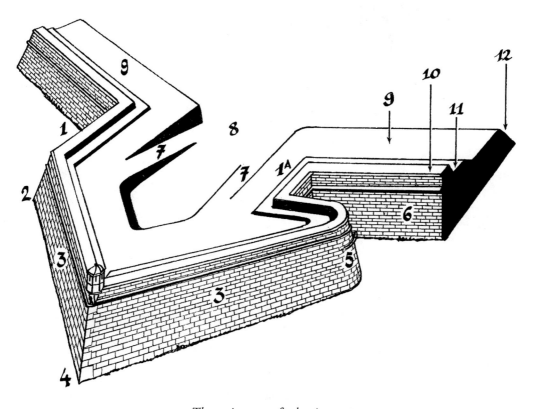

The main parts of a bastion
1: *flank*; 1a: *flank with ear*; 2: *shoulder*; 3: *face*; 4: *salient*; 5: *orillon or ear*; 6: *curtain*; 7: *ascent, sloping access*; 8: *gorge*; 9: *wallwalk*; 10: *breastwork*; 11: *banket or fire step*; 12: *interior slope.*

obstacles opposing the progression of besiegers. The *tenaille* was a low wall placed in the ditch at the foot of the main curtain between both flanks of the bastions. Its purpose was to protect the base of the curtain and flanks of adjacent bastions from bombardment and assault. The *caponier* was an open protected corridor enabling the communication between the main enceinte (enclosure) and a demi-lune. It was placed across the ditch and continued by a *postern* or *sally port* passing under the rampart. The *counterguard* was an outwork placed in front of a bastion or a demi-lune, whose purpose was to protect the salient point and both faces. Advanced works were placed ahead of the main ditch. They were projecting combat positions which occupied a portion of the glacis ahead of a curtain or ahead of a bastion. They were designed to force the besiegers to begin a siege from a greater distance and to cover parts of the ground not easily seen and defended from the main wall. A *hornwork* (*ouvrage à corne*) consisted of a bastioned front (one curtain and two half-bastions) which was linked backwards to the main ditch by two parallel *ailes* (wings or walls). A *crownwork* (*ouvrage à couronne*) was the reunion of two hornworks, thus a large unit including two bastioned fronts composed of two curtains, one bastion and two half-bastions. A *flèche*, also called *redan*, *freccia* or *arrow*, was a small arrowheaded advanced work, an entrenchment formed by two protruding faces, placed either ahead of the salient of a bastion as support of a salient place-of-arms or ahead of a re-entering place-of-arms.

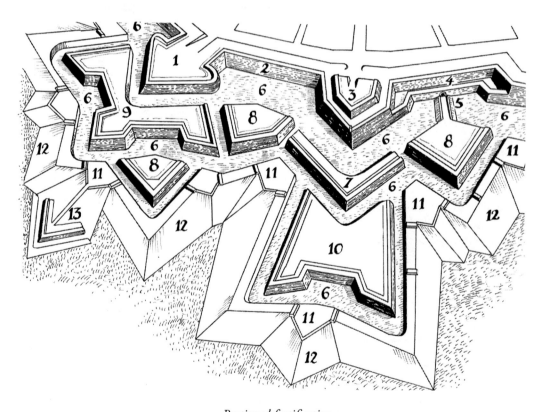

Bastioned fortification
1: Bastion with ears; 2: curtain; 3: bastion with cavalier; 4: tenaille; 5: caponier; 6: ditch; 7: counterguard; 8: demi-lune (or ravelin); 9: crownwork; 10: hornwork; 11: covered way with places of arms and traverses; 12: glacis; 13: arrow.

A *lunette* was an advanced work which often had the form of a bastion. It was placed ahead on the glacis to oppose and delay the besiegers' approaches. The lunette often possessed its own ditch and covered way, and, closed in the gorge by a parapet and only accessible by mean of a drawbridge, it often constituted a small autonomous detached fort. In addition, though only when natural conditions allowed it, the vicinity of a fortress could be flooded by *inundation*, the voluntary submersion of more or less broad zones in order to create inaccessibility. When a stream or a river was in the vicinity of a fortress, an inundation could be formed by constructing dams across the valley. The water thus swelled above the banks and overflew the country.

The bastioned front, an ensemble of elements related by rules and geometrical ratios, could be repeated at will to form a fort, an urban enceinte, or a line of defense. Endlessly, the outline of the bastioned front and its numerous advanced and outworks might vary in length and size, and be connected with each other with various angles. These infinite variations were determined by engineers according to local circumstances to adapt fortifications to the site, but

Echauguette
The echauguette was a small turret or sentry-box built of masonry. The purpose was to have an observation post to watch over the ditch. For this reason echauguettes were placed on corbels at the salients and shoulders of bastions and outworks. The jutting out turret sheltered a single standing guard from wind and rain. The sentry-box was fitted with small and narrow loopholes for observation and firing, should the occasion arise.

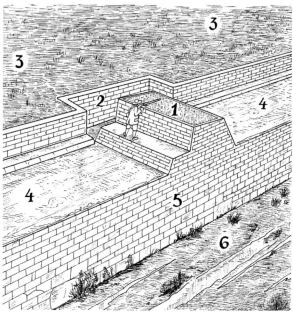

Traverse on the covered way
The traverse was an earth or masonry breastwork usually of equal height to the crest of the parapet and placed crosswise at regular intervals on the covered way. It presented the advantage of chopping the covered way into separate sections. The traverse could also be built on the capital line of a bastion, demi-lune, or lunette, for example, in order to create compartments protected from enemy fire. 1: Traverse; 2: chicane passage; 3: glacis; 4: covered way; 5: counterscarp; 6: main ditch.

can also be explained in terms of a sort of fashion created by currents, schools or movements. This phenomenon, in the 16th, 17th, and 18th centuries, gave birth to numerous theoretical bastioned fronts and endless sterile disputes between engineers of opposing cliques.

As can be easily imagined, the bastioned system demanded a very high cost to be built, and a specialized corps of engineers with knowledge of artillery, geometry and mathematics to be designed. The art of fortification became thus a sophisticated science, resulting in the definitive obsolescence of medieval private fortification and causing the standardization of military architecture as a state monopoly.

Louis XIV and Vauban

The apogee of the bastioned fortification was reached in the second half of the 17th century with the French engineer Sébastien Le Preste de Vauban (1633–1707). Vauban is generally regarded as one of the greatest military engineers of all time. He is said to have fortified about some 100 places in France (a figure widely open to discussion), and his major contribution to warfare was his methods of attacking in siege warfare.

Vauban, born in 1633 into a family of the petty Burgundian nobility, enlisted as a cadet in the rebellious army of the Prince of Condé during the Fronde, the civil war that raged during Louis XIV's minority. The young Vauban rapidly distinguished himself in several siege actions. Captured by royal troops in the spring of 1653, he was induced to change sides, and soon joined the newly-formed engineer corps in the army of Louis XIV. Taking part to several actions during this period of his early career, he rapidly climbed the promotion ladder. He was appointed King's Engineer in 1655, and was involved in the demolition of the fortifications of various places in Lorraine (e.g., Nancy), and improved new ones in Alsace on the Rhine near the German border. During the war against Spain in the Low Countries (present-day Belgium), Vauban played a significant role in the capture of several key strongholds (Tournai, Douai and Lille). When his design for the citadel of Lille was accepted in 1667, he attracted much attention, and his career began in earnest. He assumed the duties of Commissary General of Fortifications, although the title remained with Vauban's predecessor, Chevalier de Clerville, until his death, at which time (in 1677) it officially passed to Vauban. He worked closely with Louvois, Louis XIV's war minister, and became a trusted military advisor of the king. Vauban was assisted by the fact that Louis XIV took military engineering very seriously.

During Louis XIV's wars, Vauban took part in many sieges, always with much success. He designed a special method of laying siege, based on a judicious use of artillery, and the moving forward by successive parallel trenches and saps with the deepest concern for sparing as many lives as possible. Vauban's standardized system of siege warfare was eventually adopted throughout Europe and was still in use over a century later. In 1688, he developed a new artillery technique known as ricochet fire. He also introduced the socket bayonet which could fit around the barrel of the musket. During the interlude of peace, he traveled all over France and the newly conquered territories, inspecting, checking, remodeling and improving existing fortifications and surveying sites where new fortifications could be built in order to secure France's frontiers. He supported Louvois' military reforms, and also advised Louis XIV in bargaining for the exchange or dismantling of fortresses captured from the enemy in order to have safer borders. With royal support, he sketched out his plan for the famous *Pré Carré*, a defensible frontier zone based on two lines of fortified cities running across the French northeastern frontier. He also fortified naval bases at Dunkirk, Brest, Rochefort and Toulon to support Louis XIV's plan to develop a powerful navy.

Vauban never spared himself; he was a courageous soldier who was several times wounded in action. He was also a tolerant man at heart, one of the few who dared criticize Louis XIV's revocation of the Edict of Nantes (1598), which had allowed freedom of worship. By 1701, Vauban's health was deteriorating, and in his retirement he wrote a

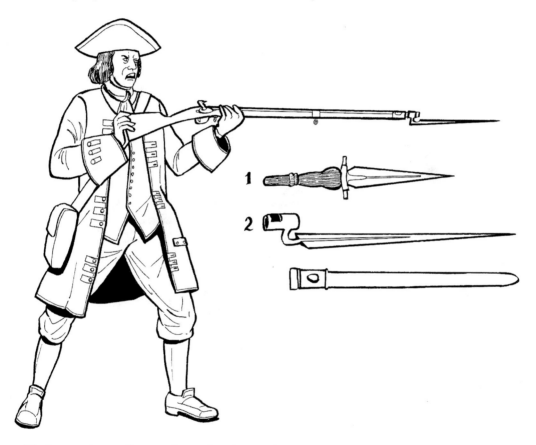

The bayonet (originally manufactured in the French town Bayonne, famous for its cutlery) was a kind of dagger (1) introduced about 1642. Originally the early plug bayonet was not entirely useful, as its haft was fixed in the barrel; the musketeer had a pike-like shock-arm but his weapon could not fire since the barrel was obstructed. Vauban is credited with the design, in 1687, of a socket bayonet (2), consisting of a sleeve fitting around the muzzle of the musket and locking into place with a slot and stud. This enabled the musket to be loaded and fired while the bayonet was fixed; the soldier could fire at one instant and stab at the next. By this means pikes could be discarded and the effectiveness of the infantry doubled. The socket bayonet came into general use in the early 18th century. It could be used in defense, the combined length of rifle and blade being long enough to reach an opponent, either mounted or on foot. The bayonet could also be used for a charging shock attack, but it required a good discipline, great courage, nerves of steel and a special, aggressive "pike mentality," which could only be acquired by intensive training.

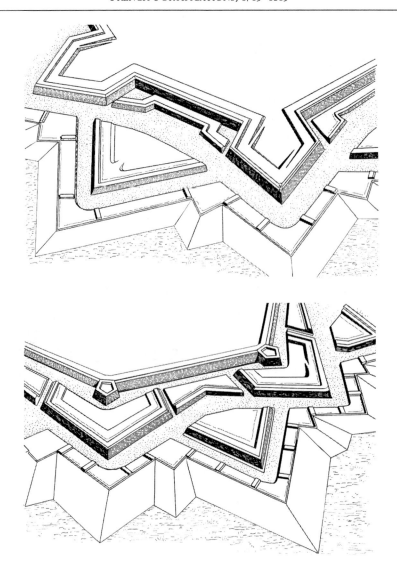

Vauban's fortification
Top: *Vauban 1st system*—The "first system" was essentially the bastioned tracé inherited from Pagan, which Vauban used in normal circumstances.
Bottom: *Vauban's 2nd system*—The so-called second system, conceived about 1687, included two autonomous parts separated by a ditch. The first external line was called enceinte de combat (fighting line). The second internal line—called enceinte de sureté (safety line)—included two-story polygonal bastioned towers, stoutly built to contain artillery within bombproof casemates and firing through port-holes. This "second system" was very expensive and not widely applied (only at Oléron, Besançon, Landau and Belfort).
It should be noted that the theoretical and highly contestable classification of Vauban's work into "system" was not done by Vauban himself but deduced and codified by laudative analysts and admirative followers in the 18th century. Actually, Vauban was opposed to strict doctrines, systems and dogmatism. He merely observed one and only rule: the skillful adaptation to the site which was one of the fundamental laws of fortification. Vauban applied one principle: to follow good sense and experience in order to achieve maximum efficiency.

number of treatises (known as *Oisivetés* = "Leisures") not only on fortification and siege warfare, but also on a wide variety of subjects such as overseas colonization, privateering, agriculture, sylviculture, and waterways. In 1703 Louis XIV rewarded his old and loyal servant by elevating him to the dignity of Marshal of France. By that time Vauban had published a highly controversial book on taxes in which he proposed a fair system.

Groundplan Neuf-Brisach

The third "system" was merely an improvement of the precedent. The curtain of the internal enceinte was casemated and its perimeter was fitted with small flanks which increased the defense of the ditch. The demi-lunes were enhanced by a reduit and its own ditch. The superior parts of the internal main walls were made of thick earth layers which reduced the volumes of masonry and offered an efficient resistance to enemy fire. Neuf-Brisach, created in 1698, is the magnificent but one and only application of the very expensive "third system." Actually, as this method was never copied, it is more appropriate to say that this "system" was an oddity or an expensive experiment.

Vauban's fiscal reform was too ambitious and too "modern" for his time. His book was forbidden by the king and he fell into a kind of half disgrace. Vauban died shortly afterwards, in March 1707.

Vauban was a good military leader, a courageous soldier extremely competent in siege warfare, a skilled fortification builder, an architect and an urbanist, a great traveler, a loyal servant with a strong commitment to the king's service, a good-hearted man involved in the public good, and an eclectic pre-encyclopedic thinker dedicated to the care of the common people, but he was certainly not the inventor of the French bastioned fortification, as an erroneous and persistent legend says. He was merely a rightful heir, a skilled and a brilliant continuator of techniques created by 16th century Italian, Dutch, German and French precursors including Beroil de La Treille, Jean Errard, François Blondel, Alain Manesson-Mallet, Antoine de Ville, and more particularly Blaise-François Pagan. As he himself readily admitted, his designs came less from genuine creation than from the adaptation of existing figures into a logical and homogenous system. Vauban was highly inspired by the heritage of the military engineers and architects that had preceded him as well as his own experience of all the techniques of siege warfare. Vauban was not necessarily a greater engineer than his contemporaries, but he happened to be Louis XIV's engineer, and Louis XIV's France was the greatest power in Europe, and the only country able to command all the resources necessary to see grandiose schemes and large-scale projects through to completion. Through theoretical studies in geometry and mathematics, Vauban had established the best form classic French bastioned fortifications should take, in such a way that French fortresses could withstand, or at least delay, the type of siege operations he himself had designed and practiced. Vauban's great talent was to weld various theories and features which had existed long before him, and to bring them together into an effective and coherent techniques. It has been objected that Vauban's work was too much based on a rigid geometry, and that he sometimes tended to consider bastioned fortification as a pure mathematical problem. Vauban was the leading military engineer of Louis XIV's reign and arguably the best known of many. His influence on bastioned fortification and siege techniques was enormous, and somehow the Barok bastioned fortification tended to be associated with his name.

Fortifications in the 18th Century

THE SCHOOL OF MÉZIÈRES

The art of fortification in the 18th century was characterized by ultra-conservatism. The stagnation of fortification after Vauban can historically be explained by several reasons. After Louis XIV's death in 1715 commenced a rather long period of peace, and the wars waged during Louis XV's reign took place abroad. Well protected by the numerous fortresses built at the time of Louis XIV and Vauban, France was not threatened by invasion. During the 18th century, Vauban's successors could not be so liberal with money, men and materials. In this background, cut from practical reality, the art of fortifying tended to theorization and unimaginative stiffness.

The French Military Engineering Academy was founded at Mezières in the Ardennes in 1748. Known as *École de Mézières*, it was headed by Chastillon until 1763, by Ram-sault de Raucourt until 1776, and by Villelongue until 1794. The institution was remarkably good by the standards of the day and covered aspects of military and civil engineering, fine arts, architecture, urbanism (town planning), geometry, and military tactics — notably artillery and, of course, siege warfare. While primarily concerned with fortifications, engineers were also expected to design churches, and civil buildings such as warehouses, windmills, and bridges. This gave them a certain independence from the army, the navy and provincial intendants. Candidates who wanted to become *Ingénieurs du Roi* ("Kings' Engineers") had to be educated, and pass a selection exam. The study course lasted for two years, at the end of which selected individuals held a royal commission and were provided with a rank, generally starting with that of captain. They formed a kind of small independent staff, which was spread all over France and its colonies. They were detached within the army and the navy as staff officers, and placed under the orders of a governor, a senior officer or a general. Famous teachers of the School of Mézières included Bossut and Monge, and famous students Borda, Coulong, du Portail, Dejean, Lazare Carnot, Marescot, Bertrand, and Rouget de Lisle, for example, all of whom played a role in the French Revolution and the Empire.

The School of Mézières acquired a good reputation, but its staff and teachers largely contributed to the exaggerated admiration and dogmatization of their famous forebear to the point of creating a "myth of Vauban" with an infallible legend, which probably would have deeply irritated the Marshal himself. Vauban's reputation, experience and authority on the art of fortification and siege warfare became military gospel — an unfortunate honor which paralyzed French military engineer corps until the second half of the 19th century. Long after Vauban's death his work was studied, analyzed, codified in "three systems," commented on, continued and perpetuated by generations of French engineers who frequently interposed their own concepts, making it somewhat difficult to see precisely what Vauban had in mind. Any military engineer who dared criticize Vauban's views was regarded an iconoclast, a foolish heretic, and an intruder who had better mind his own business. A safe course was to make a well-argued amendment to Vauban's systems.

In the 18th century there was a profusion of engineers who tried to improve on Vauban, if only on paper. Many treatises presenting new systems of permanent fortification were published, particularly in France, where engineer officers were convinced that Vauban's fatherland was the sole fountain of knowledge on that subject. Military engineers, officers, architects, professors of mathematics, students and even pupils, all claimed to be masters in the art of fortification. The claim was easily set up, since by taking the straight line and the curve an infinity of combinations could be made. Many people teaching, commenting or writing about fortifications were inclined to design systems of their own. Among many others we could cite *L'Ingénieur de Place* by Nicolas Buchotte (1673–1757); *Nouvelles méthodes pour fortifier les Places et pour remédier à la faiblesse des Anciennes* by Herbort, published in 1735; *Traité de Fortifications* by Belidor in 1735; *Le Parfait Ingénieur ou la Fortification offensive et défensive* by Deider, published in 1757; *Théorie de la Fortification* by Cugnot (1778); *Mémoire sur la Fortification* by Fourcroy de Ramecourt (1774); *Construction de la Fortification suivant une Nouvelle Disposition* by Desclaisons (in 1777); and *Nouveau Système de Fortification* by Filley (1777). Many authors, carried away by extravagant whims, tried to reduce the art of fortification to fixed rules and to processes of descriptive geometry. They fancied that by multiplying the obstacles they could attain their goal, cutting elements into a number of small parts hoping to strengthen their system by increasing its complexity. However, if we venture into these so-called "new" systems of permanent fortification we soon find out and perceive that they are not so much distinguished from each other by any essential differences as by their authors' names. Most remained extremely conservative, featuring only slight modifications, many being totaling absurd and lunatic, some of limited usefulness, and only a few rational and feasible. Besides most authors forgot the cost involved, and paid no attention to the force of the garrison and the provisioning of their impregnable paper fortresses. The design of a permanent fortification system was undoubtedly an essential point, but it was not all. Many authors forgot or underestimated the fact that a determined and ably commanded garrison could perform wonders even behind a wretched outline.

CORMONTAIGNE

The most noteworthy of these "new" bastioned systems was that designed by Louis de Cormontaigne (1696–1752). Cormontaigne had served as a volunteer at the siege of Freiburg and

Engineer officer, 18th century
In February 1732 Marquis d'Asfeld (Vauban's successor as Director-General of Fortifications) introduced a colorful uniform for the corps of King's Engineers in order to distinguish them from other officers of the army. This included a black tricorn with golden edge and white plume, a scarlet coat with blue cuffs and gilt buttons set in pairs, a scarlet waistcoat, breeches, and stockings. In December 1755 they were provided with a uniform similar to their colleagues of the artillery, including a blue coat, red collar, cuffs and lining, waistcoat and breeches.

Landau (Germany) in 1713. He became military engineer in 1715, and was promoted to the rank of Lieutenant in 1718. Between 1728 and 1733 he worked at Metz (Fort Moselle and Bellecroix double-crownwork). Now appointed Engineer-in-Chief, he worked at the citadel of Bitche, and at the fortifications of Thionville. Appointed to the function of Directeur-General des Fortifications in 1745, he continued working at Strasburg, Wissemburg, Thionville, Metz, Verdun, and Longwy. Cormontaigne, the continuator of Vauban, had written a secret treatise in 1714, *L'Architecture Militaire*, but the document was soon stolen and an unauthorized edition came out abroad in 1741. In this book, Cormontaigne defined a rather classical bastioned system directly influenced by Vauban with a few minor modifications: improved redoubts in the demi-lunes; re-entering places-of-arms turned into small independent fortlets; a strong citadel placed *à cheval* on the main enceinte; and traversed covered way given a *tracé en crémaillère* (saw-tooth edge). The double crownwork Bellecroix at Metz, designed by Cormontaigne in 1728, gives an excellent illustration of Modern French Bastioned Front which had a significant influence on

Bastioned system by Bélidor (18th century)
The military teacher Bernard Forrest de Belidor (1698–1761) was honest enough to reproduce Vauban's work, but was no more capable of resisting the urge to create his own than was any other fortification expert of the time. He published several works on siege warfare, mines and explosives, and fortifications, including the Bombardier français (1731), and Traité de Fortifications (1735), in which he designed various methods of defense. One of this system comprised a bastioned front in which the bastions were divided into several entrenched compartments. Belidor also published several works of great importance, on a wide range of subjects, including mathematics, civil engineering and the science of hydraulics.

fortifications built both in France and abroad. Slightly modified by General Noizet, and known as *Modern French System*, Cormontaigne's method of fortification was to remain the accepted standard for bastioned fortifications in France until the 1870s. Cormontaigne also worked out a "scale of comparison," a device whereby the strength of a fortress, and thus the number of days it could be expected to hold out, was calculated against an attack, provided the besieger would follow the general rules of siege warfare. The disadvantage of this scale was that once the strength of the stronghold was known, few fortress commanders would feel in honor bound to resist an attack beyond the time predicted for its success.

In June 1792, the École de Mézières was closed down and the establishment was transferred to Metz. It became the *École Centrale des Travaux Publiques* (Central School for Public Work), which in turn was transferred to Paris in 1795 and eventually became the famous *École Polytechnique*.

If the "politically correct" line in France was conservatism, abroad many engineers dared to criticize Vauban openly. A certain Rottberg published in 1744 in The Haag (Netherlands) a treatise titled *L'ingénieur Moderne*, in which Vauban's work was discussed without great esteem, and without reserve and moderation. Rottberg, of course, wrote a scholarly work that proposed an alternative in the form of an extravagant enceinte made of a belt of independent forts covered by counterguards, ditches and outer works. Much more profound in their reflections and much more influential were two theorists, Guibert and Montalembert, who did not content themselves with superficial reforms, but who

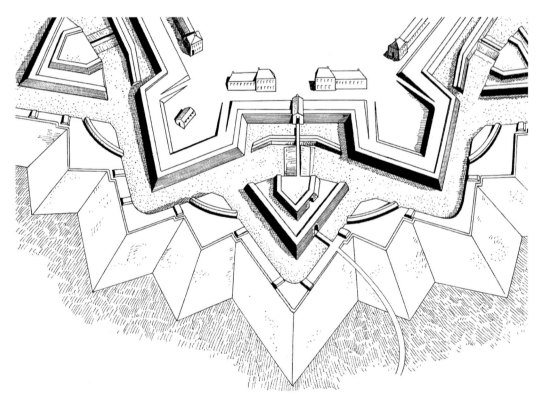

Bastioned front by Cormontaigne

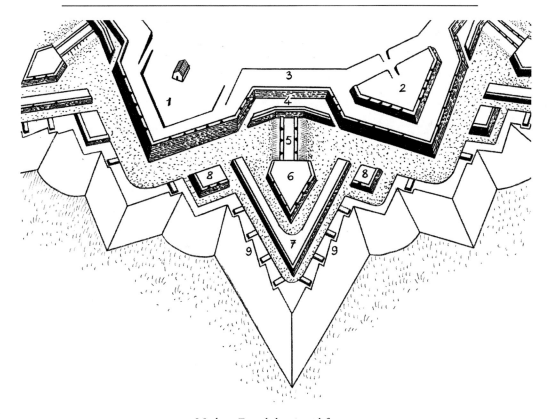

Modern French bastioned front
Designed by Cormontaigne and Noizet, the Modern front was characterized by a bastion with long faces (1) without ear and often fitted with a cavalier (2), a short curtain (3), defended by a tenaille (4), a reinforced caponier (5) connecting to a demi-lune (6), which was protected by a counterguard (7). The place-of-arms (8) was transformed into a small independent fortlet cut off from the covered way by an arm of the ditch. The covered way (9) was divided into traversed parts and was given a "en crémaillère" (sawtooth-shaped) layout.

paved the way for a new way of waging war, the former on general strategy and tactics, the latter on fortification. Both authors symbolize a renewal of French military thought in the second half of the 18th century. Although they were heavily criticized and objects of controversies, their works formed the basis of a new kind of warfare, one that was adopted and successfully put into practice by the leaders of the French Revolution and by the Napoleonic Empire.

GUIBERT

Jacques Antoine Hippolyte, Count of Guibert (1743–1790), was born at Montauban and started his military career at the age of thirteen. He distinguished himself during the Seven Years' War between 1756 and 1763, won the Cross of Saint Louis and was appointed to the rank of colonel in 1767. In 1773 he visited Germany and witnessed the efficiency of the Prussian regimental drills and army maneuvers; Frederick the Great, recognizing Guibert's ability, showed great favor to the young colonel and freely discussed military

Rottberg's fortification system (1744)
Each independent fort was planned to have a garrison of 500 men and 100 cavalrymen for sallying. It is extremely doubtful whether this complicated and expensive system would have worked in practice.

questions with him. Guibert, like all his military contemporaries, was deeply impressed by the achievements of Frederick, and as a typical aristocratic rationalist believed that the Prussian example could transform the French army into a logical instrument of state power.

In 1775 he began to cooperate with the Count de Saint Germain in a series of successful reforms in the French army. In 1777, however, Saint Germain fell into disgrace, and his fall involved that of Guibert, who had been appointed maréchal de camp (brigadier general), but was relegated to a provincial staff command. In his semi-retirement he vigorously defended his old chief Saint Germain against his detractors. On the eve of the Revolution he was recalled to the War Office, but in his turn he became the object of attack and he died, practically of disappointment, in 1790.

Guibert was a member of the French Academy from 1786, and he also wrote a tragedy, *Le Connétable de Bourbon* (1775), and a journal of travels in Prussia, France and Switzerland, but most important were his publications on military matters. In 1772, Guibert wrote *Essai Général de Tactique* (*General Essay on Tactics*) and *Défense du Système de Guerre Moderne* (*Defense of the System of Modern War*), in 1779 in which he developed original concepts. Guibert was well aware that France's military potential had greatly increased. In spite of the weakness of the French monarchy, there were more men, more food, more metals and better transportation. Arguing that the French soldier was by nature predisposed rather to attack than to passive resistance, and claiming that a modern battle should be based on mobility and movement, Guibert advocated a combination of troops into self-sufficient divisions (a concept already experimented by Marshal de Broglie in the Seven Years' War). He developed a system of simple basic movements by which troops could form quickly and without confusion from line to column and vice versa. This would allow for rapid deployment, and — once the troops were in action — he recommended the use of the *ordre mixte*, combining concentrated artillery fire, skirmishers, the line to deliver effective infantry firepower, and the column for swift assault, whose weight would deliver a decisive blow. Guibert suggested a strategy deliberately seeking battle in the open field, and ignoring fortresses which had obsessed so many 17th- and 18th-century commanders. Instead the army was to march fast and straight on the enemy's capital and major economic centers. Another part of his tactical formula was an insistence on all-out pursuit to decisive victory. To speed up the offensive, he advocated that armies should dispense with slow and cumbrous baggage-trains, and instead live off the enemy's country. He also urged commanders to pay less attention to parade-ground perfection, and to abandon the brutal and degrading discipline of the 18th-century armies, and instead to encourage performance by combining a firm and fair discipline with efficient training, appeal to personal pride, regimental élan, and spirit of nationalism. Intellectually Guibert harked back to the idea of the citizen soldier, but his social prejudices prevented him from embracing the idea as a reality.

Until the French Revolutionary Wars began in 1792, these new untried military ideas were debated and often criticized, but change was on the way. Under hard pressure, the Revolution brought into being a true citizen army which found in Guibert's strategical and tactical ideas the solutions to the problems it was to encounter on the battlefield. The French drill book of 1791, and the measures taken by Lazare Carnot to reorganize the French army, incorporated many of these new ideas. Guibert's influence on the armies of the French Revolutionary and Napoleonic Wars was profound.

Montalembert

New Fortifications

The Marquis Marc René de Montalembert (1714–1800) was an odd personality who definitely stood out among all 18th century fortification theorists. Born in Angoulême to a family with a strong military tradition, the young Marc René became a junior cavalry officer at the age of 16, and participated in the sieges of Kehl in 1733, and Philippsburg a year later. He was in the Prince de Conti's army during the wars in Austria, Bohemia and Italy. In 1747, he entered the Academy of Sciences, and in 1752, he obtained the charge of lieutenant-général in the province of Saintonge. During the Seven Years' War, the Duke of Choiseul sent him as attaché to the Swedish and Russian armies.

Although a stranger to the engineering corps, the cavalryman Montalembert was interested in fortifications. On that subject he appeared as an original mind and made important contributions to fortress design. Whereas most of the French engineers were prepared to stick with absurd obstinacy to the traditional fortification evolved by Vauban and his continuators, Montalembert searched for other means of defense and elaborated new systems making a departure from the classical bastioned fortification. Montalembert exposed his views and theories in a series of eleven books titled *La Fortification Perpendiculaire ou Essai sur plusieurs manières de fortifier la ligne droite* (*Perpendicular Fortification, or Essay on several manners to fortify a straight line*), published between 1776 and 1794. He pointed out many important defects of Vauban's traditional bastioned fortification, and justly claimed that: the ramparts and the interior of a place were much exposed to mortar and ricochet fires, which ruined the artillery of the defenses; the reverse and ricochet fires rendered the flanks of the bastions almost untenable (although it was on them that the defenses rested); cross fire from the bastion flanks did not make full use of the effective range of which the siege artillery pieces were capable; the communications between the enceinte and the outworks were badly designed, rendering sorties and offensives raids difficult; the ditches of the outworks formed openings through which the besieger could breach the main enceinte from a distance; the interior retrenchments were difficult to build when the breach was made; and the labor necessary to put a place into a state of defense and to keep it during the siege was dangerous, exhausting and often impossible for the garrison to accomplish. Montalembert's main concern was to prevent the besieger from opening a breach.

As an experienced man of war, Montalembert appears to have been one of the first to refuse the defeatist notion that a fortress invested was a fortress taken, and to realize that a siege was basically an artillery duel; his leading idea was thus firepower. For a successful outcome it was necessary for the defending artillery to be superior to that of the attacking enemy. This idea led him to the adoption of artillery fortresses (in fact huge batteries) installed within a new perimeter. In considering the defects of bastions he had arrived at the conclusion that for flanking purposes two forms of layout were preferable. In short, Montalembert's original views can be basically summed up in the following points.

First System

In a first system, designed in 1776, Montalembert reintroduced and modernized an old concept of defense called *tenailled system*. Already advocated by the German engineers Suttinger in 1670, and Rimpler in 1673, used by the Dutch Menno van Coehoorn (1641–1704), and revived by the German Heinrich von Landsberg (1670–1746) in the 1710s, this method was characterized by the abandon of curtains and bastions, which were replaced by a series of triangular structures with long faces, abutting each other and forming together in plan a saw-edged outline generally with right angles of 90 degrees, which Montalembert called *Perpendicular System*. The advantages of this method were that it was much cheaper to build than a bastioned front, it ensured a very good flanking and necessitated fewer soldiers to man. The main drawback was that the long faces could easily be enfiladed by enemy fire. The tenailled system had never really become popular. It never supplanted the bastioned method, and only a few tenailled forts and lines were built in the 18th century. Ahead of the tenailled front, Montalembert advocated two outer lines of counterguards fitted with musketry loopholed walls, and casemated artillery emplacements. Behind these stood strong, multi-storied circular towers (generally 11 yards in diameter), each housing artillery capable of firing out across the countryside for long-range defense, and acting as redoubts. His system had thus three ditches and four dis-

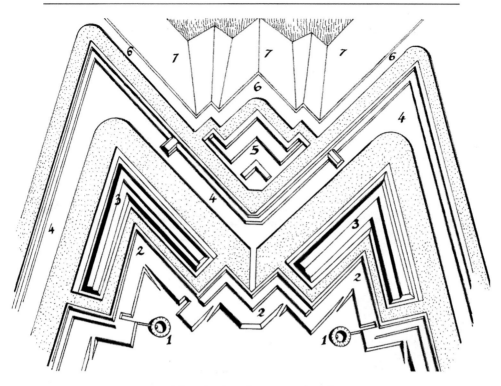

Montalembert first system (1776)
This first tenailled system designed by Montalembert in 1776 included large circular gun towers (1) for long-range fire. The main enceinte consisted of a series of casemated tenailled walls (2). Ahead of this there was a counterguard (3); an envelope (4) with casemated batteries placed in the re-entering angles; a detached lunette (5); a covered way (6); and a bare glacis (7).

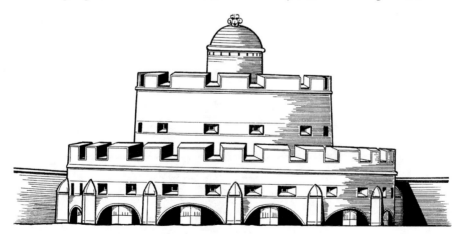

Artillery tower by Montalembert in tenaille system
A major part of Montalembert's perpendicular and tenaille systems, the multi-stories-high gun tower could command a wide field of fire. It was armed with 72 cannons, its largest diameter was 144 feet, and the superior platform was about 46 feet above ground. At ground level, it was protected by casemated riflemen emplacements fitted with loopholes for close-range fire. The top turret was used as an observatory.

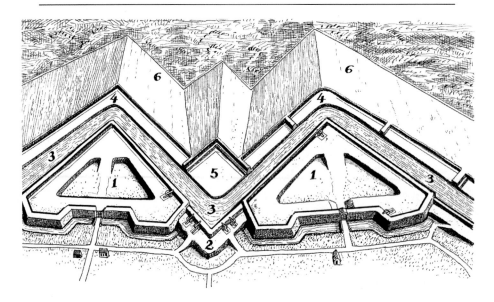

Tenailled front by Menno van Coehoorn at Groningen (1700)
The Line of Helpman was designed by the Dutch engineer Menno van Coehoorn in 1700 in the south of the city of Groningen in the northern Netherlands. It was composed of triangular redoubts called lunettes (1) and gun batteries (2) placed in the re-entering angles. Together these elements formed a saw-tooth outline. The redoubts were closed at the gorge and fitted with a ditch filled with water, and therefore autonomous and difficult to take even from the rear. The line also included a moat filled with water (3), a covered way (4) with traverses and places-of-arms (5), and a glacis (6).

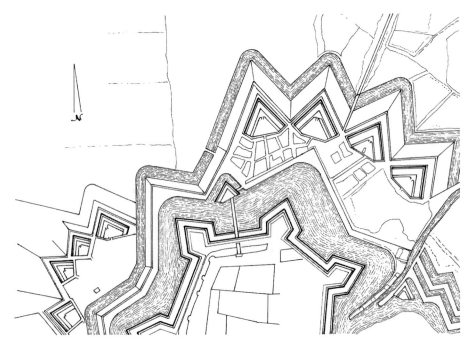

Tenaille line at Zutphen by Menno van Coehoorn

2. Fortifications of the Ancien Régime

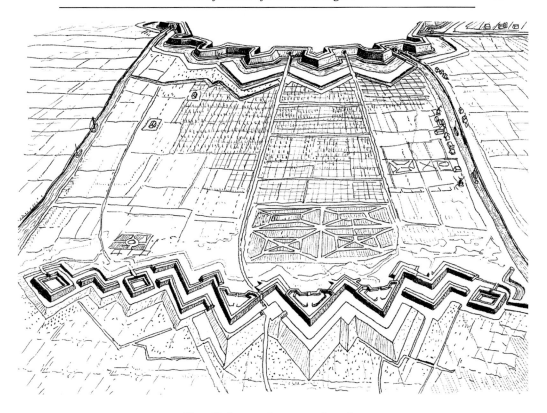

Tenaille line at Groningen (1700)
The line formed the front of a vast entrenched camp. Tenailled fortifications were also designed and built by Menno van Coehoorn at Zutphen, Nimegue and Doesburg.

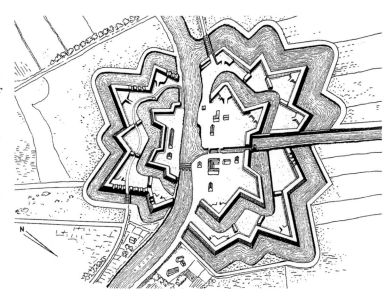

Tenailled fort Nieuwersluis (1775)
The tenaille system could also be the basis for the construction of an independent position, like Fort Nieuwersluis, built on the River Vecht near Utrecht in the Netherlands in 1673. The fort was transformed in 1849–1850 as a torenfort (a large circular masoned tower), to which were added an enceinte, a barracks, and remises (artillery shelters) in 1880–1882.

tinct enceintes (linked by bridges, posterns and subterranean vaulted passages) which, for their conquest, demanded four successive attacks. Other advantages, at least so claimed Montalembert, were that the besieger had little or no space to emplace breach batteries; that each enceinte was commanded by neighboring fire; that garrison, equipment, weapons and ammunitions were in safety under bomb-proof shelters and casemates; and that the defense would be very energetic owing to the rapidity of the communications which facilitated sorties and counterattacks on threatened points. Under a deluge of fire, attacking such a fortified place would be a bloody folly doomed to failure from the start.

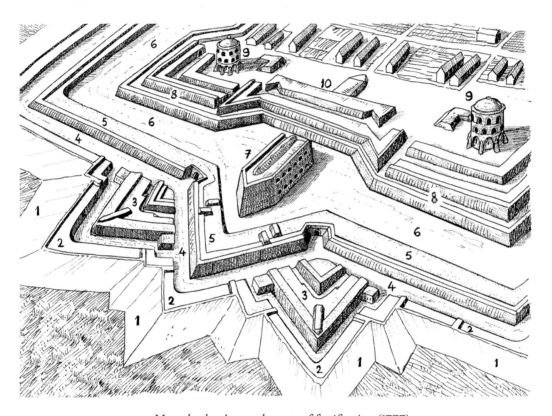

Montalembert's second system of fortification (1777)
Montalembert in his huge books had designed many defensive methods ranging from improved bastioned front to tenaille system. One of these designs, which promised to become the inspiration for 19th-century fortification, was the polygonal front. This included: a glacis (1); a covered way (2); large detached places-of-arms (3) with casemates, traverses and redoubts placed in a fore-ditch (4). Behind these was a "couvre-face général" (5), a continuous envelope fitted with casemates protecting the fore-ditch. The main ditch (6) was defended by a powerful multi-story caponier (7) bristling with guns and riflemen loopholes. The main enceinte (8) was divided into several walls which housed riflemen galleries, mortar and gun batteries. Large circular self-defensive multi-story towers (9) were intended for long-range action, bombarding and crushing the enemy before he could establish his siege works. The garrison was to be quartered into defensive barracks (10) placed near their combat emplacements. All elements of the defense, from the barracks to the advanced places-of-arms (including ammunition store and supply dumps), were linked by underground galleries, thus well-protected from enemy fire.

Second System

In a second system, designed in 1777 and named *Polygonal Fortification*, Montalembert developed a form including a main straight line, presenting its entire front (and thus its entire armament) to the enemy. Also, the primary flanking elements, instead of facing each other with overlapping/cross fire, as with the flanks of bastions, were to be placed in the middle of the exterior scarp front. The central flanking work resulting from this arrangement was the caponier. The *caponier* (a flanking work defending a ditch by extending into it or across it, designed by early 16th century Italians) was reintroduced, developed and enormously upscaled. Intended up to the time of Vauban as a secure means of communication between a curtain and a demi-lune, the caponier, in Montalembert's system, became a strongpoint in its own right. It was a massive, three-story-high structure projecting into the ditch, a sort of artillery cathedral ringed with three floors of continuous gun casemates and infantry loopholed galleries facing the ditch. The main enceinte was defended by casemated mortar and gun emplacements, infantry walls, self-defensible circular gun towers (the same as in the first system), a cavalier (emplaced along the main wall, and whose basement was arranged as underground shelters for the troops, and as ammunitions stores). Like in the first system the various elements were linked by subterranean communications. Each front, having an exterior length of about 370 yards, also included an envelope made of casemated counterguards, two strongly armed detached lunettes (each with two flanks and redoubts), a covered way with places-of-arms, and a glacis. The whole design was theoretically sound and Montalembert claimed that his system gave unity to the defense, that it enclosed a larger space than a bastioned tracing, that the enemy was compelled to execute an immense development of trenches and approaching works, and that the straight fronts could follow the irregularities of the ground, and were better armed than any other outline.

Montalembert's first and second systems, however, would

Multi-layered artillery tower designed by Montalembert
This is a close-up of (9) in the previous illustration. The tower was a large circular casemated work bristling with guns. It was to be built with extremely strong masonry, and included quarters for the gunners, as well as ammunition, supply and water stores. The top of the tower was arranged as an observatory and command post. The ground floor included riflemen loopholes for close-range defense.

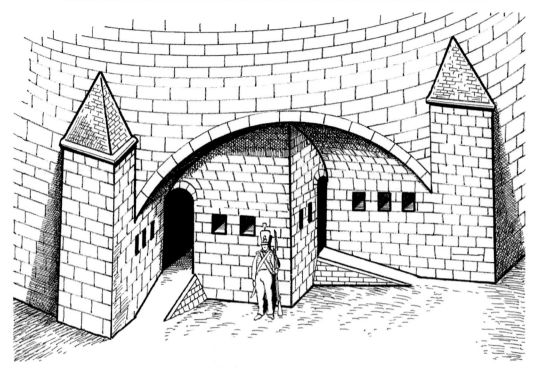

Close-up of vaulted base of artillery tower by Montalembert
Under the arch, supported by pillar and counterforts, were tenailled riflemen short range defense emplacements and bomb-proof quarters and ammunition stores.

Kufstein, Austria
Montalembert did not invent the high, thick-walled, round artillery tower. This had already been advocated by several engineers and theorists, notably Albrecht Dürer in the 16th century. The massive four-story-high artillery tower of the castle of Kufstein in the Austrian Tyrol, named Kaiserturm (Emperor's Tower), was built between 1518 and 1522. Its walls are 7.5 m thick at the base and 4 m thick at the top.

have proved ruinously expensive in both construction and fitting-out. It is doubtful whether a Montalembert fortress would have been able to hold a sufficient garrison to man all those guns, together with the necessary infantry, cavalry for sorties, and service troops and their stores and ammunition. However, with the caponier (later developed in a down-scaled form) Montalembert laid the foundation of the polygonal system of the 19th century. Montalembert allied his particular outline with a suitable design for artillery emplacements. In preference to open parapets, exposed to artillery fire of all kinds, high angle, ricochet and reverse, he advocated the use of casemates in which guns could be emplaced closer together, ranked in tiers and completely protected. Casemates, just like the caponier and the massive gun tower, were not new. They had existed since the beginning of the bastioned fortification in the early 16th century, and even before in the transitional period following the introduction of firearms after the Middle Ages. But due to ventilation problems they had fallen out of favor with the development of the bastioned fortification. Montalembert had not created the caponier, the

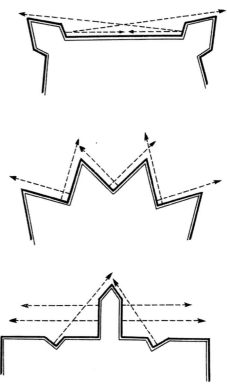

Flanking
Top: bastioned system (fire from the flanks of bastions). Middle: Tenaille system (from the angles of the faces). Bottom: perpendicular system (from the caponier)

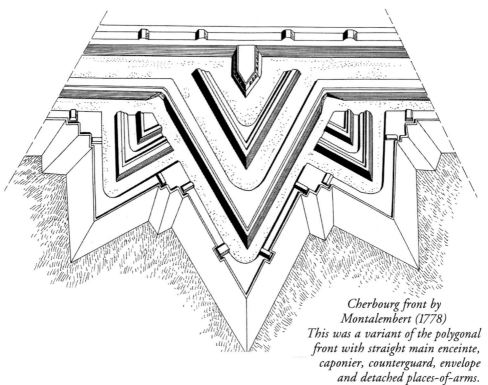

Cherbourg front by Montalembert (1778)
This was a variant of the polygonal front with straight main enceinte, caponier, counterguard, envelope and detached places-of-arms.

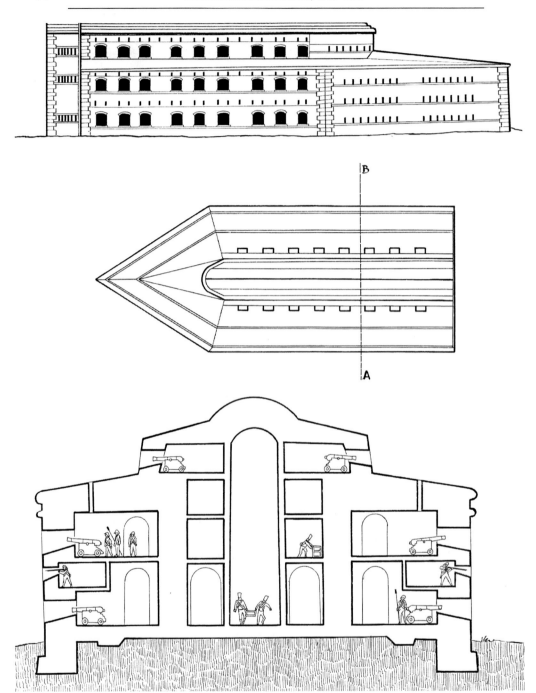

Montalembert's caponier
1: Side view; 2: Plan; 3: Cross-section A-B.
The caponier as designed by Montalembert in his polygonal front was not a small affair. Placed across the ditch, it was a large work, totally made of masonry, having the shape of a warship and built like a cathedral with a central nave. It possessed formidable firepower, including guns in casemates and riflemen's galleries.

casemate, the huge gun tower, the loop-holed riflemen's gallery, the lunette and the counterguard, but his great merit was to weld these features and adapt their use into a rather coherent scheme, at least on paper.

OTHER CONCEPTS

Montalembert was well aware that a bastioned enceinte was in due course vulnerable and practically always doomed to surrender if attacked by an army employing Vauban's siege

Caponier by Giorgio Martini Montalembert did not invent the caponier. This was already advocated by the architect and military engineer Francesco di Giorgio Martini (1439–1502) from Sienna in a treatise published in 1480, entitled Trattati dell'architectura ingegneria e arte militare.

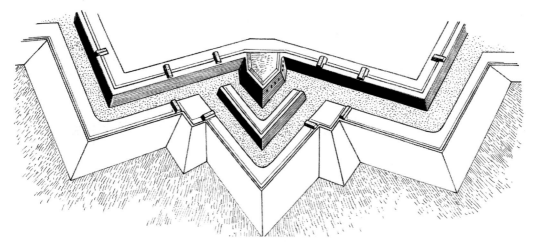

Defensive front by Montalembert (1776)
This system was a simplified variant with caponier and counterguard.

method. In fact, if a part of the fortress was breached, the whole defensive system collapsed. Montalembert was one of the first to foresee the coming necessity for a new visionary method. Montalembert therefore advocated the notion of *camp retranché* (entrenched camp already developed by Vauban, Menno van Coehoorn and others), a wide fortified perimeter established around a city or a fortress in order to complicate and increase the size of the enemy siege approach works, to delay the attack, and to put the defended object out of range of enemy artillery. For the same purpose, Montalembert also advocated the creation of a girdle of detached autonomous forts with interlocking fields of fire around cities and fortresses: if one fort was conquered, it was only a problem and not a

Profile of rampart
Top: Vauban.
Bottom: Montalembert.

2. Fortifications of the Ancien Régime

disaster, as the others works could still resist and continue the defense. It was also for detached forts that Montalembert chiefly proposed to use his caponier flanking, preferring the tenaille system for large places.

In abandoning the bastioned plan he was already committed to the principle of casemate defense for ditches, and the combination of this principle with his desire for an overwhelming artillery defense led him, over the course of years of controversial writing, into somewhat extravagant proposals. For instance, for a square fort about 400 yards wide, he proposed over 1,000 guns emplaced in vaulted casemates. Even more extravagant was his later design of a totally circular fortification. This consisted of two four-story casemated enceintes surrounded by a two-story tenailled enceinte, with a ditch, a covered way with re-entering places-of-arms, and glacis surrounding the whole. Montalembert's methods—

Project by Montalembert for a fort on Aix Island (1774)
This projected triangular fort was to include a central tower (1) forming a keep and a lighthouse, and two angular gun towers (2) heavily armed with artillery firing in the direction of the sea. The land front included a covered way with glacis (3), a counterguard (4), two demi-lunes (5) and a ditch (6). This project, which would have been extremely costly, never went further than Montalembert's drawing board.

Plan of Montalembert's circular system
This system consisted of two casemated enceintes, both four stories high with a two-story tenailled wall, ditch, covered way and glacis at the front. It is obvious at first sight that this system of fortification was a monster of very limited usefulness. It would have been impossible in practice. It would have cost fortunes to build, it would have taken crowds of soldiers to man and would have involved too many artillery. It is also evident that the inner casemated second enceinte (intended for riflemen) had no field of fire, and was doomed to destruction at the very onset. As for the effect expected from the immense armament of the first artillery enceinte, it was nothing but an illusion. The plan shows the following. 1: Inner enceinte for riflemen; 2: main enceinte for artillery; 3: outer tenailled enceinte; 4: ditch; 5: counterscarp with covered way and places-of-arms; 6: glacis.

on the whole based on an obsession with superior firepower — were quite sound on paper, but highly unlikely to be acceptable and affordable in practice because of their monstrous size.

Before Montalembert's basic multi-gun caponiers and multi-gun towers were recognized as suitable and adapted by the Germans, his work was either ignored or understandably heavily criticized in France. On the whole, his ideas faced fierced opposition from the traditionalist engineering corps. His detractors said that the marquis was an ignorant outsider, a cavalryman who knew nothing of fortifications, and that he had better mind his own business. His views on fortification gave rise to quarrels and controversies, and his progress on the ladder of promotion was prejudiced by his forthright opinions. Some of Montalembert's unconventional proposals, however, had a certain influence on

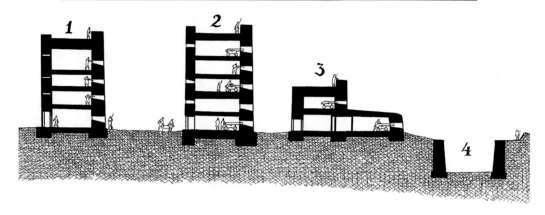

Cross-section Montalembert's circular system
1: Inner enceinte for riflemen; 2: main enceinte for artillery; 3: outer tenailled enceinte; 4: ditch.

several engineers, notably Lazare Carnot, who adopted some of his features into the French Napoleonic military architecture.

During his lifetime, the highly controversial Montalembert had little opportunity to demonstrate his theories, and no fortifications were built according to his concepts. He designed a wooden prefabricated fort, named Fort Condé, that could be embarked on ships and quickly assembled in the colonies threatened by the British. In 1773, he presented in vain a project to fortify the French-held city of Pondichéry in India. In 1779 he made an ambitious design (a huge triangular fort defended by large high round artillery towers) for the defense of the island of Aix. All these projects were rejected, and his one and only realization was a temporary wooden fort built on Aix Island, which was quickly replaced by a permanent fortified design dating from the time of Vauban. The forts of Querville and île Pelée, constructed by engineer Decaux at Cherbourg in 1786, corresponded more or less to his conception regarding coastal defense, including large roundish gun batteries turned toward the sea.

Montalembert was also interested in ballistics, in the shapes of embrasures, and in new alloys for the fabrication of cannons. With his own money he created a forge in the 1750s at Ruelle-sur-Touvre in the Charente-Maritime destined to manufacture cannons. He sold guns to the French navy, but due to financial and management difficulties, his business was taken over by the French crown. After endless lawsuits, Montalembert was reinstated as head manager and owner of his forge. Ultimately he sold it in 1776 to the Count of Artois (the future King of France, Charles X). At the time of the Revolution he surrendered a pension, which had been granted him for the loss of an eye. Persuaded by his wife (Marie Josephine de Comarieu, the hostess of one of the best-known salons of Louis XVI's time), he joined in the emigration of the noblesse, and for a time lived in England. All his possessions were thereupon sequestrated by the republican government. He very soon returned, divorced his wife, married again, and obtained the annulment of the sequestration. Carnot often called him into consultation on military affairs, and, in 1792, promoted him to general of a division. Montalembert also modeled a complete course of fortification (92 models), which he offered to the Committee of Public Safety. Montalembert, who was a prolific writer and also a playwright, has left a voluminous correspondence, short stories, poetry and three plays: *La Statue* (written in 1784), *La Bergère*

Fort on southern point of Aix Island designed by Montalembert in 1779.

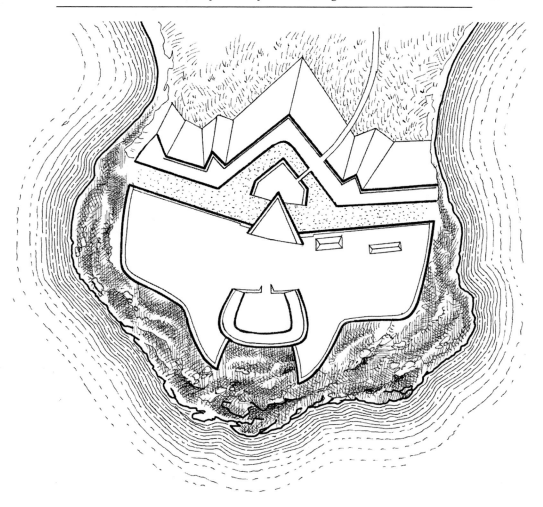

Temporary wooden fort built by Montalembert in 1779 at Saint-Catherine Cape, Aix Island.

de Qualité, and *La Bohémienne Supposée* (both written in 1786). He was proposed as a member of the Institute in 1797, and died in March 1800 in Paris.

Montalembert's Legacy

Montalembert was a man of the 18th century (he died in 1800), but his work belongs to the 19th century. Like many other innovators and fortifications experts, his advanced and sometimes extravagant concepts could have passed unnoticed and been consigned to oblivion were it not for the fact that they attracted attention and were accepted by the rising power of Prussia and soon transmitted to the other German states during a period of feverish rearmament in the 19th century. The marquis is said to have contributed more new ideas to fortification than any other man. His designs must be considered in some ways unworkable by their huge planned sizes and by the costs they would have involved, but the basic principles were sound. All the best fortification work of the 19th century rests more or less on his teaching.

The Germans, who already used the tenaille system and made free provision of bombproof casemates, took from him the polygonal front with its caponier and the idea of entrenched camp. After the Napoleonic Wars, the most important states of Germany began to strengthen their frontiers. Considering that they had not derived much strategic advantage from their existing bastioned fortresses, the Germans took up Montalembert's idea of entrenched camps, utilizing at the same time his polygonal system with modifications for the main enceintes. The Prussians began with the fortresses of Coblenz and Cologne. Later Posen, Konigsberg and other places were treated on the same lines. The Austrians constructed, among other places, Linz and Verona. The Germanic Confederacy reinforced Mainz with improved works, and entirely reorganized Rastatt and Ulm. The Bavarians built Germersheim and Ingolstadt. While all these works were conceived in the spirit strongly influenced by Montalembert, they showed the differences of national temperament. The Prussian works, simple in design, relied upon powerful

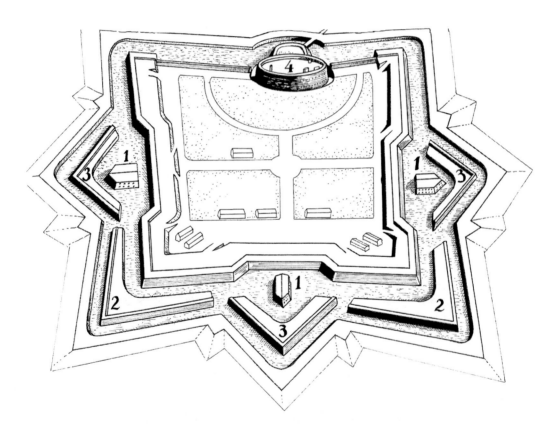

Fort Alexander, Coblence

Fort Alexander, situated south of Coblence on the Rhine River, was a part of a Großfestung (huge fortified ensemble). It was built between 1815 and 1822, and gives an excellent example of early German polygonal system in fortification directly based on Montalembert's theories. The schematic plan shows that the fort had straight or slightly broken exterior sides, flanked by casemated caponiers (1). The front angles and the caponiers, the vital points of the front, were protected by counterguards (2 and 3). The fort included a redoubt or keep (4), placed in the gorge, in which the garrison could withdraw and continue to fight even when the fort was taken.

2. Fortifications of the Ancien Régime

Dutch torenfort, Honswijk
Intended to protect the Netherlands from invasion, the so-called torenforten were built in the period 1840–1860 in the Nieuwe Hollandse Waterlinie (New Holland Water Line), a system of defense based on inundation, and on fortifications where the grounds could not be flooded. The circular towers—of various sizes—were circular or slightly oval. They housed guns, crews, supplies and ammunitions. Made of masonry, they became useless and obsolete when rifled artillery was introduced in the 1860s.

Dutch torenfort, Muiden.

German artillery tower, Ulm.
The illustration shows the large four-story redoubt/tower of Werk XIV at Ulm, designed in the 1840s.

Artillery tower at Wawel Castle at Krakow, Poland.

artillery fire, and exposed a good deal of masonry to the enemy's view. The Austrians covered part of their masonry with earth and gave more attention to detail.

The large, powerful, free-standing, multi-story, circular artillery towers bristling with guns as advocated by Montalembert enjoyed a revival. Many were built in the first half of the 19th century, for instance at Genoa and Verona (Italy), Linz and Torbole (Austria), Kozle (Prussia), Ulm (Germany), Kronstadt (Russia), and Krakow (Poland). The Dutch for their part developed the so-called *torenfort* (tower-fort), based on the same principles, at Everdingen, Asperen, Muiden and Honswijk, for example.

In France the Austro-German polygonal fortification — based on Montalembert's views — was slow to be adopted. The French would modernize their defenses and abandon the bastioned plan only after the fall of the Second Empire in 1870, when a vast program was launched by General Séré de Rivières.

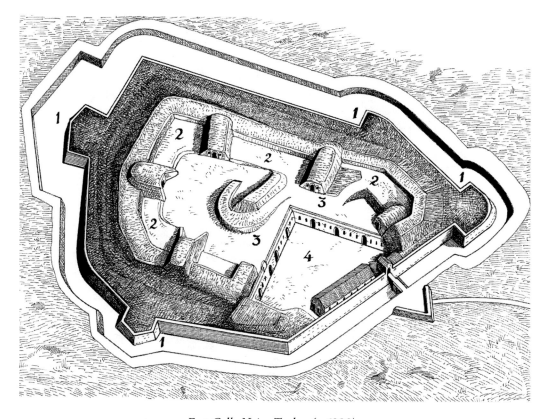

Fort Colle Noire Toulon (c. 1880)
Situated on the coast west of Toulon, the polygonal Fort Colle Noire was built in the period 1874–1914, as a part of a vast program launched by General Séré de Rivière (1815–1895), clearly showing how slow the French were to rethink their defenses and adopt new systems of fortification. The polygonal Fort Colle Noire included caponiers (1) for the close-range defense of the ditch; open gun emplacements (2) for long-range fire, compartmented by large and thick traverses; underground quarters, services, stores, and communication galleries (3); and a yard serving also as place-of-arms (4).

Siege Warfare

The art of siege warfare did not undergo major changes in the 18th century. It essentially remained the method designed by Vauban, which followed a prescribed pattern of events often undertaken in a standard and classical fashion. Though considered specialists rather than fighting soldiers, engineering officers, pioneers and sappers were particularly exposed to defenders' fire during a siege. Obviously their task was of the utmost difficulty and very dangerous. Those men risked their lives at any moment and casualties were particularly high. To reduce the number of wounded and dead among them, Vauban had thought the relevant problems over and designed a better, safer and systematic method of attacking fortifications.

When a besieging army arrived at its target, cavalry was sent to surround the city and cut all the roads leading to it, thus creating a blockade. Standard protocol dictated that the attackers demand the surrender of the defenders, but it was expected that this would be rejected for reason of honor. Next, the besiegers constructed two temporary earthwork lines. One line, called line of *countervallation* or *contravallation*, faced the besieged fortress at about 2,400 m from the defenses (out of artillery range) in order to guard against sorties from the garrison. The other line, named line of *circumvallation*, faced the open country outwards to repel a relieving enemy force attempting to break the siege. Between the two lines, the besiegers established their camps, supply stores and artillery parks. After a weak point had been selected as the main objective, saps (zigzag-shaped trenches) were dug forward to a distance of about 600 m from the defenses. There

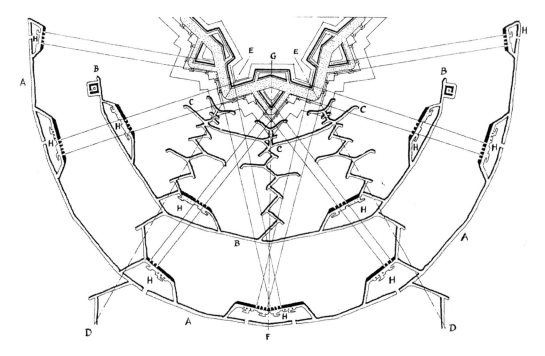

Theoretical siege approaches by Vauban
AA: First parallel; BB: Second parallel; CC: Third parallel; DE: Saps dug on the capital line of bastion; FG: Saps dug on the capital line of demi-lune; H: Artillery batteries.

the first parallel was dug, providing a base for siege artillery batteries. Just like the name indicates, the parallel was dug alongside the attacked front, and enabled the besiegers to get closer and closer to their objective in comparative safety. This pattern was repeated to about 320 m from the enemy front, where a second parallel was established for closer and more effective artillery fire. From the second parallel other zigzagging trenches were dug to a distance of about 30 m, where a third parallel was dug, forming the base for attacking the covered way. From here also a breach in the main wall could be made, either by artillery fire or by using one or more mines. When a breach was made in the defense, then storming troops gathered for the final assault. This was always the most critical and bloodiest part of the siege, and the defenders usually surrendered right before it started in order to avoid more bloodshed, and to prevent retaliation and atrocities like rape and pillaging which often ensued a successful assault. According to 17th century formalized "rules" of siege warfare, a garrison should be allowed to surrender with honor when they had shown their fighting skill and gallantry until that point. The main drawback of Vauban's method was that the establishment of the elaborate and sophisticated fieldworks was time-consuming and laborious: it demanded a huge amount of manpower and a number of troops estimated at ten times more than those of the defenders. It also pre-

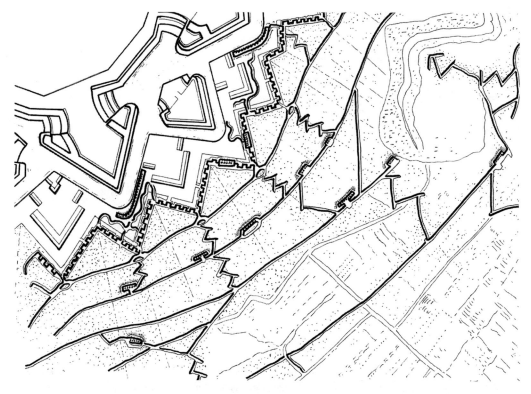

Siege of Bergen-op-Zoom in 1747
The siege lasted from July 12 to September 16, 1747, during the War of Austrian Succession. The map shows the French approaches established south of the city, composed of parallels, zigzag-shaped access trenches and gun batteries intended to attack the Van Coehoorn bastion (left), Pucelle bastion (right), and Dedem demi-lune (middle). Forty years after Vauban's death, his siege warfare method with three parallels was still used in the field.

cluded the element of surprise. Vauban's method of attacking fortified places constituted an undeniable progress, not only by reducing casualties but also for the certainty of success. Nevertheless, static fortress siege warfare remained a grueling test and a terrible ordeal, particularly for the civilian population.

Projects Under the Reigns of Louis XV and Louis XVI

ENTRENCHED CAMPS

During the 18th century, the French military authorities were content with completing some projects undertaken at the time of Louis XIV and with improving several strong-

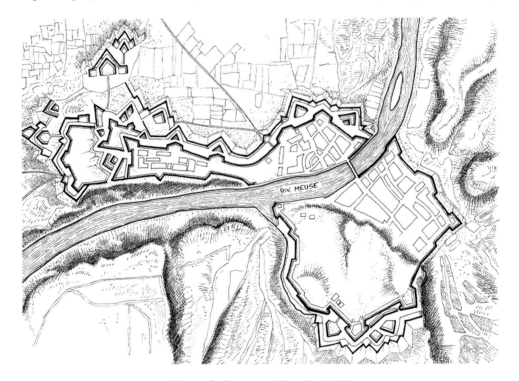

Entrenched camp at Givet (c. 1740)
A border city on the river Meuse, Givet is situated on the point of a kind of horn penetrating into Belgian territory. The fort of Charlemont was edified by order of King Carlos V of Spain between 1555 and 1560 to face the French fortresses of Champagne. The fort was built on the left bank of the Meuse on a narrow 100 m high ridge dominating the village. Givet and Charlemont were annexed by France in 1678, and the fortifications were reshaped and improved by Vauban in the 1680s. After the siege of 1696 led by the Dutch engineer Menno van Coehoorn, Vauban proposed the establishment of a large entrenched camp on the Haurs hill in 1697, but this ambitious project was completed later. The fortifications of Givet were eventually reinforced by detached works built between 1720 and 1740, including Fort Condé on the northern front. Underground quarters and stores were arranged after 1870 by General Séré de Rivières. Givet was besieged in 1815, 1914 and 1940. The urban enceinte was dismantled in 1890, but the citadel, the fort and the Haurs crownwork have been preserved and are still occupied today by the French army.

holds, principally coastal forts. The only great innovation was the creation of *camps retranchés* (entrenched camps), a strategy already advocated by Vauban, his Dutch rival Menno van Coehoorn, and Montalembert. The *camp retranché* strategy basically consisted in increasing the area to be defended, by adding fortifications (e.g., a continuous line, or a girdle of forts) around a fortress or a fortified city in order to put this target out of enemy artillery range. The *camp retranché* also provided a space to gather numerous troops for a planned offensive, or to regroup and re-form a withdrawing (defeated) force. Entrenched camps were created at Maubeuge in 1709, Givet in 1740, Toulon in 1747, Sedan and Belfort in 1792.

There were, however, a few projects carried out by the Ancien Régime, notably at the border with Germany (Thionville, Bitche, and Metz), in the Alps (Briançon), and along the coasts of the English Channel (Le Havre and Cherbourg).

THIONVILLE

Originally a Roman settlement called Theodonis Villa, then a Merovingian stronghold, Thionville (Didenhoven in German) was fortified in the 13th century with walls, towers and gates. In the 16th century the city became an important advanced stronghold defending roads leading to Metz, Luxemburg, Arlon and Namur in the Spanish Lowlands. Thereafter the medieval defenses were adapted to the use of artillery in the period 1596–1610 by the addition of Italian-styled bastions designed by engineers Jacques van Noyen and Francesco de Marchi. Thionville became French in 1643, and the Spanish fortifications were modernized by Vauban. The improvement of the fortifications was continued during the reign of Louis XV by the engineers Tardif and Duportal between 1707 and 1727, who established a series of advanced works and the double Moselle crownwork. Between 1745 and 1752, Cormontaigne ordered the construction of sluice-bridges, and the crownwork of Yutz defending the southern part of the city.

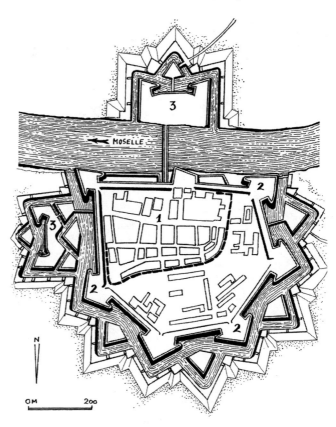

Thionville in 1673
1: Old medieval town; 2: Spanish bastioned enceinte from 1643; 3: Hornwork planned by Vauban (built in 1676).

Bitche

Bitche, situated in the department of Moselle near Sarreguemines in the north of the Vosges Mountains, has always been an important strategic crossroads controlling the access to Sarrelouis, Landau, Strasburg and Phalsburg. An old medieval town depending from the counts of Zweibrucken, and eventually a possession of the dukes of Lorraine,

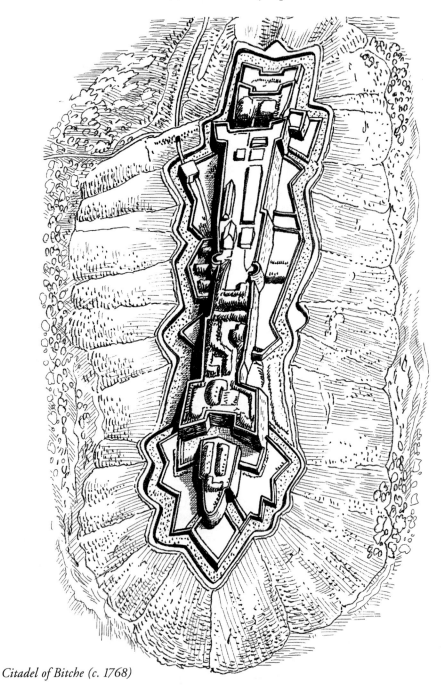

Citadel of Bitche (c. 1768)

the town was devastated by the Swedes in 1633 during the Thirty Years' War. It became French in 1676. The citadel, placed on a narrow ridge dominating the city, was improved by Vauban between 1681 and 1683. Bitche was restituted to the Duke of Lorraine by the Treaty of Ryswyck in 1697, and its fortifications dismantled. French again in the 18th century, the citadel of Bitche on its narrow and steep ridge was reconstructed in the 1730s by Charles d'Aumale and Cormontaigne. Bitche victoriously resisted two Austrian sieges in 1744 and 1793. In 1838, further improvements were added to the citadel, and the city itself was hemmed in by a bastioned enceinte established between 1844 and 1853.

METZ

Metz is situated at the junction of the Moselle and Seille Rivers. Occupied by the Gauls and the Romans, the city was the capital of the Frankish kingdom of Austrasia and one of Charlemagne's favorite residences. In the 12th century, Metz became a free city. In the following centuries, the rich bishop's town was protected by a six-kilometer-long stone wall, 38 towers and strong gate-houses.

(continued on page 90)

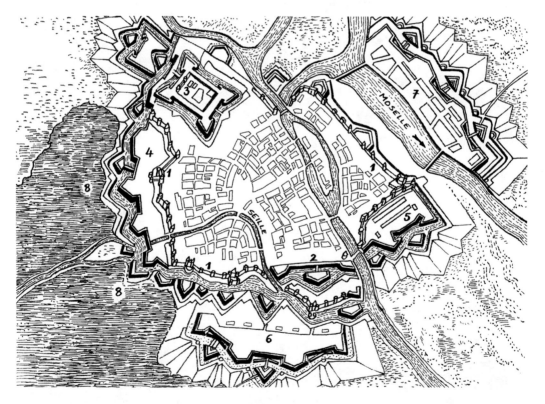

Metz circa 1752
1: Medieval walls with towers and gates; 2: entrenchment built by the Duke of Guise in 1552; 3: citadel erected in 1560; 4: Saint-Thiebault front; and 5: chambière front, both started by Vauban in 1676 and completed in 1752; 6: double crownwork Bellecroix; and 7: double crownwork Front de Moselle, both built by Cormontaigne between 1728 and 1740; 8: floodings.

Fortifications of Briançon
This overview displays the 18th century fortifications of the town, designed by Lieutenant-General d'Asfeld, Director of Fortifications of Dauphiné Tardif, and Chief Engineer Nègre between 1721 and 1734.
    1: Briançon, urban enceinte and citadel, improved by Vauban in the 1690s. On the gentle

slope of the northern Champs de Mars, Vauban had the Pignerol gate protected by a strong curtain, two casemated redans and a demi-lune. On the northwest front, he built two bastions and one traversed demi-lune, and he designed the Notre-Dame-et-Saint-Nicolas Church. On the western Embrun front, he created a terraced position including bastions and curtains, a traversed fausse-braie and a covered way. In front of the southwestern Embrun-gate, Vauban set up a place of arms and a chicane. On the abrupt and inaccessible southern front, plunging into the canyon of the Durance, a single stone wall was sufficient. On the eastern front, Vauban proposed to dismantle the medieval castle and to erect a bastioned citadel, but due to lack of funds, this part of his project could not be realized. Vauban completed the ensemble by constructing a barracks and two powder houses.

2: Fort des Têtes. On the Têtes plateau, which dangerously overlooks Briançon on the southeast, Marshall de Berwick put a design by Vauban in concrete form by establishing a large entrenched camp in 1709. Between 1724 and 1734, the camp became the Fort des Têtes, the central pivot of the defense of Briançon until 1870. The fort is even larger than the city of Briançon itself, and is one of the greatest achievements of Louis XV's reign. Today it still testifies of the extraordinary skills of the royal engineering corps regarding mountain fortification. The fort is basically a large bastioned triangle with a base of 900 m and a length of 300 m. It is pierced with three gates and is divided into three distinct fronts, each utilizing the mountainous terrain: The eastern Royal Front, the strongest and most heavily armed, turning towards Italy; the northwestern Durance Front, turning towards Briançon; and the southern Front de Secours, turning toward the Randouillet fort. The Têtes fort included four barracks for a garrison of about 1,000, an arsenal, a powder house, a food store, the governor's house and a chapel. The Fort des Têtes saw combat in June 1940 and in September 1944. The communication between the city and the forts situated on the left bank of the Durance demanded the construction of a bridge. The Asfeld Bridge, defended by a redan, and with a 40 m span arch, constituted an achievement of audacious technical prowess when it was opened in August 1734.

3: Fort du Randouillet. To hold the southern peak of Randouillet which dominates the Fort des Têtes, another work was built between 1724 and 1734: the Fort of Randouillet, originally a gun tower, transformed into a Haxo casemated battery in 1836. The artillery tower was protected by a large bastioned enceinte built on the downhill slope, which included several gun emplacements, a barracks, a powder house, and a cavalry stable.

4: Communication Y. The small valley between Forts des Têtes and Randouillet was fitted with a unique and original work called Communication Y. This was a 200-m-long vaulted passage fitted with doors, pierced with loopholes for infantry fire and hemmed with two bastioned walls, enabling the protection and connection between the two forts in case of a siege. The urban enceinte of Briançon, the Fort des Têtes, the covered Communication Y and the Fort of Randouillet thus formed a strong fortified line intended to stop any attack from Italy. In addition there were other works forming an advanced position.

5: Fort d'Anjou. This fort was built in the 1720s as an advanced work defending the valley of the Cerveyrette torrent. The small hornwork-shaped fort included a barracks, and a store for food and ammunition.

6: Redoute du Point du Jour. On a peak dominating the Fort of Anjou, a masoned three-story tower was built between 1724 and 1734 as an advanced sentry.

7: Fort Dauphin. This fort, intended to directly defend the road to Italy, was placed as another lone sentry on a flat ground dominating the Fort des Têtes. Built between 1724 and 1734, it is roughly a bastioned rectangle (about 200 x 350 m), fitted with a classical gatehouse, a two-level gun battery, a casemated barracks, and a dry ditch defended by bastions.

8: Redoute des Salettes. This work was built between 1709 and 1712 by engineer Tardif after a design made by Vauban on a plateau on the right bank of the Durance dominating the northeast of the city and the road to Italy. Originally composed of a simple casemated redoubt hemmed by a ditch, it had the same task as Fort Dauphin. The redoubt of Salettes was enlarged in 1815, and transformed into a Haxo-casemated fort between 1830 and 1854.

Metz was the third Evéché (bishopric town), together with Toul and Verdun, annexed by force by King Henri II of France in 1552. Besieged the very same year by Carlos V of Spain, the Duke François de Guise ordered the construction of new fortifications adapted to firearms. A square citadel with four bastions was built in 1560 by the governor, de Vieilleville. During Louis XIV's reign, Vauban was particularly devoted to the defense of the town and made projects in 1675, 1680 and 1698. He designed a cunning system of flooding and planned the establishment of a huge entrenched camp. However, Vauban's ambitious projects were only realized in the 18th century by his follower, Louis de Cormontaigne. From 1728 to 1752, the fortifications of Metz were greatly reinforced by the construction of the Moselle double-crownwork (erected between 1728 and 1732) and the Bellecroix double-crownwork (built from 1736 to 1740), which both gave a good example of Cormontaigne's modern bastioned front. With medieval and bastioned fortifications, 19th-century polygonal French forts, German Festen and 20th-century Maginot Line bunkers, Metz displays today the whole evolution of military architecture.

Briançon

Briançon is the highest town in France (average altitude is 1,326 m). Situated upon the Durance River on the road leading to Italy via the pass of Mont-Genèvre, it has always been a strategic crossroads in the Upper Alps. The site was occupied as early as the Iron Age, about 800 B.C. It became eventually a Roman settlement called Castellum Virgantia, then a possession of the counts of Dauphiné, until annexation by France in 1349 under the reign of King Philippe VI. Since it was placed close to the dangerous and often

Briançon: urban enceinte

Fort des Salettes, Briançon

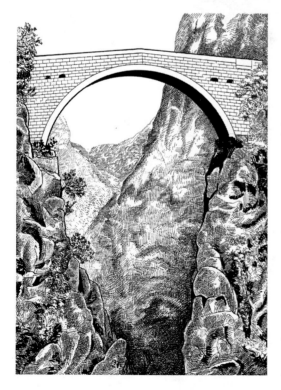

The Asfeld Bridge, Briançon
The Asfeld Bridge, defended by a redan, and with a 40 m span arch, enabled the connection between Briançon and the forts situated on the left bank of the Durance.

hostile Duchy of Savoy, fortification works for Briançon were undertaken, notably by the counts of Dauphiné, who built a castle on the spur dominating the town, including a square 24-m-high keep and a stone wall with three towers. During the Italian Wars (from 1495 to 1559) and the Wars of Religion (from 1562 to 1598) the city was looted several times. In 1580, Constable Lesdiguières added two bastions to the castle and built a hornwork on the existing Champ de Mars. In 1624, Briançon was destroyed by fire and king's engineer Persens rebuilt and enlarged the town. In 1692, the Duke of Savoy Victor-Amédée joined the anti–French coalition

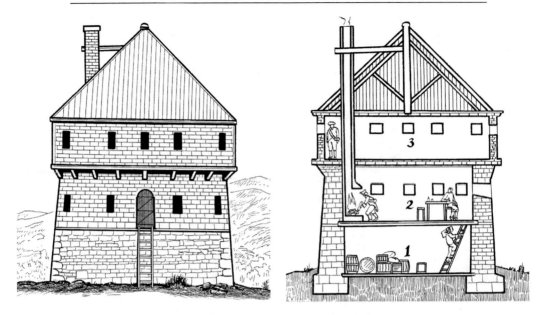

Redoute du Point du Jour at Briançon
Note the door placed about 2 m above the ground only accessible via a ladder. The cross section (right) shows the food and ammunition store (1), the garrison quarter (2) with fireplace, and the combat floor (3).

Fort Dauphin, Briançon

(League of Augsburg) and took the cities of Embrun and Gap. Briançon, menaced by invasion, was then hastily fortified by engineer d'Angrogne and victoriously defended by Dauphiné's governor, Marshal Catinat. Unfortunately another fire damaged the town again. When Vauban came on inspection tour, he found Briançon in a pitiful state, and he immediately made new designs for the town. After Vauban's death in 1707, his work was continued, particularly after the signature of the Treaty of Utrecht in 1713. Then France lost the eastern part of the province of Dauphiné, including the valleys of the rivers Doire Ripaire, Cluson, and Varaita. As a compensation she acquired the valley of the

Fort Randouillet, Briançon

Ubaye River with the city of Barcelonette, thereby making Briançon an important first-line frontier town facing the aggressive and expansion-minded House of Savoy. During the three following centuries Briançon was therefore transformed into an exceptionally strongly fortified site, including 17th- and 18th-century bastioned works, late 19th-century Séré de Rivière forts, and 20th-century Maginot bunkers. All of them are well-preserved today and display a unique summary of military architecture located in a sublime mountain landscape.

Le Havre

On a small and modest fishermen's site chosen by the Grand Admiral of France, Guillaume de Gouffier de Bonnivet, Le Havre-de-Grace was founded in 1516 by order of King François I to replace the silting-up haven of Harfleur. The marshy site, located on the right bank of the Seine estuary, did not look promising at first except that the floodwaters at high tide remained there for two hours or more, and this, in fact, proved decisive in Le Havre's development. The ambitious project was essentially military and intended to provide the French navy with a harbor to protect navigation in the English Channel and to avoid an English invasion on the river Seine. Under the direction of Monsieur de

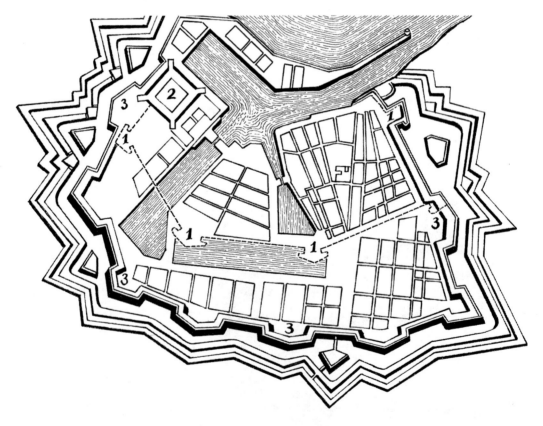

Le Havre c. 1787
1: Enceinte of 1541 designed by Jeromino Bellabarto; 2: emplacement of d'Argencourt's citadel; 3: urban enceinte built in the late 1780s.

Chillon, works proceeded quickly, and the brand-new city and its port, defended by two artillery towers, were ready by 1533. The city developed, attracted people from the neighboring Montvilliers, Harfleur and Granville, and was fortified by the Italian engineer Jeromino Bellamarto in 1541. The port and the land-front were fitted with Italian-style bastions with ears, and a triangular citadel was erected east of the town in 1564. Under Louis XIII's reign, the citadel was enlarged and outworks were added by engineer Pierre d'Argencourt in 1628.

The bombardment of Dieppe and Le Havre by the British fleet in 1694 demonstrated the weakness of the old fortifications. Vauban, aware of the harbor's importance, presented a design in October 1699; this project was refused by Louis XIV, probably because of the high cost involved. Vauban's plan, only slightly modified, was carried out during Louis XVI's reign. Le Havre's importance as a trading and transatlantic port began during the American War of Independence, when it supplied the rebels. Eventually all produce such as cotton, coffee, sugar, tobacco and exotic woods from the one-time colony were distributed from Le Havre to all parts of Europe, bringing considerable prosperity to the port.

The citadel and the early fortifications were dismantled in 1784, and replaced by a new and larger enceinte constructed between 1786 and 1790. This was composed of ten bastions, a wide wet ditch and a double covered way. At the same time new urban neighborhoods, an arsenal, and a new dock were established, a new jetty was built and a canal connecting to Harfleur was dug. Le Havre, a close parallel to Liverpool in many senses, became a synonym for the powerful international commercial and banking organization which had developed in the town. Napoléon called Le Havre the "port of Paris" and visited it twice, in 1802 and 1810. He ordered the construction of a new dock (Bassin de la Barre) and made ambitious development plans, but his fall in 1815 prevented them from being carried out. Le Havre was heavily damaged during the Battle of Normandy in the summer of 1944, and the town was rebuilt with impressive perspective according to a design by the urbanist August Perrot, the pioneer of reinforced concrete construction. Today all fortifications have disappeared; only two forts (Sainte-Adresse and Tourneville, built in the 19th century) are preserved.

CHERBOURG

In 1692, Admiral Tourville's fleet was partly destroyed in a sea battle against the British and Dutch off La Hougue, lacking a port and a refuge on the Cotentin Peninsula. This disaster was at the time of the creation and development of the village of Cherbourg as a major maritime military arsenal and eventually as a transatlantic port. The aim of this fortified harbor was to counter the British bases of Plymouth and Portsmouth at the other side of the Channel. Vauban was the first person to see the possibilities offered by Cherbourg as an Atlantic military port, but nothing happened until the 18th century. Another British attack in 1758 and increasing tension with Great Britain at the beginning of Louis XVI's reign marked the start of a huge construction program. The French hesitated between La Hougue, which had already been fortified by Vauban in 1683–84, and Cherbourg. Finally it was the latter that was chosen, and huge works were started in 1776. Under the supervision of engineer Alexandre de Cessart, the construction of a huge artificial dike was undertaken. The frame of the dike was composed of ninety enormous

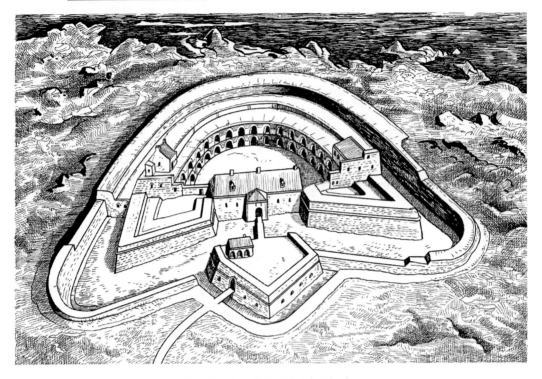

Fort Royal on Pelée Island, Cherbourg

Project for Cherbourg by Montalembert (c. 1778)

wooden cones, built on the mainland, filled with earth and rubble, towed in position in the bay and sunk down to a depth of 20 m. The works were thwarted by violent storms in 1784 and 1788, which swept away most of the underwater conical structures placed on the seabed. At the same time, Louis XVI ordered the construction of coastal works to defend the future port: Fort Royal on Pelée island; Fort de Querqueville, west of the town; and Fort d'Artois on the Homet rocks, were built in the 1780s. With their casemated semicircular gun batteries, these forts were directly inspired by Montalembert's theory. When the French Revolution broke out, the port and the dike of Cherbourg, as well as the coastal defenses, were far from being completed. Work stopped only to be continued under the Consulate and the Empire (see Chapter 4).

French Fortifications in Overseas Colonies

FRENCH COLONIES

European civilization had always shown a tendency to expand, but in the 16th, 17th, and 18th centuries (with the exception of the American continent, where a new cutting of the white race and of Western civilization was taking root), no European powers yet wished to subject Asia and Africa to their political control. Most were usually content with a few influential coastal trading stations. The older empires of the pre-industrial centuries were maritime and mercantile. The European traders simply purchased the wares brought to them by native merchants, on a kind of cash-and-carry basis. They had no territorial ambitions beyond the protection of way stations and trading centers, and — on the whole — they did not venture far in the hinterland, at least in Africa and Asia. In the 18th and 19th century, France possessed the following territories: Canada from 1608 to 1763; Acadia, Newfoundland and Hudson Bay until 1713; Cape Breton Island until 1758; Sainte-Lucie Island from 1650 to 1803; several islands in the Caribbean Sea, including Martinique (colonized in 1635) Guadeloupe (annexed in 1674) and Saint-Domingue (Haiti, from 1697 to 1804); the Malouines Islands (Falklands), temporarily held during the reign of Louis XIV; the Seychelles Islands from 1742 to 1804; and Maurice Island from 1764 to 1814.

Project of coastal fort by Montalembert (1793)

In addition, France possessed Louisiana from 1682 to 1803. In the late 17th century, French expeditions established a foothold on the Mississippi River and the Gulf Coast. With its first settlements, France lay claim to a vast region of North America and set out to establish a commercial empire and French nation stretching from the Gulf of Mexico to Canada.

The French explorer Robert Cavelier de La Salle named the region Louisiana to honor France's King Louis XIV in 1682. The first permanent settlement, Fort Maurepas (at what is now Ocean Springs, Mississippi, near Biloxi), was founded in 1699 by Pierre Le Moyne d'Iberville, a French military officer originally serving in Canada. The large French colony of Louisiana, as already seen, claimed all the land on both sides of the Mississippi River and north to French territory in Canada. Most of the territory to the east of the Mississippi was lost to Great Britain in the French and Indian War, except for the area around New Orleans and the parishes around Lake Pontchartrain. The rest of Louisiana became a possession of Spain after the Seven Years' War by the Treaty of Paris of 1763. Despite the fact that it was the Spanish government that now ruled Louisiana, the pace of francophone immigration to the territory increased swiftly, due to another significant after-effect of the French and Indian War. Several thousand French-speaking refugees from the region of Acadia (now Nova Scotia, Canada) made their way to Louisiana after being expelled from their home territory by the newly ascendant British. They settled chiefly in the southwestern Louisiana region now called Acadiana. The Acadian refugees were welcomed by the Spanish, and descendants came to be called *Cajuns*. In 1800, Napoléon Bonaparte reacquired Louisiana from Spain in the Treaty of San Ildefonso, an arrangement kept secret for some two years. Documents have revealed that Napoléon harbored secret ambitions to reconstruct a large colonial empire in the Americas. This notion faltered, however, after the failed French attempt to reconquer Haiti following its revolution. As a result of his setbacks in Haiti, Bonaparte, as already pointed out, gave up his dreams of an American empire and sold Louisiana to the United States in 1803.

In the 18th century, France also possessed important territories in India. Started under the reign of François I, the French presence in India was greatly extended with the creation of the *Compagnie Française des Indes orientales* (CFIO, French East India Company) formed under the auspices of Cardinal Richelieu in 1642, and reconstructed under Louis XIV's minister, Jean-Baptiste Colbert, in 1664. The maximum extent of French influence in India was in the middle of the 18th century under the governorship of Joseph François Dupleix. French ambition, however, clashed with British interests in India, and a period of military skirmishes and political intrigues began. By 1761, after a series of unfortunate local wars, the French had lost their hold in South India. In 1816, after the conclusion of the Napoleonic Wars, all was lost except the five enclaved establishments of Pondichéry, Chandranagore, Karaikal, Mahe and Yanam (Yanaon) and the lodges at Machilipattnam, Kozhikode and Surat.

COLONIAL FORTIFICATIONS

As individual settlements had to provide for their own defense, forts were the first structures built in the overseas colonies. They were constructed for protection by European rivals for land and influence, but also to guard settlers and traders against those natives who reacted with hostility to the intrusion into their homelands. Although many forts were only temporarily built, and although many were eventually destroyed, abandoned to deteriorate and swallowed up by nature and vegetation, the sites of many of these early forts often decided the locations of settlements that became permanent villages, cities, towns and ports. These early forts were usually quite simple in design, mainly small trading posts and garrison places from which soldiers could operate, rather than truly fortified structures. They were usually built with perishable earthwork, timber and logs, mud or adobe, but as time went by, larger and more significant fortified places were constructed of more durable stone whenever skilled personnel, manpower, money and stone were available. The builders often attempted in their designs to reproduce examples familiar to them from the Old World so far as the materials available to them permitted. Although no systematic pattern of defensive construction was adhered to, and although elaborate European formalism was of little practical value to guard a sparse population against raiders and rivals, most of these forts were built upon the traditional bastioned system developed in Europe, though in a most rudimentary fashion.

Engineers operating in the colonies were attached to the French navy as this corps was charged to discover, explore, develop and protect overseas territories. In the 17th and 18th centuries French engineers (e.g., Jacques Bourbon, Robert de Villeneuve, Jacques Levasseur de Néré, Josué Berthelot de Beaucours, Gaspard Chaussegros de Léry, Nicolas Sarrebrousse de Pontleroy, Jacques Lhermite, Joseph-François de Verville, Louis Franquet, and many others) were active in North America.

Ouiatenon Fort

Fort Ouiatenon was the first fortified European settlement in what is now called Indiana. It was a French trading post at the joining of the Tippecanoe River and the Wabash River, located approximately three miles southwest of modern-day West Lafayette. Fort Ouiatenon was originally constructed by the French as a military outpost to protect against English western expansion. Its location among the unsettled woodlands of the Wabash River Valley also made it a key center of trade for fur trappers. In 1717, Ensign François Picote de Beletre arrived at the mouth of the Tippecanoe and Wabash with four soldiers, three men, a blacksmith and supplies to trade with the nearby Wea people, an Algonquian-speaking nation closely related to the Miami people. They built a stockade on the Wabash, eighteen miles below the mouth of the Tippecanoe. François-Marie Bissot, the Sieur de Vincennes, assumed command of the fort sometime in the 1720s. The

Blockhouse at Ouiatenon Fort

French settled on the north bank, with Wea villages on the south bank. In order to convince the Wea to trade exclusively with the French, the Governor-General of New France, Philippe de Rigaud Vaudreuil, issued permits for trade at Ouiatenon. Traders immediately began to bring a steady flow of goods to the new post. Soon the officials in Louisiana sent more men to help Vincennes to hold the Wabash River. At its peak level of activity during the mid–18th century Fort Ouiatenon was home to over 2,000 residents. After the surrender of New France to the British in September of 1760, a contingent of British soldiers led by Lieutenant Edward Jenkins arrived in 1761, capturing and occupying the fort.

Fort Beauséjour

Situated near Aulac, New Brunswick, Canada, Fort Beauséjour was built in 1750 to check the nearby Fort Lawrence built by the British. The fort was attacked by British troops led by Lieutenant-Colonel Robert Monckton in June 1755. Although the commander of Fort Beauséjour, Marquis Louis Du Pont Duchambon de Vergor, defied the British for two weeks, there was little the French could realistically do against the numer-

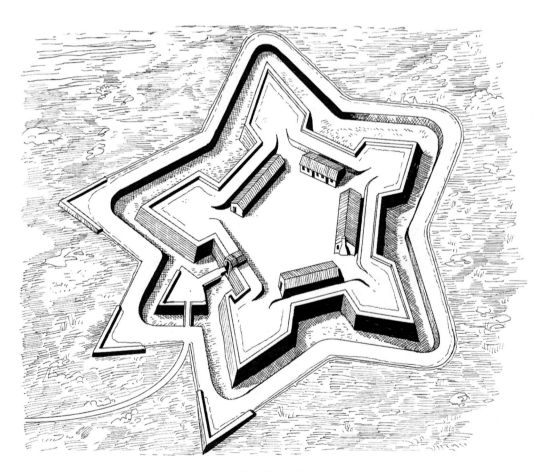

Fort Beauséjour

ically superior British forces. On June 16, when British mortar fire breached defective fortification works and badly mauled the French garrison, de Vergor surrendered. The Battle of Fort Beauséjour is often considered the first major British-American offensive action of the French and Indian War (Seven Years' War in North America). Called thereafter Fort Cumberland, it was abandoned and destroyed a year later.

Québec

Quebec City, situated on an imposing 300-foot cliff (Cape Diamond) on the St. Lawrence River, was founded in 1608 by the French explorer Samuel de Champlain. It was at first only a fortified trading place called the Habitation. Agriculture soon expanded and a continuous flow of immigrants, mostly men in search of adventure, increased the population. Over time, it became the capital of French Canada and all of New France (in 1627 encompassing Acadia, Quebec, Newfoundland, and Louisiana). In 1690 the city, now defended by wooden palisades, ditches and redoubts, was attacked by the British. The siege was repulsed, and improvements to the fortifications were made. In the early 18th century various engineers (notably Levasseur de Néré and Gaspard Chaussegros de Léry) designed and built a bastioned enceinte on the land front and divided the city into regular blocks for urban purposes.

In the middle of the 18th century, British North America had grown to be almost a full-fledged independent country, something they would actually become a few decades later, with more than 1 million inhabitants. Meanwhile New France was still seen mostly as a cheap source of natural resources for the metropolis, and had only 60,000 inhabitants. Nevertheless, New France was territorially larger than New England. When the

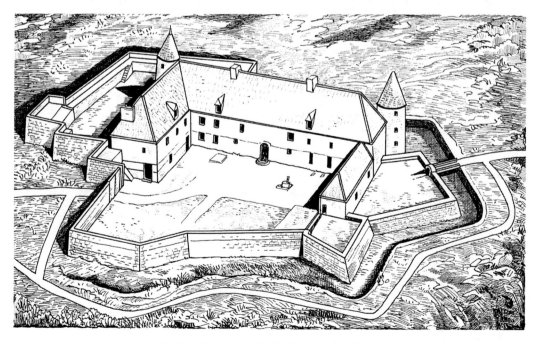

Québec (Canada), the Habitation (c. 1626)

Seven Years' War started, it was an obvious and easy target for the English. In September 1759 the British General James Wolfe, leading a fleet of 49 ships holding 8,640 British troops, laid siege to the fortress of Québec. The French forces under Marquis de Montcalm, for disputed reasons, did not use the protection of the city walls and fought on open terrain, in what would be known as the Battle of the Plains of Abraham. The battle was short and bloody. Both leaders died in battle, but the British easily won. The capture of Quebec marked the culmination of the British campaign in Canada during the French and Indian War. Now in possession of the main city and capital, and further isolating the inner cities of Trois-Rivières and Montreal from France, the British found that the rest of the campaign was only a matter of slowly taking control of the land. The last battle was fought in Montreal in 1760. Following the capitulation of the government of New France in September 1760, Canada was put under British military rule. The fortress of Quebec might have looked impressive, but actually its defenses were quite poor. The gates were inadequately defended, there was neither a proper glacis, nor a covered way, nor a suitable ditch, nor outworks. Besides, the defenders and their guns were easily commanded from hills located in the vicinity of the walls. The weakness of the defenses probably induced Montcalm to fight a pitched battle in the open plain.

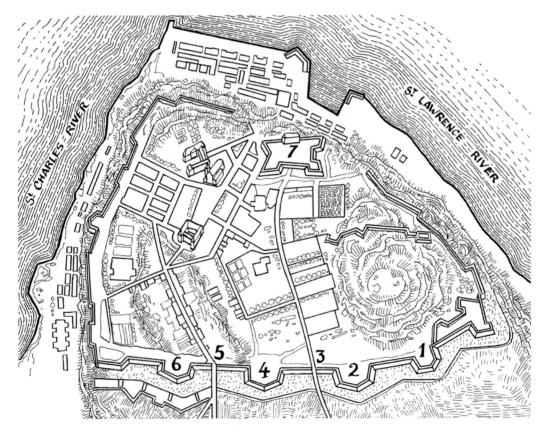

Quebec (c. 1759)
The sketch shows the following. 1: Glacière Bastion; 2: Saint Louis bastion; 3: Saint Louis Gate; 4: Saint Ursula Bastion; 5: Saint John Gate; 6: Saint John Bastion; 7: Saint Louis Citadel.

Montreal

The first post–Nordic European to reach the area of Canada was Jacques Cartier in 1534, but it was not until 1642 that a permanent settlement, named Ville-Marie, was created on the large island of Montreal by a group of French fervent Catholic settlers under the leadership of Paul Chomedy de Maisonneuve. After many vicissitudes, the colony became a center for fur trade. The town was fortified in the late 1680s by a simple wooden wall, and many forts were erected on the shores of the island (e.g., Forts Varennes, Le Tremblay, Longeuil, Saint-Lambert, La Prairie, Sault Saint-Louis, Sennevile, Ile Saint-Bernard, Gentilly, Rolland, Rémy, Cuillerier, Verdun, Saint-Gabriel, de la Montagne, and several others). The city defense was enlarged and replaced by a bastioned stone enceinte in the 1720s.

The Treaty of Paris in 1763 ended the Seven Years' War and ceded Canada and all its dependencies to the British. Ville-Marie then became known as Montreal.

Louisbourg

The French came to Louisbourg in 1713, after they were forced to cede Acadia and Newfoundland to the British by the terms of the Treaty of Utrecht, which ended the War

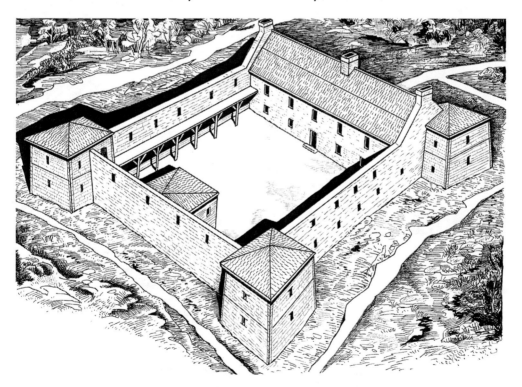

Fort Senneville, Montreal
Fort Senneville was one of the forts defending the island of Montreal. Located at the western point of the island (the area near Lake Deux-Montagnes, most exposed to Iroquois raids), the fort comprised four straight stone walls flanked by bastioned towers and a manor built between 1692 and 1702 by Jacques Le Ber.

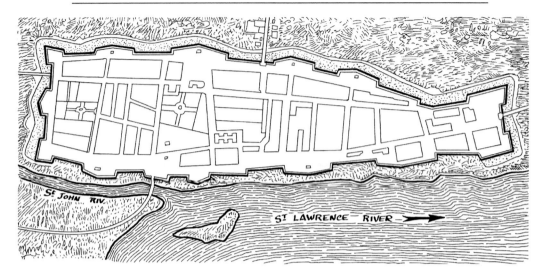

Montreal, Canada (c. 1745)

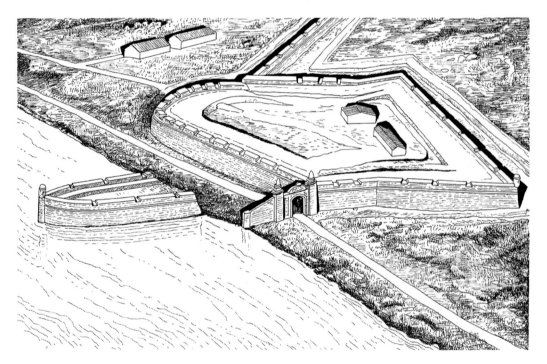

Louisbourg, Cape Breton Island

of the Spanish Succession. France's only remaining possessions in what is now Atlantic Canada were the islands of Cape Breton and Prince Edward, which were then named Isle Royale and Isle Saint-Jean. The French used these islands as a base to continue the lucrative cod fishery of the Grand Banks. In 1719 they began to construct at Louisbourg a fortified town, which was only completed on the eve of the first siege in 1745. A seaport and capital of Ile Royale (Cape Breton Island), the town and settlement along the harbor shore, protected by the fortress, soon became a thriving community, and a hub of commerce trading in manufactured goods and various materials imported from France, Quebec, the West Indies and New England, as well as one of the busiest harbors in North America and one of France's key centers of trade and military strength in the New World. The first attack came in 1745 following a declaration of war between Britain and France. After a siege of 46 days the fortress was taken. But three years later the town was given back to France by the Treaty of Aix-la-Chapelle. In 1758 Louisbourg was besieged a second time. Without a strong navy to patrol the sea beyond its walls, Louisbourg was difficult to defend. Attacking with 16,000 troops supported by 150 ships, a British army captured the fortified town in seven weeks. Determined that Louisbourg would never again become a fortified French base, the British demolished the fortifications. In 1961 the government of Canada decided to reconstruct approximately one-quarter of the original town with fortifications, buildings, yards, gardens and streets recreated as they were during the 1740s, immediately preceding Louisbourg's first siege.

Mobile

The settlement of Mobile, Alabama, then known as Fort Louis de la Louisiane, was first established in 1702 as the first capital of the French colony of Louisiana. It was founded by French Canadian brothers Pierre Le Moyne d'Iberville and Jean-Baptiste Le Moyne, Sieur de Bienville, in order to establish control over France's Louisiana claims, Bienville having been made governor of French Louisiana in 1701. An earth and palisade

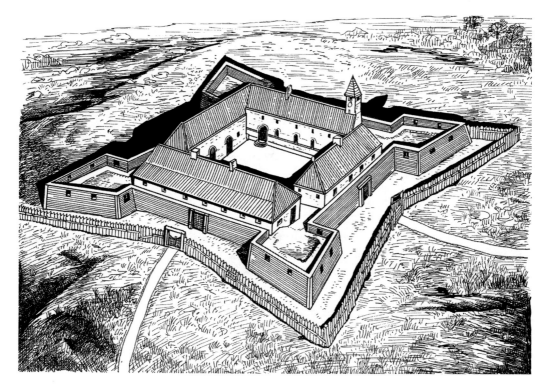

Fort Louis at Mobile

Fort Louis was constructed in 1712, when Antoine Crozat took over administration of the colony by royal appointment, and the colony boasted a population of 400 persons. The capital of Louisiana was moved to Biloxi in 1720, leaving Mobile relegated to the role of military and trading outpost. In 1723 the construction of a new brick fort with a stone foundation began and it was renamed Fort Condé in honor of Louis Henri, Duc de Bourbon and Prince of Condé. Mobile would maintain the role of major trade center with the Native Americans throughout the French period. In 1763, the Treaty of Paris was signed, ending the French and Indian War. The treaty yielded Mobile and the surrounding territory to Britain, and it was made a part of the expanded British West Florida colony. The British changed the name of Fort Condé to Fort Charlotte, after Charlotte of Mecklenburg-Strelitz, King George III's queen. The fort was abandoned and dismantled by the U.S. government in 1820.

New Orleans

The area of present-day New Orleans was originally inhabited by Native Americans who took advantage of Bayou Saint John to develop an important trade place on the Mississippi River. French explorers, fur trappers, and traders arrived in the area by the 1690s, and an encampment called Port Bayou St. Jean and a small Fort St. Jean were established in 1701.

New Orleans was founded in August 1722 by the French as Nouvelle-Orléans, under the direction of Jean-Baptiste Le Moyne de Bienville. The city was named in honor of

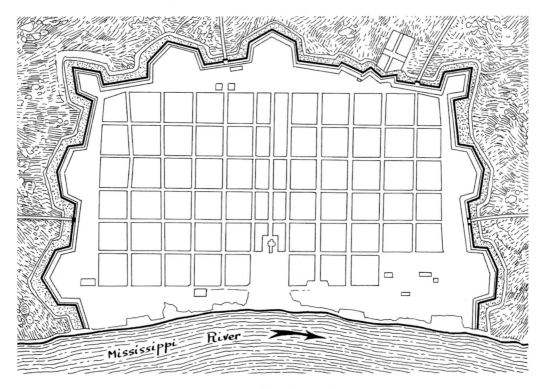

New Orleans (c. 1759)

the then Regent of France, Philip II, Duke of Orléans. Soon Nouvelle-Orléans was made the capital of French Louisiana, replacing Biloxi in that role. Louisiana, today reduced to a single American state, as already said before, was then enormous, covering the whole of the U.S. Midwest to the Canadian borders and the territories bordering the Gulf of Mexico from Texas to Florida. After a hurricane destroyed most of the settlement, the city was rebuilt following a grid pattern still seen today in the streets of the city's French Quarter. In the 1730s, the town was redeveloped and enclosed with a wooden palisade, a ditch, small earthen walls and gun batteries. In the late 1750s the French made several designs to protect the city with masoned bastions and pentagonal-shaped stone walls. After two massive fires in 1788 and 1794, the city was rebuilt in the Spanish colonial style with bricks, firewalls, iron balconies, and courtyards replacing the simpler wooden buildings constructed in the French style. In April 1803, Napoléon sold Louisiana to the United States in the so-called Louisiana Purchase.

Fort Duquesne

Situated in Pennsylvania, at the forks of the Ohio on the point of land where the Monongahela and Allegheny Rivers join to form what the French called La Belle Rivière (at the site of present-day Pittsburgh), the French Fort Duquesne was built in 1754 under the direction of Captain Lemercier, who headed a Compagnie Franche de la Marine (Marines company) and a group of Canadian militiamen. The fort was part of a line

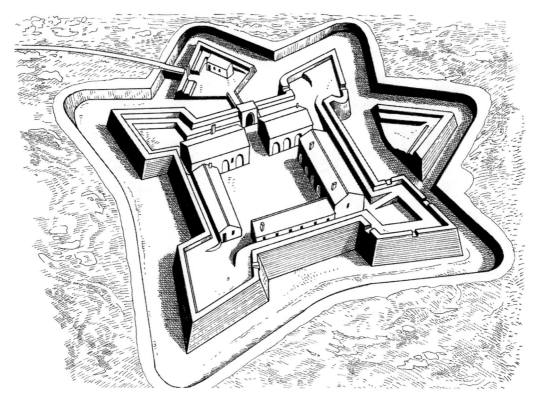

Fort Duquesne

including other forts (e.g., Le Boeuf, Marchault), that stretched along the line of communication back to Lake Erie at Fort Presquisle. A key strategic military and trading point, the compact square fort with four bastions at the angles was built partially of horizontal, squared, oak and chestnut timbers laid in criblocked walls with tamped earth and rock fill on the land side and upright stockade walls on the sides abutting the rivers. The garrison of the fort repulsed two British attacks in September 1758. They held the fort until November, when the French retreated and the fort was abandoned and burned. The site was occupied by the British, and a second fort was built in 1759 named Fort Pitt (after the contemporary Prime Minister William Pitt).

Fort de Chartres

Fort de Chartres, situated on the Mississippi River 18 miles north of Kaskaskia, was completed in 1720. Named after Louis, Duke of Chartres (son of the Regent Philippe d'Orléans when Louis XV was too young to rule), the fort consisted of a palisade (walls of square logs) defended by four bastions at the angles and a dry ditch. Buildings inside the enclosure included a storehouse used by the Indies Company, quarters, services, a prison, a stable, a powder magazine, and a chapel. The wooden fort, subject to frequent flooding, deteriorated quickly. So it was decided to rebuild it in stone. The construction of the new fort was delayed, however, and proceeded slowly. Limestone was quarried from the bluffs north of Prairie du Rocher and conveyed across lake by raft before it was hauled to the site by oxen. Completed in June 1760, the fort served at France's Illinois Country headquarters for only ten years. France surrendered Illinois along with most of

Fort de Chartres, Illinois

her North American possessions to Great Britain in the Treaty of Paris in 1763 that brought an end to the Seven Years' War. British troops took possession of the fort in October 1765, and renamed it Fort Cavendish. Soon the British authorities deemed the fort (already weakened by erosion from the Mississippi) of little practical use and ordered it abandoned in 1771.

Fort Carillon

The French Fort Carillon (named after a former officer, Pierre de Carrion, who established a trading post at the site in the late 17th century) is situated at the border of the United States (New York and Vermont) and Canada (Quebec) on a bluff overlooking the west side of Lake Champlain. It was constructed in 1755 with the aim of protecting French fur trade in the area and to prevent the British from getting a toehold on Lake Champlain. The fort was taken by the English during the French and Indian War, rebuilt in the 1760s, and renamed Fort Ticonderoga. In 1775, the stronghold was captured by an American force led by Benedict Arnold and Ethan Allen, marking the first victory of the Revolutionary War. In later years the place was abandoned and fell into ruin, until 1908 when the Pell family restored and reconstructed it. Today the privately-owned Fort Ticonderoga is open to the public, and stands as a fine example of an 18th-century star-shaped bastioned fortification.

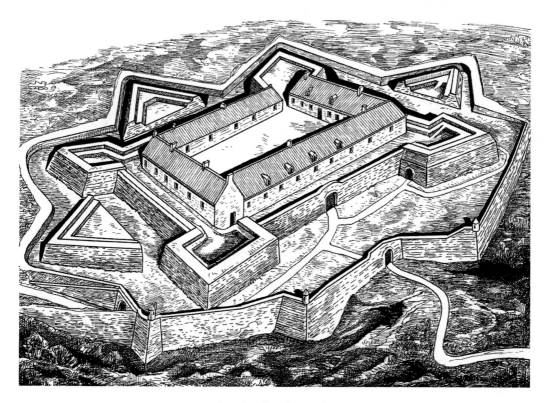

Fort Carillon (c. 1757)

Fort Bourbon

In 1638, Jacques Duparquet, first governor of Martinique in the Caribbean, decided to have Fort Saint Louis built to protect the city against enemy attacks. The fort was soon destroyed, but was rebuilt in 1669, when Louis XIV appointed the Marquis of Baas as governor-general. Under his orders and those of his successors, particularly the Count of Blénac, the settlement was built. Originally named Fort-Royal, the administrative capital of Martinique was shadowed by Saint-Pierre, the oldest city in the island, which was renowned for its commercial and cultural vibrancy as "The Paris of the Caribbean." The name of Fort-Royal was changed to a short-lived "Fort-La-Republique" during the French Revolution, and finally settled as Fort-de-France sometime in the 19th century. The city has a fine natural harbor defended by a fort with an irregular bastioned design: Fort Bourbon, built from 1763 to 1780. It was called Fort la Convention in 1793, Fort George during the British occupations (1793–1802, 1809–1814), and Fort Desaix since 1802. This name was given by Napoléon Bonaparte after General Desaix (1768–1800), administrator in Egypt, who was killed at the Battle of Marengo. Today the fort houses the headquarters of the French forces in the Caribbean and the 33rd Regiment of Navy Infantry (Marines).

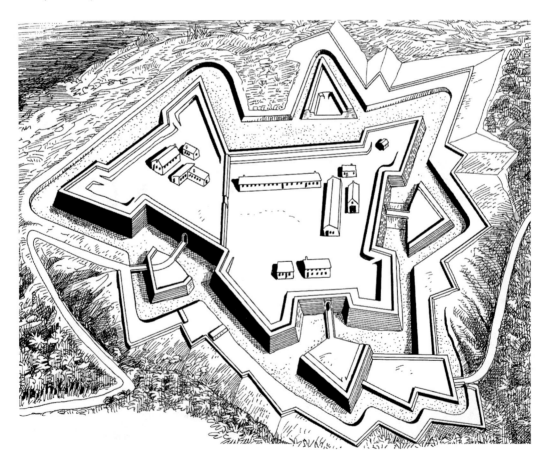

Fort Bourbon, Martinique Island (1788)

Fort Saint-Charles

Fort Saint-Charles at Basse-Terre on Guadeloupe Island in the Caribbean Sea originated from a small fortified place built in 1650 by Governor Charles Houël. In the 1720s, the place was enlarged and then comprised two parts: First, the site with the remains of Houël's castle (destroyed in 1703); second, the Basse-Terre bastioned front facing the city. The fort was besieged, taken and temporarily occupied by the British from 1759 to 1763 and renamed Fort Royal. After the departure of the British, the fort was enlarged again by the addition of a bastioned enclosure, built between 1763 and 1780, and the construction of the main entrance, and various service buildings (barracks, powder house, kitchen,

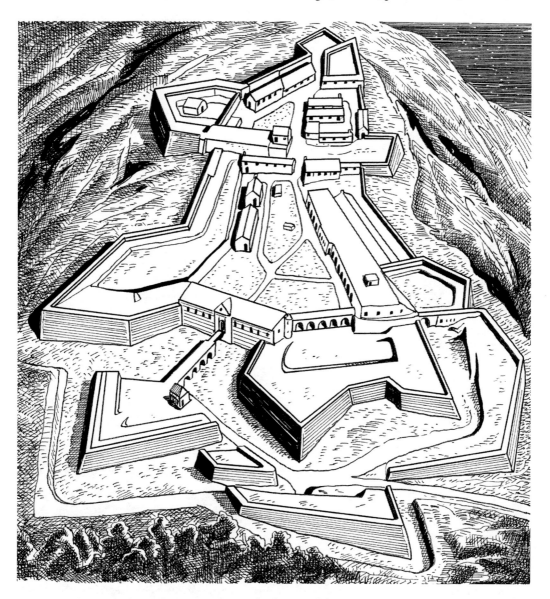

Fort Saint-Charles, Guadeloupe

cisterns). Since 1989, the work has been called Fort Delgrès, in honor of Louis Delgrès (1766–1802), an experienced and courageous French officer who led an armed movement resisting the reinstitution of slavery in the colonies, ordered by Napoléon. After a spirited but hopeless resistance, Delgrès and his followers found themselves trapped on the Matouba Volcano. There, Delgrès and most of his followers chose to commit suicide by detonating their own gunpowder stores. This act, though it effectively ended Guadeloupe's native resistance to French authority, had powerful symbolic value and continues to be heralded as an example of exceptional heroism and dedication to the cause of emancipation of black people in Guadeloupe, France, and elsewhere.

Pondichery

The simple village of Putuceri was acquired by the French Compagnie des Indes from a local Tamil ruler in 1674; they established a trading post, which was renamed Pondichery. Between 1693 and 1697, the post was occupied and fortified by the Dutch before being handed back to France. In 1740, when France and Britain were at war, the resource-

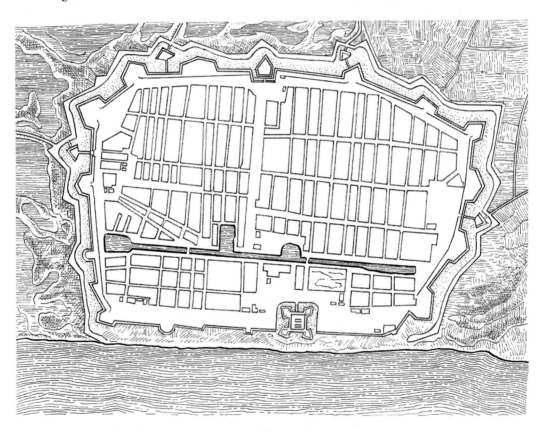

Pondichery, India
The plan shows the situation of the fortifications by the end of the 18th century. In 1771 the engineer Fourcroy de Ramecourt made an ambitious design to build a fortified city extension in the nearby Ile aux Cocotiers (Cocotrees Island). Two years later, Montalembert proposed a project to construct a large casemated fort. Neither plan was carried out.

ful Governor Joseph François Dupleix succeeded in repelling the British and extending French influence in South India. France gradually lost the initiative, however, and Lally-Tollendal, Dupleix's successor, was eventually obliged to surrender Pondichery to the British in 1761. The settlement was handed back to the French in 1816 and was held by them until 1954.

3

Imperial Fortifications

Napoleonic Style

Looking to the past and to the future simultaneously, Napoléon often thought how posterity would evaluate his life and work. Like all the great propagandists, he realized the importance of outward form, or as today's public-relations men would put it, of the *image* created. Talent was rewarded but safely placed under government control. For his own glorification, Napoléon encouraged the creation of the Empire Style, which drew influences from the ancient Roman Empire and its many archaeological treasures which had been rediscovered starting in the 18th century. Originally the Style was sober and clean-cut in its neoclassic lines, but soon became ornate and fussy, degenerating into an absurdly overburdened and pompous fashion. The Imperial Style, popularized by the inventive designs of Napoleon's architects, Percier and Fontaine, was considered to have "enlightened" architecture just as Napoléon "liberated" the peoples of Europe. In civilian architecture Greek and Roman (and even Egyptian) influences were expressed by massive colonnades, overabundant cornices and medallions, gilding, symmetrical designs, triumphal arches, impressive columns, and upscaled temples imitating antiquity and evoking and glorifying the Emperor's exploits. At the same time steel industry made great strides forward. For the first time in Paris, great metal structures were set up: the Pont des Arts in 1803 over the Seine, and the cupolas of the Grain Market in 1811. If many other projects never went further than the drawing board, it was because Napoléon's ceaseless military campaigns left him without sufficient time and funds for construction, urbanism and architecture.

The Napoleonic era is, above all, the expression of the will to create grandeur. This was paralleled in painting. What had been a revolutionary style congealed into rigid dogma, endorsed by Napoleonic government and backed by the weight of conservatism. The highly talented Jacques-Louis David (1748–1825), Antoine-Jean Gros (1771–1835), Théodore Géricault (1791–1824), and Jean-Auguste Ingres (1780–1867) were ardent Bonapartists, and the chief painters of the Napoleonic myth: the irresistible man of destiny depicted in romantic and neoclassical style. After Napoleon lost power, the Empire Style continued to be in favor for many decades, with minor adaptations. There was a revival of the style in the last half of the 19th century in France, again at the beginning of the 20th century, and again in the 1980s.

The will to create something virile, severe, and virtuous is evident in most of the works of French Napoleonic military engineers. This has often produced architectural

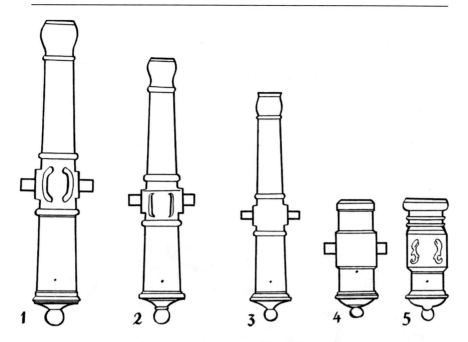

Gribeauval gun barrels
Cannons were categorized by the weight of the solid shot they fired, given in pounds. Howitzers and mortars were categorized by the size of the diameter of their projectiles given in inches. 1: twelve-pounder; 2: eight-pounder; 3: four-pounder; 4: six-inch howitzer; 5: eight-inch howitzer

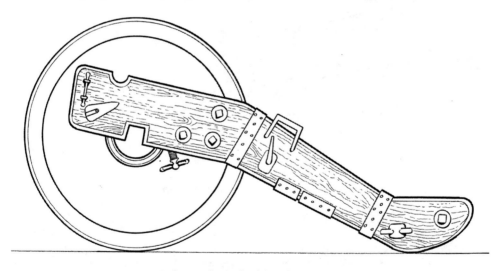

Gribeauval standard howitzer carriage
Guns of different calibers were carried on standard types of carriage. The gun carriages had large wheels, permitting relatively easy movement over irregular terrain. The trails were composed of two straight frames almost parallel to each other, but narrowing slightly to the rear. An ammunition chest was often carried, supported by its handles, between the trail frames when the gun was limbered up. Six- and eight-inch howitzers had a slightly different carriage with only one trunnion rest, but otherwise this was very similar to that of the eight- and twelve-pounder cannons. Note that the left wheel has been omitted for the clarity of the sketch.

dreams on paper totally unconcerned with what might be or could not be executed. This will is particularly evident in Montalembert's grandiose and upscaled fortification designs.

Fortifications of the time of Napoléon, at least those that were completed, are not well-known for several reasons. They are obliterated behind vast campaigns characterized by mobile warfare punctuated by large pitched battles whose names are inscribed on the Arch of Triumph in Paris. Many Napoleonic fortifications were built outside France

Gun crew

1: Gun commander and firer. This man had overall command of the gun and crew. He was responsible for giving orders and ensuring that crew members executed their tasks correctly and safely; he was often, but not always, also the firer maintaining the lintstock and touching off the charge. *2: Vent tender.* This experienced gunner stopped (or tended) the vent, making sure no air escaped during the operations of worming, sponging and loading. He picked open the charge with a priming wire; he had a leather thumbstall to protect his thumb from the heat of the gun while tending the vent. *3: Ram and sponge man.* This gunner sponged and rammed home the cartridge; he often wore heavy-duty leather gloves while performing his duties. *4: Worm and loader.* This man had to extract the spent cartridge casing, and to place the new round in the muzzle for #3 to ram; he would help aim the gun with #5. *5: Powder handler.* This gunner's job was to remove the powder box to a secure position before the gun was fired, and to bring each round forward to #4 for loading; he was also responsible for manning the tiller for aiming the gun. For practical reasons the powder had to be kept close to the gun, and to protect it from chance sparks the powder keg had a leather lining which was gathered and tied at the neck.

in the conquered territories; many were dismantled after the fall of the Empire or incorporated and modernized in the 19th century. The rapid collapse of the French Empire also prevented many projects from being completed, but the period offered to the military engineer corps a vast field of experimentation. The realizations, some of them remarkable and impressive, displayed a style of their own. In its form, Napoleonic fortification was severe and martial, complying with ideals of grandeur, robustness, solidity and economy. In its principles, it was comparatively uncreative, being basically classical and making a general use of the traditional bastioned system. It was also characterized by a curious return to some medieval forms like the standardized *tour-modèle* with its machicoulis balconies. These traditional and backwards elements were, however, mixed with innovations influenced by Montalembert's concepts like the massive artillery tower, the general use of stone and masonry for vaulted casemates, and an increased use of caponiers, subterranean passages and riflemen's galleries concealing the defenders from enemy sight and fire. The French imperial military architecture rejected obsolete forms such as the horn- and crownwork, but it made a general use of advanced works like the demi-lune, the lunette and the counterguard to develop defense in depth. Thereby it took account of the significant artillery improvements that occurred during the 18th century.

Artillery

The Heritage of the Ancien Régime

The artillery used during the Napoleonic Wars remained that developed under the Ancien Régime. It was the best element of the early Republican army, the nucleus of the

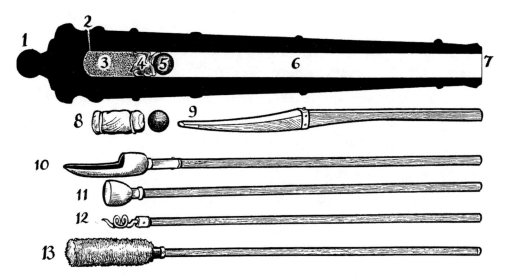

Cross-section gun and tools

The gun is shown here loaded and ready to fire. 1: breech; 2: vent; 3: powder charge; 4: wad; 5: shot; 6: smooth bore; 7: muzzle; 8: cartridge (fabric bag containing both powder and shot); 9: lever, tiller or handspike; 10: ladle (when loose powder was used); 11: rammer; 12: worm; 13: swab. Rammer and swab could also be fixed at both ends of the same staff.

Loading the gun
Until the second half of the 19th century, guns were smooth-bored and muzzle-loading. Muzzle loading was a rather dangerous and time-consuming procedure. The successive steps were carefully carried out on the gun-commander's order, under direction of the battery-commander. The cartridge or round (consisting of shot and propelling charge both in a canvas bag prepared in advance to quicken the rate of fire) was driven into the bore with a wooden rammer. If powder and shot were loose, the projectile was wrapped in a wad (material immediately at hand, like old cloths, paper, mud, grass or hay) to avoid gas dispersion and to keep the round shot from rolling out. The powder bag was then pricked with a spike or a wire from the vent (a narrow ignition-hole pierced in the upper side of the gun). The final step of loading was priming the gun; that is, pouring some powder into the vent either by using a powder horn or by inserting a quill (a small hollow tube filled with powder) into the vent. The piece was then ready to shoot and set back into firing position. The loaded gun had then to be aimed at the target. Until the late 19th century land service field guns were used in the direct fire mode; that is, the layer could see the target at which he was required to shoot. Aim was adjusted horizontally by manually moving the gun to the right or to the left with heavy levers (handspikes), and vertically by adjusting one or more wooden wedges (called coins) under the breech, or by adjusting the elevating screw when available. Aiming was done by direct sight or with the help of instruments such as a quadrant, a pendular level or a marlinspike, but accuracy, especially in case of a moving target, was poor. The final step was firing the gun. The propelling charge was ignited with a slow-burning match or a lintstock which brought a flashing flame through the vent. The gunpowder charge exploded and produced an enormous burst of energy which propelled the cannonball toward the enemy with flames, a loud and awful noise, and such violence that the gun abruptly moved backwards; this sudden movement (recoil) made re-aiming necessary after each round had been fired. Firing also produced bad-smelling clouds of toxic smoke which soon hung thickly over batteries or filled the casemate, and obscured gunners' view on windless days. The poor combustible quality of impure black powder resulted in

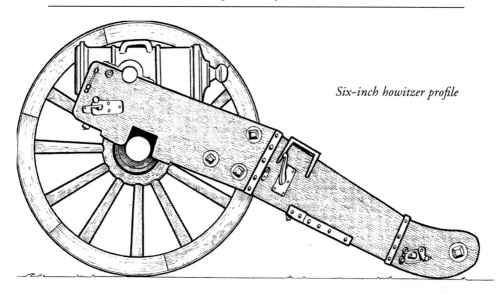

Six-inch howitzer profile

old Royal artillery serving with distinction in the early battles such as Valmy. The French artillery had seen a number of technical improvements owing to several senior artillery officers, notably Vallière, Belidor and Gribeauval.

The general of artillery, Jean-Florent de Vallière (1667–1759), had been inspector of Klingenthal weapons manufacture from 1721 to 1726, and director and general-inspector of the weapons manufactures of Saint-Etienne, Charleville and Maubeuge from 1727 to 1739. He had led the siege of Freiburg (Germany) in 1744, and eventually became lieutenant-general of the French artillery. In this function he was able to reform and reorganize the French artillery, together with his son Joseph-Florent de Vallière (1717–1776).

Bernard Forrest de Bélidor (1693–1761) was an officer and teacher at the artillery school of La Fère. He took part in the War of Austrian Succession and ended his career as general-inspector of the French artillery. Bélidor contributed to the renewal of the French army by publishing several theoretical books such as the *Bombardier français* (1731) and *Traité de Fortifications* (1735).

But the man who brought the most important changes in French artillery was Lieutenant-General Jean-Baptiste Vaquette de Gribeauval (September 1715–May 1789). Gribeauval is remembered as an innovative military officer who introduced many needed reforms that made him a leader in artillery development. Born in Amiens the son of a magistrate, Gribeauval entered the French army in 1732 as a volunteer, and was promoted to the rank of lieutenant in 1735. Interested in scientific work and engineering, he became captain of a company of miners in 1752. During the Seven Years' War (1756–1763), he was attached

a great deal of residue, and it was a constant problem to keep the barrel clean, especially of burnt-on, still glowing encrustation. Therefore, right after every shot the barrel was searched; that is, scraped with a spiral or worm (a sort of large corkscrew fixed on a wooden pole) to remove fouling. Right after worming, the barrel was vigorously scrubbed with a swab, a wet sponge attached on a wooden staff that fitted tightly to the barrel in order to extinguish all smoldering residues of wad or burning embers that may have remained from the previous shot. Worming and swabbing were usually done twice to ensure a clean barrel. This whole loading procedure was employed as long as smooth-bored muzzle-loaders were used; i.e., until about the middle of the 19th century.

to empress Maria-Theresa's Austrian army as a general of artillery and established the Austrian sapper corps. He led the mining operation at the siege of Glatz, and defended the city of Schweidnitz against Frederick the Great in 1762. The empress rewarded him for his work with the rank of lieutenant-feldmarschall and the cross of the Maria Theresa Order.

Returning to France as a lieutenant general in 1764, Gribeauval put to good use the knowledge he had gained in Austria to improve France's obsolete and chaotic artillery

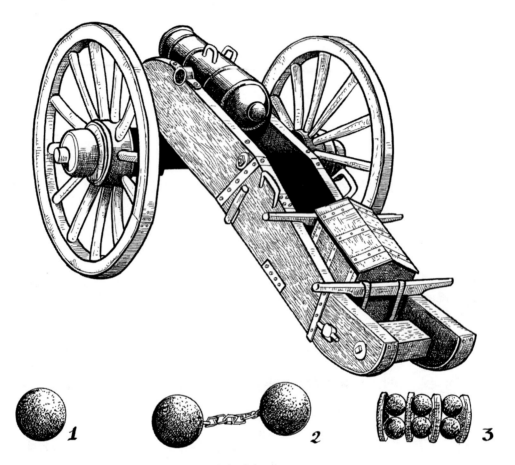

8-inch howitzer

The howitzer was invented in Sweden towards the end of the seventeenth century. At the time of Napoléon, it was a type of artillery piece that was characterized by a relatively short barrel and the use of comparatively small explosive charges to propel projectiles at trajectories with a steep angle of descent. Mounted on wheels, the howitzer was an inherently flexible weapon that could fire its projectiles along a wide variety of trajectories. It stood between the field gun (which was characterized by a longer barrel, larger propelling charges, small round shots, higher velocities and flatter trajectories) and the mortar (which had the ability to fire projectiles at even higher angles of ascent and descent). The howitzer had thus qualities of both weapons, which fitted it when the large caliber of the mortar and the maneuverability of the field gun were needed. Ammunition—1: Simple solid shot made of plain metal, this could slice through any man of horse in its path. 2: Two-chained shots, particularly effective against rigging of a warship but also devastating when whirling among infantrymen. 3: Grapeshot, an early form of anti-personnel shrapnel, composed of a bunch of small shots about the size of snooker balls arranged in tiers.

system. At first Gribeauval met with resistance from government officials when he tried to apply what he had learned in the field. In 1765, influenced by the artillery he had encountered in Austria, he began to consider implementing standard specifications for guns, designating guns according to their use (field, siege, fortress, and coastal), and ensuring that the army used lighter guns for greater ease of handling. In 1776, Gribeauval was assigned to the position of general of artillery and given a free hand. In this capacity, he trained

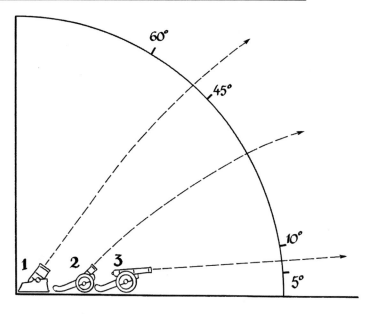

Artillery trajectories
1: Mortar (superior or equal to 45 degrees). 2: Howitzer (between 10 and 45 degrees). 3: Gun (between 5 and 10 degrees).

younger officers, including one young cadet with a pronounced Italian accent named Napoléon Bonaparte, and was able to implement his artillery reforms on a broad scale. Gribeauval achieved greater mobility by designing lighter gun carriages and having the guns and limbers drawn by paired horses, an improved harnessing pattern enabling the transport of more equipment. He was responsible for improving the hardware which

Profile and cross-section 10-inch mortar
A mortar had a fat short barrel for a high trajectory fire, secured to a timber carriage which directly passed the recoil force to the ground. Range was adjusted by altering the elevation, and also depended upon the power of the propelling charge. A mortar was extremely bulky — it weighed 1,500 to 2,500 kg, depending on the caliber — and was transported in two loads.

helped French guns to be mounted and used more effectively. Efficiency was improved by hiring more trustworthy wagon and cart drivers, and by having field artillery served by soldiers — not hired civilians, as had been the case before. Gribeauval increased the wages given to soldiers and improved the living quarters of lower-ranking men. He developed specialized training for officers that incorporated aspects of career management. In addition, Gribeauval was able to modernize the materials. He standardized the caliber of

Loading the mortar

Loading the mortar was a dangerous business. The procedure was basically the same as loading a field gun, but the ignition was twofold. First the mortar barrel was placed in a vertical position. Next a prepared powder bag and then the bomb (carried by two or more men, depending on the projectile's weight) were inserted. The range could be adjusted by varying the quantity of the powder charge. Then the mortar was aimed with the help of coins (triangular-shaped wedges) placed between the tube and the mount. Next the bomb's fuse was lit and the mortar charge ignited. The operation demanded great skill (and sometimes a dose of good luck), and therefore mortars were served by a specialized class of experienced and fearless gunners, forming an elite troop known as bombardiers. The tools used included the following:

1: Swab, used to wash out the barrel to prevent any live embers from igniting the next charge prematurely; the wet swab drenched with cold water also helped to cool the barrel. 2: Rammer, used to ensure that the powder charge was securely packed home into the barrel. 3: Pricker, used to clear the touch hole of any powder residue. 4: Bag, containing a pre-measured powder charge. 5: Bomb. 6: Scale, placed into the barrel to determine its angle of elevation. Although theorists promised a certain accuracy, the poor quality of gun and mortar casting and powder production, uneven distribution of exploding gases, combined with the effects of wind and weather, made gunnery a primitive and unreliable art. Most of the time accuracy was nearly random.

3. Imperial Fortifications 123

Gunners' uniforms (c. 1809)
Left: Officer's service dress from Foot-Line Artillery. Right: Gunner's field dress from Guard Foot Artillery.

cannons, which was indicated by the weight of the shot in French livre (pound, roughly 500 grams): 6, 8, 12, 18, 24, 36 and 48 pounds. Gribeauval also increased mobility by reducing the lengths and weights of the guns' barrels. He brought into general use the prefabricated cartridge (holding both propelling charge and solid shot) in place of the old method of using loose powder, wad and shot. The Gribeauval guns usually had tangent scales, and elevating screws, improving accuracy and rate of fire. He improved the quality of gun barrels, and introduced standardization on a large scale: wheels, axle-trees, screws, bolts and other spare parts were interchangeable and fitted for carriages, guns, caissons, wagons, ambulances, and carts. This enabled thus mass production and quick repair on the field. Gribeauval designed waterproof ammunition wagons that were lighter than their predecessors, and introduced mobile field forges for quick repair. He also introduced a new gun, the howitzer, which was commonly used by other armies of the time. Gribeauval's reforms made the French army a leader in the use of artillery. It remained a superior European fighting force into the nineteenth century. Gribeauval died on May 9, 1789. His book, *Tables des Constructions*, was published in 1792.

Gunner, Foot Artillery of the Line (c. 1814)
The artilleryman wears a shako, a short blue coat close to the waist with scarlet piping and red shoulder straps, blue breeches and black knee gaiters.

View and cross section of bomb
1: fuse; 2: match; 3: powder

Projectiles fired by mortars were of two kinds: bomb and carcass. The bomb was a heavy hollow spherical metal ball weighing 50 to 75 kg, filled with powder and lit by a fuse. The bomb was fitted with two rings intended to ease transport and loading with the help of a lever, chains and S-shaped hooks. The fuse was a hollow pipe made of wood and filled with an

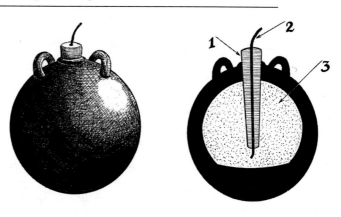

inflammable mixture whose density and burning length were estimated by the artificer. If the timing of the fuse was calculated correctly, the projectile would explode in the air over the enemy, sending a shower of dangerous splinters across a large area. The carcass was an oval metal frame containing incendiary materials wrapped in a thick canvas envelope. The mixture was difficult to extinguish and caused great destruction by setting ablaze wooden houses and buildings. Bomb and carcass were employed in siege warfare rather than on a battlefield.

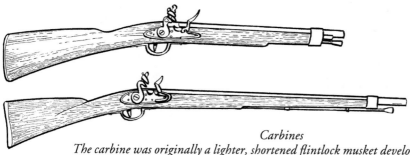

Carbines
The carbine was originally a lighter, shortened flintlock musket developed for artillerymen, and for cavalrymen, for whom a full-length musket was too heavy and awkward to fire from horseback.

Swords

Although much of the work was not directly attributable to him, the systems of organization and standardization in ordnance have been called *système Gribeauval*.

Field Artillery

Napoléon retained a high level of interest in artillery, and the Gribeauval system greatly contributed to the victories of the French Revolution, the Consulate and the

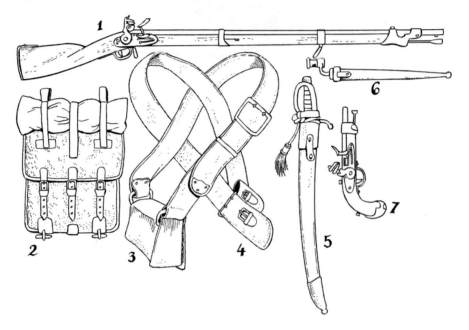

Artilleryman's weapons and equipment
The status of specialist did not dispense artillerymen of their responsibility to be proficient in operating the infantryman's basic weapon.
    1: Flintlock musket model 1777. Issue arm of the infantry during the French Revolution, the flintlock musket model 1777 was the result of the modifications made to the various models previously produced. Particular attention was given to the interchangeability of parts from one weapon to another, the precursor of modern mass production techniques. The model 1777 was slightly improved, and—then known as Fusil modèle 1777 Corrigé An IX—was the basic arm of the Napoleonic infantry. The weapon weighed about 5 kg, it was accurate up to a range of 80 m, and its spherical ball, with a caliber of 17.5 mm, was lethal up to 200 m. Rate of fire was about three to five shots per minute. The loading drill consisted of several main actions: Biting open the cartridge (a paper bag containing powder and ball); priming the pan; pouring powder and ball into the muzzle; ramming them down home; setting the lock to full cock; aiming; and firing. By modern standards, the smoothbore muzzle-loading model 1777 was inaccurate and slow to load, but the infantry tactics of the time allowed for these defects. Ranks of men fired disciplined volleys, one sub-unit firing while others were loading. Thus an effective hail of bullets could be delivered at brief intervals before the soldiers attacked with the bayonet. The weapon was fitted with a leather sling for carrying it slung over the shoulder or the back. Other items included the following. 2: Backpack of cowhide with the greatcoat rolled and strapped on top. 3: Cartridge pouch (made of black leather, the flap being embossed with a brass crowned eagle over two crossed cannon) and belt. 4: Shoulder belt holding saber and bayonet; both belts were made of whitened buff leather. 5: Saber briquet in scabbard. 6: Bayonet in scabbard. 7: Officer's pistol.

Empire. In Napoléon's hands, the mobile horse-drawn Gribeauval artillery system, organized on the same line as the rest of the army, became integrated into the general scheme of battle. It was no longer an accessory but an essential part of the combined arms on the battlefield. It must be remembered that Napoléon was originally a professional artillery officer. He placed great reliance on mobility and converging fire, and knew that artillery had to be collected in mass to achieve decisive result: at Austerlitz he had 80 guns, 100 at Wagram, 120 at the Moskova, and 200 at Eylau. An artillery battery could fire more than an infantry battalion and to a much greater range (about 600 m). However, battlefield tactics of artillery was extremely primitive, for—in spite of Gribeauval's reforms and Napoléon's military skills—tactics required movement which, due to the weight of the artillery pieces, was difficult once the battle had begun. Because most artillery fire on the battlefield was direct with a flat trajectory, the guns had to be placed among or interspersed between units, or in front of the infantry, which made them vulnerable if suddenly attacked by cavalry, for example. With any luck, troop movement would place a large number of enemy formations in line with the guns, so shots could mow them down. Besides, large field gun batteries were difficult to control. Gunners were shrouded in their own smoke, and often became isolated.

Garrison and Coastal Artillery

From the Ancient Régime, Napoléon inherited some hundred companies of *Canonniers-Gardes-Côtes* (Coast-Guard-Gunners), about 10,000 strong, who defended the French coasts. He restructured this force into hundred mobile companies. There were also twenty-eight companies of *Canonniers Sédentaires* (Static Gunners) for manning the garrison artillery in forts, batteries and fortresses. On the whole, Napoleonic fortress artillery remained of the Gribeauval system. Cannons for permanent fortifications were of various sizes and calibers depending upon the terrain that had to be defended. Unlike the field artillery, garrison guns incorporated foreign captured models, older designs and

48-pounder naval gun
Found too heavy for use aboard a warship, the 48-pounder, mounted on naval truck, was often placed in batteries for coastal and fortress defense where weight was not an issue.

16-pounder mounted on Gribeauval garrison carriage and platform
This kind of fortress mount, designed by Gribeauval for recoiling the gun, included two wooden rails for the front wheels, and a central rail for the smaller back wheel. Designed in the late 1740s, it was still used at Napoléon's time.

heavy pieces (notably 8-, 12-, 16-, and 24-pounders) as their lack of mobility due to their weight was not an issue for a static defensive role. Besides, the heavier the caliber, the longer the range; the 16-pounder, for example, could fire on a target up to 4,300 m away. But as mobile field artillery had top priority, garrison guns often served longer than the normal 1,200-round life of an iron piece. All guns and related equipment were painted in the same colors: olive-green for the wooden parts, and black for metalwork.

The principal adaptation was the carriages on which garrison guns were mounted. These were quite different from field and siege guns. An often-encountered carriage was the navy mount, a simple, robust, wooden truck fitted with four small wheels; this consisted of two cheeks of several thick planks, strongly jogged or mortised together. The small wheels gave a limited mobility but that was not an issue on a ship deck or on a rampart. In the Gribeauval system, the *affûts de place* (fortress carriages) were redesigned in order to improve aiming the gun and speeding the rate of fire. A solution was to put the gun on a three-wheeled mount, and have the wheels running into three groves made of wooden rails. The rails allowed the gun to recoil whilst keeping it pointed in the same direction, thus increasing the rate of fire. The traversing platform designed by Gribeauval in the 1790s was a further refinement; a ship's carriage without wheels was simply put on a strong wooden track that could rotate owing to back wheels running into a section of curved rail fixed in the gun platform.

Garrison cannons were not moved around on their carriages. If the gun had to be taken any long distance, it was dismounted and chained under a sling wagon or on a block carriage with big wheels.

Fortress guns fired with a relatively flat trajectory, and used the same projectiles as field guns, including solid shots, canisters and grapeshot used against personnel. Against ships, a variety of devices were used for coastal defense purposes, including shot with chain, bars and split shots, with the aim of doing as much damage as possible to the enemy's masts and rigging. Red-hot shots were introduced in the late 1570s and still used in the Napoleonic era. More useful against ships and property than against soldiers, they required great skill to use without the gunners doing themselves harm. The iron shot was

Top: *Cannon on fortress mount. This 36-pounder garrison gun is mounted on the later pattern of Gribeauval traversing platform, allowing the gun to swing from one side to another in order to follow its target.*

Bottom: *Carronade. The carronade was developed by the Scottish Carron Company and introduced in the British Royal Navy in 1779. It fired a large-caliber shot from a rather short and light gun, enabling a more effective use of the powder that enhanced close-range firepower. It was especially intended to arm warships for firing against enemy rigging and crew. It had a range of about 300 m and a rate of fire of about three shots a minute. The French copied the design in 1794 and put them on gunboats, frigates, and ships-of-the-line. Carronades, never forming an important part of French artillery, were also used as fortress guns in coastal forts and batteries.*

heated to redness in a furnace; the gun was loaded with a charge of powder and a tight-fitting dry wad rammed down on top; then with great rapidity, a wet wad was rammed down, followed by the red-hot shot, whereupon the gun was quickly fired before the shot burned its way through the wads and did the job itself. Primitive as it sounds, incendiary red-hot shots were standard ammunition in coastal defense and siege warfare.

Fortress artillery emplacements

The fortress artillery emplacements included two main modes: either in the open air or inside a casemate. In the first case the gun was placed on an open platform behind an epaulement, also named *parapet* or *breastwork*, a strong man-high wall made of masonry revetment holding a thick earth cover. This disposition was known as *en barbette* ("like a small beard"). The term is said to have derived from the French, due to the resemblance of the parapet to a beard beneath the gun muzzle. A refinement was to cut an opening in the parapet. Known as an *embrasure* or *gun port*, this was an opening made in the upper part of the rampart in the parapet to allow artillery fire. It gave servants, guns and ammunition some protection, but though given a widening-out shape, the traverse was reduced. In both cases, the gun's being placed in the open allowed for a rapid dispersion of toxic gases generated by firing.

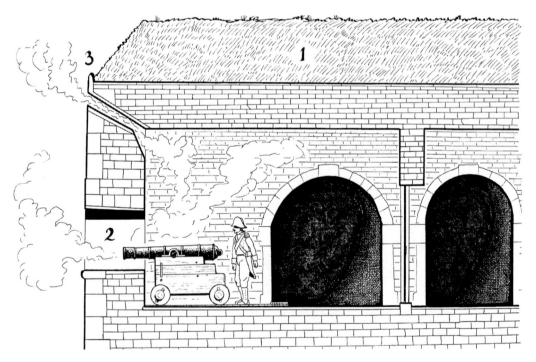

Cross-section of casemate (gun chamber)
A casemate was a vaulted gun chamber built in the rampart with a port to permit artillery to be fired from it. It gave excellent protection to the weapon and the gunners but the main disadvantages were: Poor observation possibility; limited traverse; problem of ventilation and light. In cross-section the main parts were the following. 1: Thick layer of earth covering strongly masoned walls and ceiling; 2: gun port; 3: air-duct to allow toxic smoke and fumes to escape.

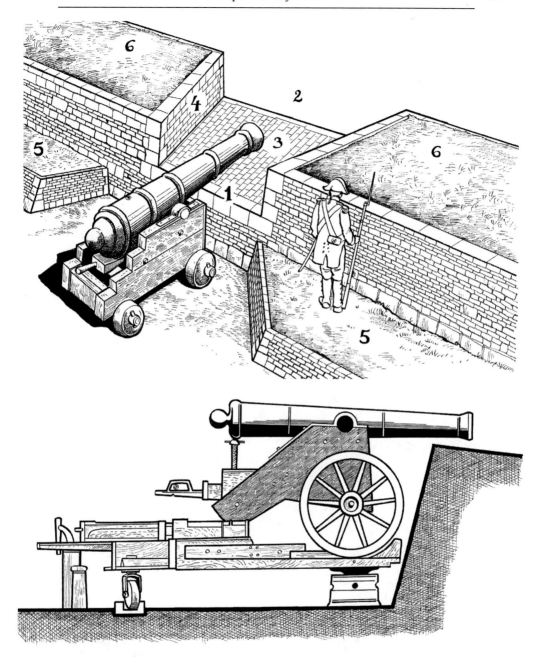

Top: *Embrasure.* An embrasure included the following components. 1: Throat, the interior opening wide enough to admit the muzzle of the gun. 2: Mouth, the exterior opening governed by the amount of lateral coverage required. 3: Sole, the bottom surface, the outward slope. 4: Cheek, each vertical side wall of the opening. 5: Fire-step for infantry musket fire. 6: Merlons, often made of comparatively thin layers of bricks filled with earth; it was observed that brick splinters were less dangerous than stone splinters.

Bottom: *Barbette firing.* The gun was fired above the parapet. The depicted cannon is mounted on a traversing carriage designed by Berthelot allowing a few men to move, aim, fire and recoil the gun with relative ease.

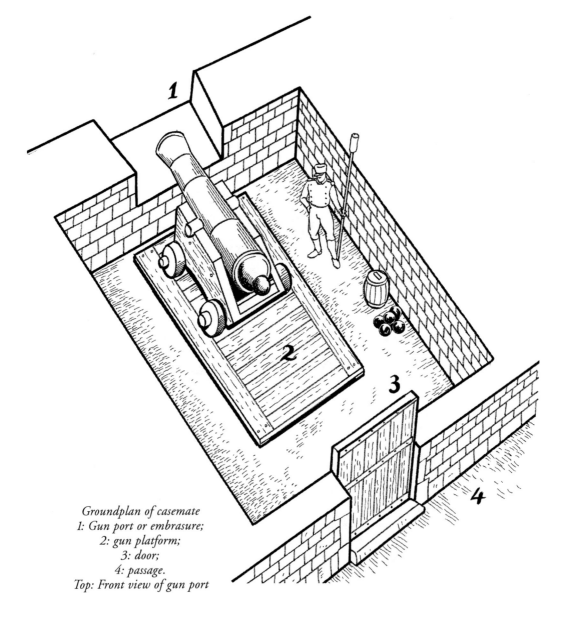

Groundplan of casemate
1: Gun port or embrasure;
2: gun platform;
3: door;
4: passage.
Top: Front view of gun port

Haxo casemate
The gun chamber was open at the rear and usually measured 3 m in height and 8 m in length.

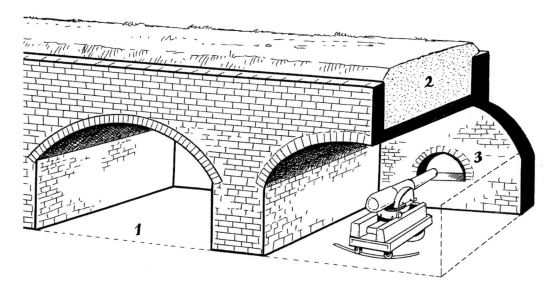

Cross-section of Haxo casemates
1: Opening at the rear; 2: earth cover; 3: gun port

The second mode of placing artillery was in a casemate. A *casemate* was a closed vaulted gun chamber. In a fort it was usually built with strong masonry covered with a thick layer of earth. It was obviously fitted with a port to permit the gun to be fired from it. The casemate gave excellent protection to gunners, cannons and ammunition, but the angle of fire was considerably reduced and observation was extremely limited. The casemate was a dark, humid and cold cave, and its ventilation was also a difficult problem to

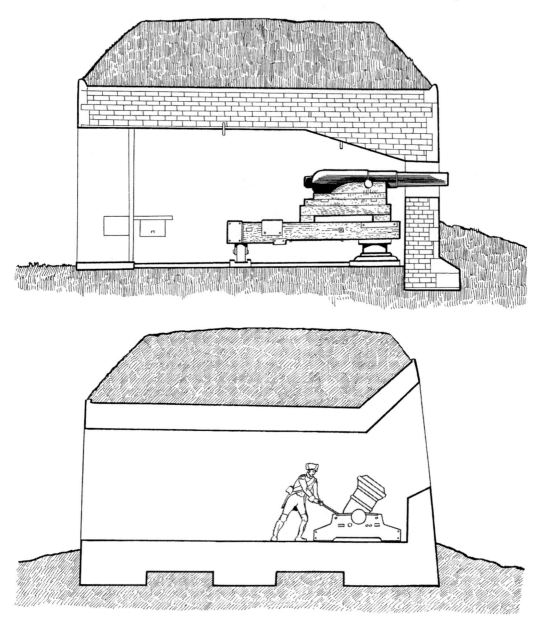

Top: *Cross-section of Haxo casemate.* Bottom: *Cross-section of Haxo casemate for mortar.* The Haxo casemate could also be adapted to house a mortar. In that case, the port was enlarged and directed slightly upward to match the high-angled trajectory of the weapon.

solve. In spite of vents, chimneys, ventilation shafts, and other air-ducts intended to evacuate smoke, the chamber was usually full of choking fumes after a few shots. A solution was developed by the French officer François-Nicolas-Benoit Haxo. This type of gun emplacement, which was eventually widely adopted in European fortification in the 19th century, was called a *Haxo casemate*. It was a classical gun chamber, fitted with a port, and arched with strong masonry covered with earth. The innovation was that the casemate was open at the rear to the terre-plein so as to reduce the usual smoke problem by enabling ample ventilation. Other advantages were that it allowed mobile guns to be run in and out easily, and that natural light could enter the dark casemate.

Military Engineering Corps

The Engineering Corps was (and still is) charged with conception, construction and maintenance of fortifications. Marching with the army, the corps' mission was also to collaborate closely with artillery and to establish temporary siege works. For centuries, engineers were civilian architects, master-builders or artists (such as Albrecht Dürer, Michelangelo or Leonardo da Vinci) who earned money by contributing their researches, experiences and skills to military authorities. The first organization of what would become the *Génie* (French Engineer Corps) was created during François I's reign. The conception and execution of defensive permanent works were entrusted to civilian architects or to infantry or artillery officers who were temporarily placed under command of the Director of the Fortifications. During Henri IV's reign, Maximilien de Béthunes, Baron of Rosny and Duke of Sully, further organized the administration of the department by clearly defining attributions and geographical limits of the corps. This task was continued by Richelieu by the time of Louis XIII. In 1659, under Louis XIV's reign, Mazarin created the charge of Commissaire Général des Fortifications and the engineering service progressively began to get specialized and militarized.

The infantryman had his musket, the cavalryman his saber, and the artilleryman his cannon. These front-line soldiers showed some contempt and little regard for the engineering soldier armed with pick and shovel. This was, of course, wrong and unfair, as the engineering corps gradually played an important role in warfare with a significant impact both on and off the battlefield. The engineer eventually became the professional technologist in the military world, a specialist practicing a black art which the "real" soldier could not aspire to, but without which the war could not be fought: bridges to be built, defenses constructed, fortifications designed and built, attacked and mined. These activities all required special skills. Engineers had to have knowledge of mathematics, geometry, architecture and construction techniques. At the same time, they were fighting men, ready to take an active part in the battle when the need arose; they thus had to have a good understanding of strategy, tactics, artillery, and military matters at large. In short, they needed to combine general engineering knowledge with a sound military education.

At the time of Louis XIV, engineers were empirically formed by senior colleagues, by participating in sieges and by working on military constructions. Further theoretical education was done by reading and studying a number of books, treatises and manuals, mostly Italian translated works and a few French theoretical treatises such as those of Jean

French Fortifications, 1715–1815

Sapper-miner (c. 1800)
Left: Embroidered red arm badge (symbolized grenade above, or crowned eagle holding, two crossed axes) for sappers worn on right upper sleeve. This existed also in metal form on headgear.

3. Imperial Fortifications

*Geographic Military engineer (c. 1800)
The uniform was blue, epaulettes gold, waistcoat
and breeches white.*

Errard, Antoine De Ville and Blaise De Pagan. Engineers also studied and drew maps, constructed scale models and copied experienced colleagues' illustrations, designs and notes.

When their education was completed and successfully tested at war, candidates obtained a brevet of *Ingénieur Ordinaire du Roi* (King's Ordinary Engineer). Artillerymen and engineers began to come into their own largely through the exertions of Vauban, who made use of them in siege warfare as it became the principal feature of 17th century warfare. Vauban can be regarded as the actual founder of the Génie in 1669, by recruiting a permanent brigade of specialized officers, and by drawing up the main rules and instructions concerning tasks and organization of works, as well as the administration regarding pay, advancement and pensions of the men. An Ordinary Engineer was posted in every important fortified place. These local engineers were supervised by a Provincial Director Engineer, and the structure was directed at national level by the Commissaire General of the Fortifications. For siege warfare, Vauban created companies of pioneers who specialized in digging trenches, and sappers and miners using underground explosives. In spite of Vauban's efforts, though, the Engineer Corps was only organized along precise military lines in the late 1740s, when engineer-officers, as said before, were formed at the *École de Mézières*, a specialized engineer academy founded in 1749 in the town of Mézières in the French Ardennes.

Just like the rest of the French army, the engineering corps was greatly disorganized by the French Revolution of 1789. In the Ancient Régime, the function of army officer was exclusively reserved for and monopolized by the nobility. When the Revolution broke out many officers were dismissed, many refused to serve the new regime, and many nobles emigrated to combat the revolutionaries from abroad. The *Comité Central des Fortifications* was hastily created by the law of July 10, 1791. Its members were to decide which old fortifications were to be dismantled, which were to be improved, and where new ones should be built. On the short term, in an emergency, with economic chaos and political confusion inside France, and with enemies at the gates of the country, the Comité was tasked to reorganize the corps by recruiting educated civilian bourgeois (e.g., geographers, teachers, architects and engineers), enabling a renewal of personnel. The Committee was maintained during the Consulate and the Empire, and carried out important reforms. In December 1793 the engineering corps was given an autonomous existence. It was separated from the artillery, and twelve independent specialized battalions of sappers and miners were created. Each battalion included eight companies of 200 men led by a staff of 400 professionally qualified officers and engineers, formed at various technical academies such as the Polytechnic School and the School of Application. In Egypt, Bonaparte had 800 sappers and miners, under the leadership of General Cafarelli-Dufalga. During the Consulate and the Empire, the Corps was enlarged, reaching a peak of 20,000. For example, in 1812, for the campaign of Russia, the Génie included eight sappers battalions (of which three were composed of foreigners, mainly Dutch, Italians and Spaniards) plus two battalions of miners, a grand total of 13,000 men.

Rather well-equipped, well-organized and skillfully led, the Napoleonic Génie enjoyed a great reputation. Responsible for the design and construction of offensive, defensive and logistical structures for warfare, the Génie was entrusted with more and more specific missions (including mapping and surveying), resulting in increasingly specialized roles, notably the combat or *assault engineer* who operated during battle, often as spearhead of the attack under enemy fire. *Sappers* (from Italian *zappare*, to pick) and *ouvriers* were basically men who excavated trenches and built fortifications. The *pompiers* ("pumpers" = fire brigades) created by Napoléon were attached to them, as still illustrated today by the designation *Sapeurs-Pompiers* (firemen).

The *Imperial Guard Engineers* were formed in July 1810; their function was that of firemen for Napoléon's residence with six horse-drawn pumps.

Miners were an elite troops using explosives in sieges but also in demolition. In 1808 they were reorganized into two battalions of five companies.

Pioneers were used for fortress and fortification building, but also for building and repairing public roads. Some of these units were composed of conscripts who had mutilated themselves to avoid service. Others were made up of prisoners of war. There were also the so-called Pioneer Companies of *Hommes de Couleur* (colored men) who were refugee Negroes from Egypt and San Domingo; this battalion of black pioneers was transferred in 1806 to Neapolitan service, where it formed the basis of the Royal African Regiment.

Rivers have always constituted major obstacles to armies in campaign, and bridges were of prime importance. *Pontoniers* therefore specialized in the building and repairing (and possibly destruction when retreating) of bridges both permanent and temporary with rafts and pontoons. The Napoleonic Génie also included units of *Génie Maritime* (naval engineering battalions) which specialized in building mooring facilities, gunboats, landing barges, floating batteries and pontoons.

In addition a battalion of Guard *Ouvriers d'administration* (Administra-

Pontonnier (c. 1806)

tion workers) was constituted in 1806 including companies of bakers, butchers and medical personnel (doctors, surgeons and pharmacists).

There briefly existed a *Companie d'Aérostiers* (Aërostiers Company) created in March 1794, with specialists operating hot-air observation balloons. This company, which opened the era of air warfare (notably at the Battle of Fleurus in 1794), was, however, too far ahead of its time. Most military authorities did not appreciate the potential, and the company was disbanded in 1799.

Engineers and supporting services were much less celebrated than the fighting infantry, Imperial Guards and cavalry. They were, however, indispensable units without which the Napoleonic armies could not have operated. All these men often worked under difficult conditions. The constraints of time, schedule, finance, labor, and materials, which affect civil engineering projects, weigh especially heavily on military engineering in time of war with the added complication that activities may be hampered by hostile actions, sometimes conducted even under enemy fire. These highly specialized personnel — and this also applied to artillerymen — were well-drilled and trained in order to retain efficiency on the battlefield, where operations had to be conducted under conditions of confusion, noise, bad visibility, stress and intense nervousness. In 1809, General Bertrand's engineers

Sapper (c. 1813)
This combat engineer wears a heavy metal helmet (with visor and cheek plates) and a bullet-proof armored cuirass intended to protect him in siege-work when digging saps, trenches and parallels under enemy fire. In some ways the last link with the armored medieval knight, the Napoleonic sapper and the cavalry cuirassier were the only soldiers of the time to wear protective body armor.

built several large bridges connecting the south shore of the Danube River with the Lobau Island, a major technical achievement which enabled the victory. At the Beresina River in 1812, General Eblé's pontonniers (French, Polish and Dutch) saved the remnants of the badly mauled and retreating *Grande Armée* by plunging naked into the icy river, and working in water up to their armpits to construct the two famous Beresina bridges.

Napoleonic Génie Leadership

Napoléon was not a major military reformer, since he operated with the weapons and tactics developed in France when he was a young cadet, but he could draw upon the progress made in the French royal army of the *Ancien Régime* and on the fervor of the Republican armies, representing the nation in arms from 1792. He was careful to continue the Revolutionary practice of careers open to talent and promotion by merit for bravery in battle. As a skilled propagandist, he was adept at artfully exploiting the revolutionary *élan* of his troops as well as their desire for booty and honor. Napoléon certainly attracted intense loyalty from his soldiers as he played skillfully on their desire for comradeship, military glory and recognition of their bravery. But, always impatient for change—which was not always synonymous with improvement—Napoléon wanted collaborators and yet trusted only servile associates who, unequal to the conflict of loyalties, eventually betrayed their master. Although it depended upon a high degree of personal control by the Emperor himself, who dictated both strategy and tactics, the Napoleonic Génie leadership was, on the whole, brave, efficient, creative, and determined. Engineers were formed at the previously described School of Mézières, and at two newly created institutions. The *École Nationale des Ponts et Chaussées* (ENPC) ("National school of Bridges and Roads"), often referred to as *les Ponts*, was created in 1747. It is the world's oldest civil engineering school and remains to this day one of the most prestigious French *grandes écoles* of engineering. The *École Polytechnique*, often referred to as *X* (from the two crossed cannons featuring on its emblem) was founded in 1794, and was (and still is) the foremost French *grande école* of engineering. Napoleonic fortification was thus designed and carried out by a new generation of rather young and talented military engineers.

Pioneer helmet

Bertrand

General Henri Bertrand (1773–1844) was an engineer by training and his great success in the field was the construction of the Danube bridges during the Austrian campaign of 1809. Immensely loyal to Napoléon, he was appointed Grand Marshal of the Palace. Bertrand accompanied him to his first exile on Elba Island, was present at the Battle of Waterloo, followed him during his second exile, and was, with his wife and child, at the Emperor's bedside when he died on Saint-Helena Island on May 5, 1821.

Bousmard

Henri Jean Baptiste de Bousmard (1749–1807) entered the corps of engineers in 1768. Deeply Royalist, he rejected the Revolution and emigrated to Wiesbaden (Germany) in 1792. From 1792 to 1796, during his forced retirement, he wrote his celebrated work *Essai Général de Fortification*, published in 1797, and which he dedicated to the King of

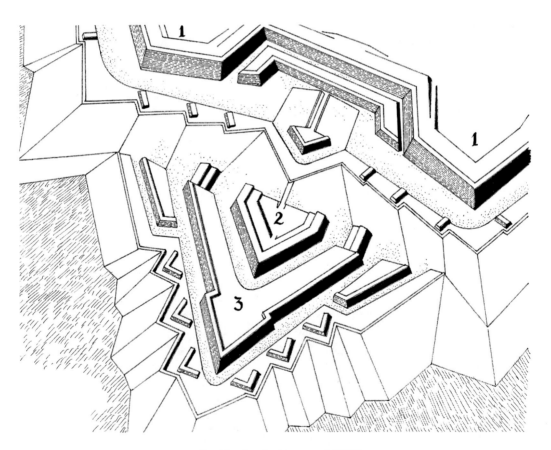

Fortification by Bousmard (1797)
Basically, Bousmard's fortification included a classical bastioned front (1) with the addition of a detached lunet (2), an advanced counterguard (3), casemated batteries and underground passages for subterranean communication. The covered way of the main enceinte was traced en crémaillère with traverses, and that of the counterguard included a series of redans.

Prussia. Compelled by poverty to take service, the noble French émigré accepted the rank of major in the Prussian Engineering Corps. He served his new king with loyalty and was killed in action in 1807 while defending Danzig. Bousmard is often regarded as Chasseloup-Laubat's inspiration (vide infra).

CACHIN

Joseph-Marie-François Cachin (1757–1825), after attending the School of Ponts-et-Chaussées in 1776, travelled to Great Britain and to the United States of America. Back in France he became an engineer specializing in naval engineering. He proposed the construction of a canal parallel to the River Seine between Quilleboeuf and the sea. The French Revolution of 1789 thwarted the realization of this project but eventually the Directoire charged him with improving the port of Honfleur and appointed him Engineer-in-Chief for the *département* of Calvados in Normandy. Cachin envisaged the construction of a canal linking Caen to the sea, and was charged by Napoléon to participate from 1805 in the development of Cherbourg. Cachin made a tremendous work at Cherbourg: he improved the port of commerce, and directed the digging of the military port, the building of the new arsenal, and the construction of an enormous artificial dike intended to shelter the port. Cachin, who was appointed General-Inspector of Ponts-et-Chaussées and General-Director of Naval Construction, wrote a number of *Mémoires* (essays) about maritime building and canals, and also made designs for the improvement of the port of Antwerp in Belgium. He was granted the prestigious *Légion d'Honneur* medal, and made a Baron of the Empire in 1813.

CAFFARELLI-DUFALGA

Louis Maximilien de Caffarelli-Dufalga (1756–1799) was a student at the Royal School of Mézières, and became a military engineer. Appointed captain in April 1791, and artillery officer in the Rhine army a year later, he refused to recognize the forfeiture of Louis XVI and therefore was imprisoned for 14 months. Reinstated in the army in 1795 with the rank of *chef de batallion* (major) and supervisor of the fortifications of the Sambre-et-Meuse army in Belgium, he was severely wounded and had his left leg amputated. Appointed brigadier-general, the now one-legged Dufalga took command of the engineering unit of the Eastern army heading for the Egyptian campaign. He participated in the conquest of Malta, worked on the protection of Cairo, improved the road between Alexandria and the Nile River, and participated in all kinds of scientific activities, notably the creation of the Egyptian Institute. A rash, brave and gallant soldier, the highly-regarded "Wooden Leg" Caffarelli-Dufalga also took part in the Battle of Salheyeh, in the siege of Jaffa, and in that of Acre, where he was mortally wounded in April 1799. Bonaparte had a special affection for him, and named a Dutch fort near Den Helder after him.

CARNOT

Lazare Nicolas Marguerite Carnot (1753–1823) was born into a bourgeois family of lawyers. He volunteered in the army in 1771, aged 18, and after graduation from the École de Mézières in 1777, became a regular engineer officer in the Ancient Régime army. In 1789 he adopted the principles of the French Revolution with enthusiasm. He was elected deputy of the department of Pas-de-Calais in 1791, became a member of the Legislative Assembly and the Convention, and joined the Committee of Public Safety in August 1793. He was among those deputies who voted for Louis XVI's death. Carnot's contribution to the French Revolution cannot be overestimated.

Concentrating on military matters, he soon recognized that a new way of waging war was required if France was to fight off foreign invasion. Greatly influenced by the theories of Guibert, Carnot took the first steps toward creating a truly national army by bringing about the amalgamation which combined the old royal army with the new republican and revolutionary troops. He created fourteen armies, reorganized the supply of weapons, and instituted proper magazines and factories for the materiel of war. At a time of great national peril in the autumn of 1793, he took the field with Jourdan and defeated the Austrians at the Battle of Wattignies near Maubeuge in October. Carnot exposed his views in 1794 in a book entitled *Système général des Opérations* in which he advocated the principle of a "nation in arms." He wrote several essays on strategy and tactics which, together with Guibert's theories, had a significant influence on Napoleonic warfare. Despite invaluable service to the Revolution — for which he was nicknamed the "Orga-

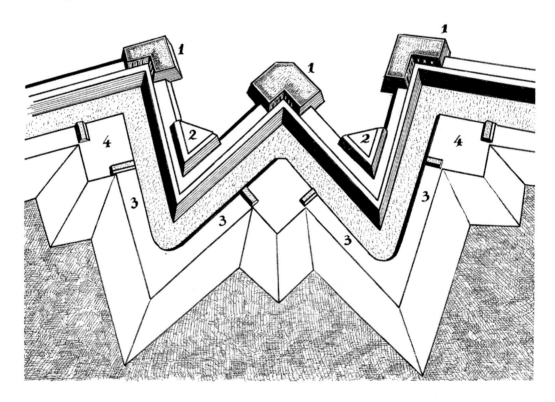

Tenaille system by Lazare Carnot (1797)
On the main tenailled enceinte Carnot advocated the construction of artillery and mortar casemated batteries (1) and cavaliers (2). The counterscarp had a gentle slope with a covered way (3) and places-of-arms (4).

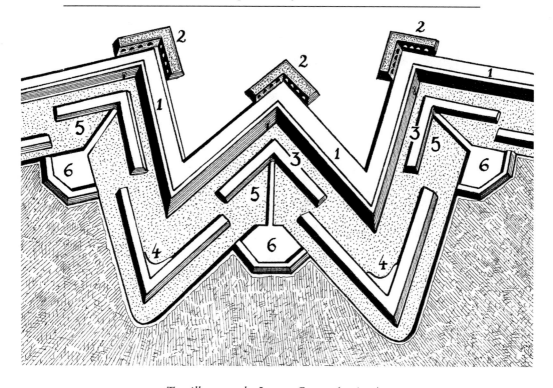

Tenaille system by Lazare Carnot (variant)
This variant included a main tenailled enceinte (1) with mortar casemated batteries (2). In the ditch there were outworks in the form of tenailles (3) and counterguards (4). From the re-entering angle of the tenaille a covered passage (5) led to a sort of redoubt/place-of-arms (6) emplaced on the counterscarp without covered way.

nizer of Victory"—Carnot became ideologically suspect after the fall of Robespierre and was obliged to go into exile for two years. He returned to France in 1800, and Napoléon appointed him Minister of War. In 1802, faithful to his republican political principles, he refused to serve the First Consul Bonaparte and retired into private life. In 1814 he accepted service and was entrusted with the defense of the port of Antwerp, and was reinstated as Napoléon's War Minister during the Hundred Days in 1815. With the Monarchic Restoration following Napoléon's fall, Carnot was banished. He spent his last years in exile in Poland and Germany and devoted his last energy to studying modern geometry. He died at Magdeburg in August 1823. His ashes were transferred to the Panthéon in Paris in August 1889 during the septennat (seven-year term) of his grandson Marie François Sadi Carnot (president of the French Republic from 1887 to his assassination in 1894). Lazare Carnot is one of the seventy-two scientists whose names are inscribed on the Eiffel Tower in Paris.

Carnot was not only a revolutionary politician, a devoted patriot, a brave soldier and a skilled administrator who participated in the creation of the Polytechnic School. He was also a mathematician: he published *Métaphysique du Calcul Infinitésimal* in 1797 and *Géométrie de Position* in 1803. Carnot excelled as a military organizer; he also wrote poetry, and he possessed sufficient foresight to accept innovations. As early as 1783 he encouraged the use of captive hot-air balloons for observation and artillery ranging, for

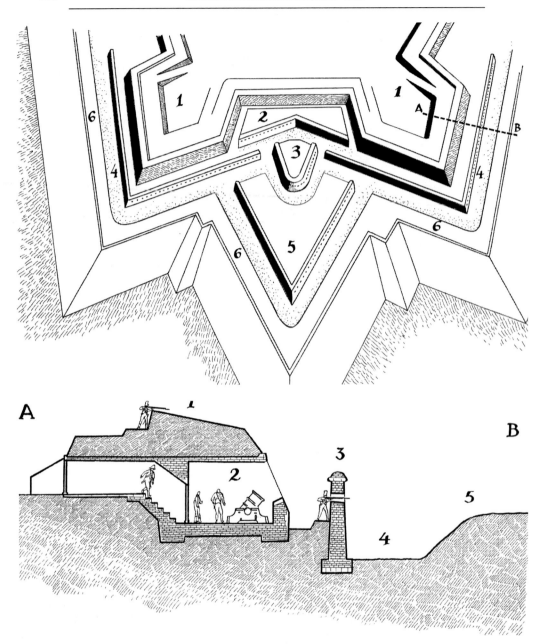

Top: Bastioned front by Lazare Carnot. This design included bastions (1); a tenaille (2); a demi-lune (3); a loopholed couvre-face (4); a loopholed counterguard (5); a covered way (6) and the usual bare glacis.

Bottom: The cross-section AB shows Carnot's profile including the main rampart (1); the mortar's casemate (2); the so-called Carnot's Wall (3); a detached scarp wall made of masonry and pierced with riflemen's loopholes; the ditch (4); and the sloping counterscarp (5).

instance. On the subject of fortification, he was a warm supporter of new theories and innovations expressed by Montalembert. In a letter to the latter, he wished that "posterity would render the justice that is due to you." As an expert on fortifications, Carnot published a book in 1810, *De la Défense des Places Fortes*, at the request of Napoléon. In this book he reminded fortress commanders of their responsibilities, criticized the general conservative attitude of the French Génie, and offered several systems of permanent fortification. For a dry and level site he recommended a bastioned system; but for wet ditches and for irregular ground, tenaille fortifications. Carnot showed a particular interest in the profile of the scarp and advocated the construction of casemates with mortars and guns, and the replacement of the covered way by a gently sloping non-riveted counterscarp. This was commanded by the so-called *Carnot's Wall*. This free-standing feature was a detached, buttressed and arched masoned wall pierced with loopholes for musketry defense. One advantage claimed by Carnot was that, since his wall was concealed at the edge of the ditch, the besiegers would not be able to bring artillery fire to bear upon it until they had crowned the covered way and established guns there. Besides, should his wall still be destroyed by enemy artillery, the main curtain was not yet breached. The whole arrangement, fitted with sally ports, was intended for an active offensive role: during a siege, infantrymen, instead of sitting passively behind their ramparts, would be deployed in Carnot's Wall, and would make frequent sallies and counterattacks against enemy approaching trenches; the sorties, which would greatly disrupt the besiegers' plans, would be supported by the fire of guns and mortars in the casemates. Carnot's key idea

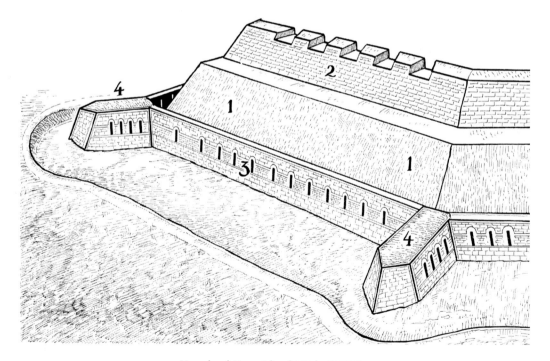

Yaverland Fort, Isle of Wight (1863)
The British Yaverland Fort featured a sloping rampart (1); gun emplacements (2); a loopholed Carnot's Wall for riflemen (3); and downscaled Montalembert's caponiers — vaulted fortified positions projecting from the wall for flanking the ditch (4).

was based on sorties and plunging fire to stop the progress of attack. He was indeed a strong believer in the power of mortar fire, and he expected great results from a 13 in. mortar throwing 600 iron balls at each discharge. He endeavored to prove mathematically that the discharge of these mortars would in due course kill off the whole of the besieging force. These mortars he emplaced in open-fronted casemates, in concealed positions, either standing free from the main enceinte or incorporated in it. These casemates were borrowed from a work published in 1781 by a Swedish engineer named Virgin. Carnot's ideas were good in theory, but in the practice the profile of his arrangement was not completely sound. Indeed, the masoned infantry wall that bore his name was rather vulnerable to enemy artillery fire, and — being parallel to the main wall — it gave a poor flanking. As for the almighty mortar fire, Carnot greatly overestimated its efficacy, his calculations were only paper expectations, and the whole theory of constant sorties was dangerous and not always feasible, particularly for a small garrison. Carnot's ideas, like those of Montalembert before him, were not well received by the French Engineering Corps, but they had a certain influence abroad. After the fall of the Empire, when the frontiers of Europe were stabilized and realigned, new fortifications were called for.

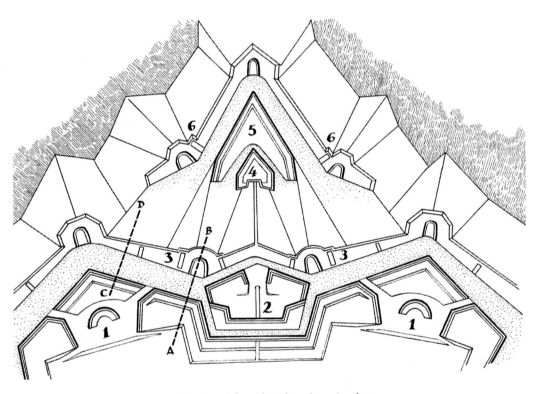

Bastioned front by Chasseloup-Laubat
Chasseloup-Laubat's theoretical view, eventually known as Front d'Alexandrie (Alessandria Front), included entrenched bastions (1); a tenaille merged into a wide demi-lune (2) mirroring Montalembert's caponier; a main ditch about 20 yards wide; and a traversed covered way (3) defended by masoned casemated fortlets, rendering the defense more energic. Advanced works in the glacis, intended to protract a siege, included a sort of lunet à la Arçon (4); a counterguard (5); and a second covered way (6) with flanking casemates.

Carnot's scarp profile and concealed mortar batteries, in combination with some of Montalembert's principles, were eventually adopted in English and German fortifications until the 1860s, when the introduction of new rifled artillery and powerful shells filled with explosives rendered them totally vulnerable and obsolete.

CHASSELOUP-LAUBAT

Count François de Chasseloup-Laubat (1754–1833) was born from a noble family traditionally dedicated to the career of soldier. In 1770, aged 16, he volunteered to serve in the artillery. After attending the School of Mézières, he entered the French engineering corps in 1774. Still a junior officer at the outbreak of the Revolution, he became captain in 1791. Chasseloup-Laubat, although a young nobleman, accepted the principles of the Revolution and refused to emigrate. His ability as a military engineer was recognized in the campaigns of 1792 and 1793 at Givet, Montmédy, Longwy, and Arlon. In the following year he won distinction in various actions, notably at the siege of Maastricht in June 1794, and was promoted to the rank of major and soon colonel. He was engineer-in-chief at the siege of Mayence in 1795, and, promoted brigadier-general by the end of the campaign, was subsequently employed in fortifying the new French Rhine border. His work as engineer-in-chief in the army of Italy (1799) had good results: he participated with success in the sieges and battles of Milan, Mantua, Lonato, Castiglione, Arcole and Rivoli, resulting in his elevation to the rank of division-general in 1799.

Top: Close-up gun-ports of masoned casemates.
Middle and bottom: Cross-section C-D showing casemated salient point of bastion, ditch, counterscarp, covered way and glacis. Cross-section A-B showing casemated bastion shoulder, subterranean passage under the ditch connecting to counterscarp casemated fortlet, and covered way with breastwork.

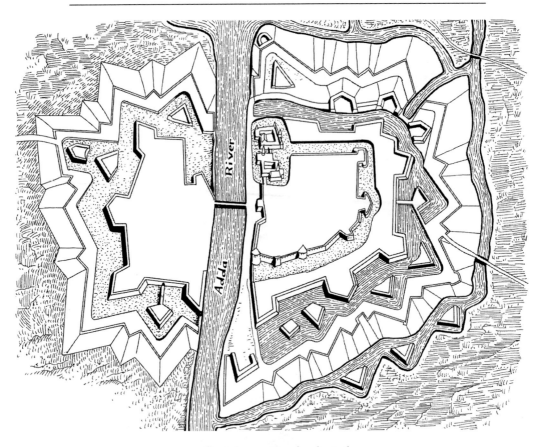

Pizzighettone Lombardy, Italy
Situated in the province of Cremona north of Piacenza in Lombardy, the fortifications of Pizzighettone were modernized by Count Chasseloup-Laubat in the 1800s.

When Napoléon began his new campaign in 1800 to retrieve the 1799 disasters, Chasseloup-Laubat was again chosen as chief engineer. During the period of peace from 1801 to 1805, he was mainly ordered to reorganize the defenses of northern Italy, and, in particular, those in Mantua's region, including the formidable Rocca of Anfo (1800) as well as works at Pizzighetonne, Peschiera, Mantua, Legnano, Tarente, and his masterpiece, the fortress of Alessandria, built on the Tanaro River between 1801 and 1808. In 1805 he remained in Italy with André Masséna, but at the end of 1806, Napoléon, leading the Polish Campaign, called him to his *Grande Armée*, with which he served during the campaign of 1806–1807, directing sieges at Colberg, Danzig and Stralsund. During the Napoleonic domination in Germany, Chasseloup-Laubat reconstructed several fortresses, in particular Magdeburg and Marienburg, as well as Thorn in Limburg (Netherlands). In the 1809 campaign he was again in Italy inspecting the fortifications, notably the completion of Alessandria. As a reward for his service Napoléon made him Count of the Empire, senator and state counselor. His last active campaign was the Russian of 1812.

Retired from active service, he espoused the Bourbon cause and took no part in the events of 1815. He refused to join Napoléon during the Hundred Days. He was occasionally engaged for inspections and construction of fortifications by the restored monarchic regime. Louis XVIII made him a Peer of France and a knight of the Saint Louis order. He died in October 1833, aged 79. His name is inscribed on the southern side of the Arc de Triomphe in Paris.

Chasseloup-Laubat wrote several *Mémoires sur l'Artillerie* (*Essays on Artillery*). As an engineer, he was a supporter of the classical bastioned system, though with some modern views borrowed from other theorists. These were expressed in a book published in 1798, titled *Mémoire sur quelques changements à faire à la fortification moderne* (*Essay about Several Changes to be done on Modern Fortification*). Chasseloup-Laubat proposed several systems, but basically he followed in many respects the engineer Henri Jean Baptiste de Bousmard, whose work (titled *Essai Général de Fortification*), published in 1797, advocated the use of advanced work (e.g., a kind of lunet borrowed from Arçon), a carefully entrenched bastion in Belidor's style, and casemated works in Montalembert's fashion. His ideas were applied at Alessandria (Italy), which had many upgrades of the bastion outline, with, in particular, an important number of advanced works. Chasseloup-Laubat's fortification system possibly gives the best illustration of what French Napoleonic fortification actually was: basically a classical bastioned system à la Vauban-Cormontaigne mixed with modern features and adaptations influenced by Montalembert's systems.

Dode de la Brunerie

After graduation at the Engineering School of Mezières, Guillaume Dode de la Brunerie (1775–1851) served in the Rhine army and took part in the campaigns of Egypt and Italy. Appointed colonel in 1805, and general of brigade in 1809, he distinguished himself at the siege of Saragossa in Spain. As general of division in 1812, he was charged to command the engineering corps on river Elba in 1813. After Napoléon's fall Dode la Brunerie faithfully served the Restoration, was elevated to the dignities of Peer of France and Marshal of France. Also fulfilling the function of general inspector of fortifications, he was particularly known for the design of the fortification of Paris (the so-called Thiers's enceinte) built between 1841 and 1845.

Eblé

Jean-Baptiste Eblé (1758–1812) started his military career in his father's artillery regiment at the age of nine. In 1791 he was promoted to the rank of captain, and served in General Dumouriez's army in 1793 during the campaign in the Low Countries. In September 1793, now general of brigade, he served with General Moreau in the Rhine army and in Italy with General Championnet. He served in Germany and commanded an artillery brigade at the Battle of Austerlitz in 1805. He was appointed governor of Magdeburg in 1806 and minister of war of the realm of Westphalia (whose king was Jérome Bonaparte) in 1808. He commanded the French artillery in Spain, serving in the army of Marshal Masséna at Ciudad Rodrigo and Almeida in 1809. In 1811 Eblé was put in command of the pontonniers of the Grande Armée, and during the disastrous retreat from Moscow in November 1812, Eblé's men worked feverishly in the dangerous ice-cold water of the river Berezina (which marked the Russian boundary) to complete two bridges, allowing the remnants of Napoléon's army to escape just in time. The campaign of Russia had taken a heavy toll on Eblé's health and he died in December 1812 in Konigsberg shortly after returning from Russia. Today, his name has been given to a Génie barracks and museum at Angers (department of Maine-et-Loire).

Haxo

François Nicolas Benoît Haxo (1774–1838), after an education at the Navarre grammar school at Paris and the artillery school at Chalons-sur-Marne, entered the French army. Promoted Lieutenant at the age of 19, and Captain at 22, he participated in the campaigns of 1794 and 1795, and took part in the sieges of Mannheim and Mayence. As an engineering officer in the Army of the Rhine, he commanded in the Alps in 1798, and distinguished himself in 1801 at the Grand-Saint-Bernard pass, at the capture of the Fort de Bard, and in combat at Mouzanbano and Caldiero. Haxo worked at Venice, Mantua, Peschiera and Rocca of Anfo, and acquired such a good reputation as a fortification builder that Sultan Selim of Turkey (then allied to France) asked him to fortify Constantinople and the Strait of Dardanelles in 1807. Haxo took part in the Spanish campaign, at the siege of Saragossa, Lerida, Mequinenza, and Tortosa. In 1811 Napoléon made him Baron

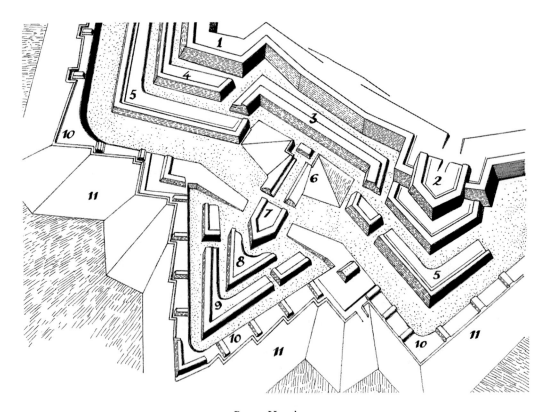

Baron Haxo's system
Haxo's system was rather conservative and traditional. It included a bastioned front with a void bastion (1) and bastion fitted with a cavalier (2); a tenaille (3) covering the curtain; couvre-face (4); and counterguard (5). Outer works included a covered passage (6), connecting to a bastionet or caponier (7); a demi-lune (8) and a counterguard (9) with great saliency; a covered way (10) traced en crémaillère with traverses and places-of-arms; and a glacis (11).

of the Empire, and appointed him at the head of the Génie in Germany, where he fortified Moldin and Dantzig, and where he designed the famous "Haxo casemate" which was eventually widely adopted by most nations in the 19th century. During the ill-fated campaign of Russia, he was Napoléon's aide-de-camp and fought at Mohilow. In 1813, he was appointed general of division, governor of Magdeburg and commanding officer of the Génie of the Imperial Guard. After the Battle of Kulm near Dresden, Haxo was wounded, captured and held as a prisoner in Hungary until 1814. By that time, Haxo's loyalty to Napoléon was wavering. Particularly servile to the Bourbons, he was one of the first to suggest capitulation after the Allies arrived on the outskirts of Paris. After Napoléon's first abdication, Haxo turned coat and entered service of the restored monarchy as commanding officer of the Génie in the French Alps. During the Hundred Days, Napoléon apparently forgave Haxo's lack of fidelity and reappointed him commanding officer of the Génie of the Imperial Guard. Haxo then fought at the Battle of Waterloo. After Napoléon's second and final abdication, the unreliable Haxo fell in disgrace for a while but, due to his talent and reputation, was reintegrated into the new royal French army in 1819 with the rank of general inspector of fortification. He then started a huge work, improving the fortifications of Grenoble, Besançon, Dunkirk, Saint-Omer, Sedan, Bitche, Fort l'Ecluse and Belfort, and hereby gained the nickname of "Vauban of the 19th century." After the revolution of 1830, he distinguished himself at the siege of Antwerp in 1832. For his service, he was made a Peer of France by King Louis-Philippe in 1832, and was elevated to the dignity of Grand Croix de la Légion d'Honneur a year later. The man who had survived and served successively the Ancien Régime, the Revolution, the Directory, the Consulate, the First Empire, the Restoration, and the Monarchy of July died in June 1838 at Paris. His name was carved on the Arc de Triomphe, and since 1865 a street in the 20th arrondissement of Paris has borne his name.

As a military engineer, Haxo was a conservative who remained faithful to the classical Vauban-Cormontaigne bastioned system. Haxo had designed a fortification system but did not publish it until 1826, when he had a plan of it engraved. This was distributed to a few selected French engineers on condition of not rendering it public. No fortress was built on his system, but his casemate was a success that was adopted all over Europe in the 19th century.

JULIENNE DE BELAIR

Pierre-Alexandre Julienne de Bélair (1747–1819) was an engineering officer, a military teacher, and a general of the Empire. His main contribution to the art of fortification was a book published in 1792, titled *Nouveaux Eléments de Fortifications*, in which he supported Montalembert's perpendicular fortification system.

MANDAR

Charles-François Mandar (1757–1844), the son of a grocer, was a student at the Royal Military School at Paris between 1722 and 1777, and became a teacher at the same school and at the School of Architecture between 1783 and 1786. As a civilian architect he designed several houses in Paris in the 1790s. Between 1796 and 1820, he was teacher at the School of Ponts-et-Chaussées in Paris. Mandar, essentially a civilian engineer and teacher, also contributed to military architecture by publishing, in 1801, a pedagogic work titled *De l'Architecture des Forteresses* (*Fortress Architecture*) in which he summed up the history of fortifications and described in detail and accuracy the works of the greatest military engineers.

Le Michaud d'Arçon

Jean Claude Elénore Le Michaud d'Arçon (1733–1800) was born in a family of lawyers at Pontarlier. Destined to become a clergyman, the young Arçon preferred the career of arms and convinced his father to let him follow the course of military engineer at the School of Mézières in 1754. Le Michaud d'Arçon distinguished himself during the Seven Years' War, particularly at Cassel in 1761. In 1774 he was charged to make a survey map of the Jura and Vosges Mountains. Attached to the army led by Marshal de Broglie in 1780, he designed armored naval batteries intended to take Gibraltar. The attack, which took place in September 1782, was a failure, but the creative Le Michaud d'Arçon was not discouraged. In 1795, he proposed to the Committee of Fortifications a small, standardized, detached, and independent fort. Named *Lunette d'Arçon*, this triangular fort had a circular réduit-tower in the gorge, covered by a pitch roof and defended

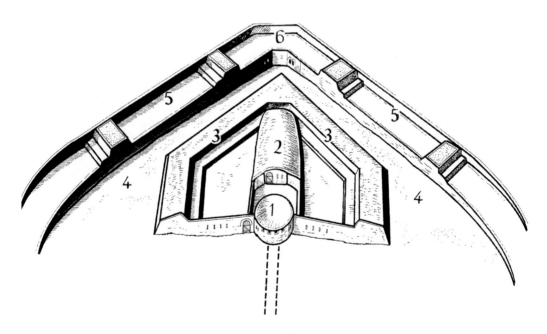

Lunette d'Arçon
The lunet designed by Le Michaud d'Arçon was a self-supporting fortlet including: a round fortified tower in the gorge (1) used as quarters for the garrison and as defense for the rear of the work; a bomb-proof vaulted ammunition store forming traverse (2) on the terre-plein; two faces forming a scarp wall with parapet and barbette gun emplacements (3); a ditch (4); a counterscarp with a covered way (5) fitted with traverses; and, under the covered way, a flanking coffer (6) consisting of two masoned casemates for enfilading fire. Placed in the reverse slope of the ditch, these elements enabled the defenders to bring fire to bear upon attackers who had got into the ditch; they were accessible from the lunet via an underground passage.

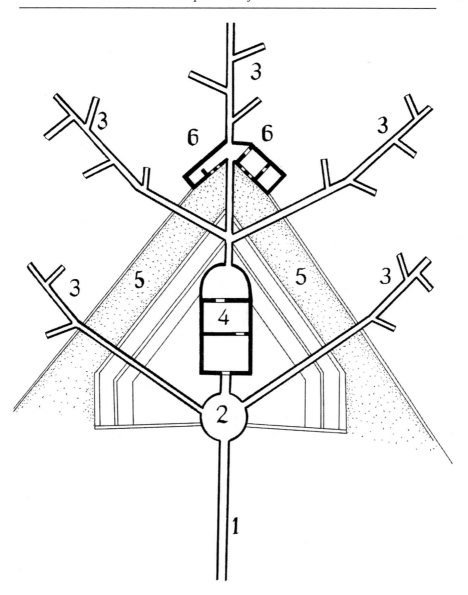

Underground Lunette of Arçon

The lunette of Arçon was a detached work that reckoned with underground mine attack, an important factor in siege warfare. A tunnel would be driven under the defenses, sacks or barrels of gunpowder placed and exploded. As a result the practice grew up of driving countermines beneath the work, usually running far out beneath the glacis. These galleries were often quite substantial masoned tunnels, some 6 feet high and 3 feet wide. During a siege they would be patrolled by sharp-eared miners alert for sounds of enemy digging. When such activity was detected, a gallery could be cut from the nearest main tunnel until it was close to the approaching mine. The countermine tunnel was then packed with explosives and fired with the intention of destroying the enemy attackers. The Arçon lunet could be accessed by a main underground gallery (1) linking the main body to the gorge tower (2). Under the glacis of the lunet, several countermine tunnels (3) were dug. The traverse-store (4) connected via a subterranean passage built under the ditch (5) to the counterscarp coffer (6).

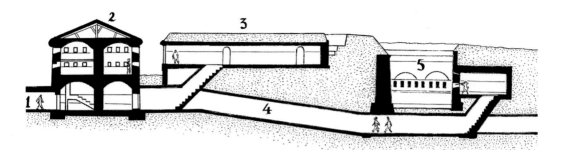

Cross-section Lunette d'Arçon
1: Gallery to the main place. 2: Round tower, about 15 feet in diameter. 3: Bombproof traverse. 4: Gallery leading to counterscarp casemate. 5: Casemate constructed under the covered way at the salient of the counterscarp for the defense of the ditch.

through musketry loopholes; to be used for a last stand by the garrison, it also had a bombproof store and quarter, and reverse fire casemates under the counterscarp. Possessing already most of the features of the future 19th century polygonal fortification, the self defensive *Lunette d'Arçon* was accepted by the Committee, and became a success of Napoleonic fortification. Arçon's fortlets were built in Italy, Poland, the Low Countries and France, notably at Metz, Perpignan, Besançon and Montdauphin. Arçon's lunet formed the basis for Fort Tigné in Malta designed in 1792 by the French engineer Etienne de Tousard. By that time, now promoted to the rank of general, Le Michaud d'Arçon took part in the siege of Breda in Holland. As his health deteriorated, he was withdrawn from active service, wrote several essays on military matters and fortifications, and was appointed fortification teacher at the Central School of Public Work, a function he held until his death in July 1800.

Marescot

Armand Samuel Marescot (1758–1832), born in a rural gentry family traditionally dedicated to the career of arms, followed the course of college of La Flèche, the School of Mézières, Military School at Paris and entered the French army in 1784 with the rank of lieutenant. The young Marescot fought and was nearly killed in combat in April 1792 at Pas-de-Besieux in northern France. He contributed to making combat ready the city of Lille, where he was wounded in October 1792. He took

Tower in the Arçon Lunet at Montdauphin.

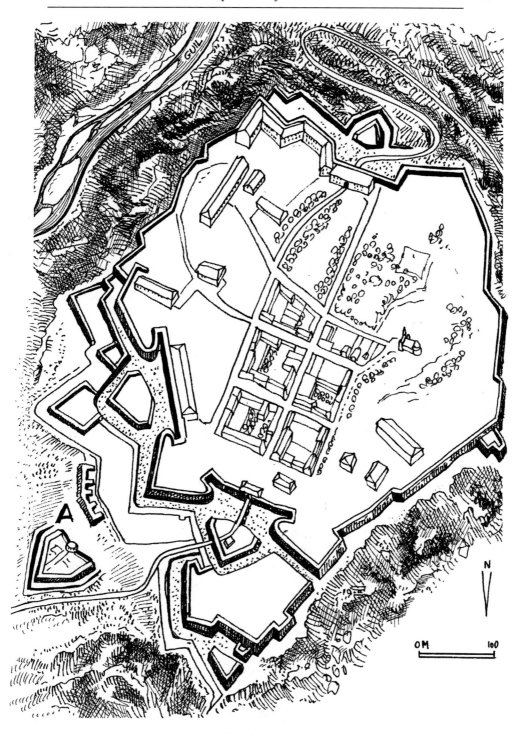

Montdauphin
The fortress of Montdauphin, situated near Embrun in the department of Hautes-Alpes, was designed by Vauban in 1693. A Napoleonic lunette (A) was designed by Le Michaud d'Arçon, and built in 1803.

part in the siege of Antwerp (November 1792), in the Battle of Nerwinden, and in the siege of Toulon in 1794, where he met a certain Bonaparte, then artillery officer. Marescot fought as a field and siege engineer at Maubeuge, Charleroi, Landrecies, Fleurus, Le Quesnoy, Valenciennes, Condé, and Maastricht. Appointed inspector-general of the French Engineering Corps in March 1795, he then defended Landau and Fort Kehl in Germany. In September 1799 he became governor of Mayence, and promoted to the rank of general-inspector of the Comité Central des Fortifications in 1800 and commanding general of the Engineering Corps in 1802. In this top function, Marescot became the most important officer of the Napoleonic Génie, directing (under the supervision of Napoléon) and inspecting all projects in France and in the annexed foreign territories, and still participating in the campaigns. He took part in the Battle of Austerlitz and was made a Count of the Empire in 1805. When he was at the top of his power, his decline was sudden and his fall rapid. Captured at the Battle of Bailen (Spain) in June 1808, he took the initiative to negotiate the capitulation without orders from Napoléon. When liberated from the Spanish jail, he was immediately arrested, condemned as a traitor, stripped of all his ranks, functions and dignities and imprisoned until April 1814. Marescot was reinstated in his rank during the Restoration. He soon retired from active service, and was made a marquis in July 1817, and a Peer of France in March 1819. He died in December 1832, aged 74. His name is inscribed on the eastern side of the Arc de Triomphe in Paris.

Siege Warfare

In the French Revolutionary and Napoleonic Wars new techniques stressed the division of armies into all-arms corps that would march separately and only come together on the battlefield. The less concentrated army could now live off the country and move more rapidly over a larger number of roads. Fortresses commanding lines of communication could be bypassed and would no longer stop an invasion. However, since armies could not live off the land indefinitely, Napoleon always sought a quick end to any conflict by a highly decisive pitched battle. This military revolution had been designed, described, and codified by two great and influential military thinkers: Guibert and Clausewitz. Advances in artillery made previously impregnable defenses less effective. For example, the walls of Vienna that had held off the Turkish armies in 1529 and in 1683 were no obstacle to Napoléon. Although much less known than famous battles like Austerlitz, Wagram or Waterloo, the Napoleonic period saw a number of important sieges which had significant influence on the campaigns.

Toulon 1793

The siege of Toulon, a military engagement in the French Revolutionary Wars, was caused by French Royalists who handed over the naval base and arsenal to an Anglo-Spanish fleet in August 1793. The French Revolutionary army began a siege to recapture the port city and, after months of preparations, they successfully assaulted the allied-held forts commanding the anchorage in December 1793. A battery of French guns, set up on an ideal place, spotted and commanded by the 24-year-old Bonaparte, fired on the British fleet and forced it to evacuate the inner harbor, though British and Spanish troops blew up the arsenal and burned 42 French ships before leaving. For his key role in the victory, Napoléon Bonaparte attracted much attention, was promoted to the rank of brigadier general and started his brilliant career.

DANZIG 1807

The Siege of Danzig (now known as Gdansk) in Poland, during the War of the Fifth Coalition, lasted from March 19 to May 24, 1807. The French, with a force of about 27,000 men, lay siege to about 11,000 Prussians and Russians. Danzig held an important strategic position in Poland. As well as being an important heavily fortified port with 60,000 inhabitants at the mouth of the river Vistula, it was a direct threat to the French left— it lay within Prussian lands but to the rear of the French army as it advanced eastward. It was also a potential dropping-off point for allied troops that could threaten the French army by opening another front to their rear. Danzig was also difficult to attack, being only accessible from the west—all other directions being covered either by the Vistula (in the north) or wetlands (in the south and east). Furthermore, it had precious resources and supplies of great interest to the Grande Armée in planning a substantial campaign in the east. The mission of capturing the city was entrusted to Marshal François Lefebvre's 10th Corps. The marshal was assisted by Generals Chasseloup-Laubat, who headed the engineering works, and Gaston de Lariboisière, who commanded the artillery. Together they were the two best specialists in their respective fields in the French army.

In March 20, the city was encircled, in April siege trenches and batteries were dug, and the defenders were subjected to heavy fire. Attempts to relieve the city by boat failed and the bombardments and mining continued. On May 21 Marshal Mortier's corps arrived, making it possible to storm the fort on the Hagelsberg. Seeing that he could no longer hold out, the Prussian commander Kalckreuth sued Lefebvre for peace, and Danzig capitulated on May 24, 1807. The terms of the surrender were generous (stipulating that the garrison could march out with all the honors of war, with drums beating and standards waving) because Napoléon was eager to put an end to the siege since the summer (and the fighting season) was approaching and he needed to remove the threat to his rear and to engage his troops elsewhere. The defenders had suffered many casualties during the siege, compared to the French losses of roughly 400 men. In recompense for Lefebvre's services, Napoléon granted him the title of Duke of Danzig. In September 1807 Napoléon instituted the Free City of Danzig as a semi-independent state. From late January to November 19, 1813, Russian forces laid siege to the city, and the French occupying forces withdrew on January 2, 1814.

ALMEIDA 1810

The fortress of Almeida in Portugal had been primarily fortified in the 17th century in order to protect the crossings of the River Coa, which formed a natural barrier between Portugal and Spain. The city played a key role in the Peninsular War (1804–1814). In January 1808 it fell to the French General Junot, whom Napoléon subsequently made Governor of Portugal. When the French retreated following the Convention of Sintra in August 1808, the Portuguese reoccupied the city. The Napoleonic army returned in 1810, occupied Ciudad Rodrigo in Spain and besieged Almeida. This siege lasted from July 24 to August 28, 1810. The city was well fortified with an enceinte including six bastions, six demi-lunes, a dry ditch cut in the solid rock and a covered way. It had casemates completely proof against bomb fire, and large enough to cover the whole garrison. It was well supplied, and the garrison — about 4500 men — was well armed with over 100 guns.

In mid–1810, the Anglo-Allied forces under Lord Wellington were deployed in the vicinity of Ciudad Rodrigo. Wellington knew that he was not strong enough to prevent the French from invading Portugal. His plan was to stay forward along the border as long as possible, and once the French began to move, he would retreat to the Lines of Torres Vedras. There extensive belts of field fortification were being built and he would have a secure supply line. His plan called for the fortresses of Almeida to delay the French as long as possible, causing them to expend valuable supplies and men. Wellington placed the defense of Almeida into the hands of the experienced Colonel William Cox. The siege of Almeida began on July 24, 1810, when French forces under Marshal Ney attacked General Crawford's Light Division in what is known as the action on the River Coa. This attack pushed the remaining British forces back across the Coa and the garrison of Almeida was on its own. The French began to dig siege works on August 15 southeast of the town

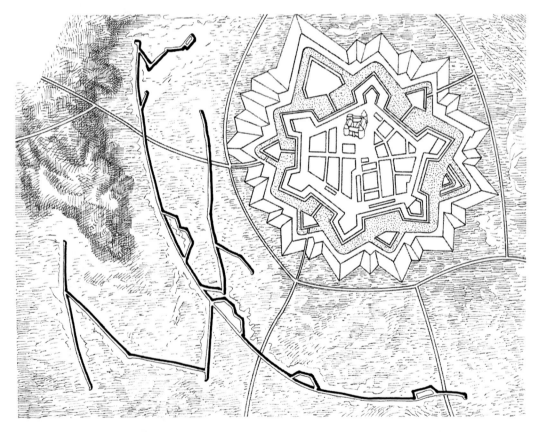

Siege of Almeida (1810)
Napoleonic siege warfare used basically the same method designed by Vauban a century before, with a lot of digging work: parallels, trenches, saps, and gun batteries.

and by August 26 they had 11 batteries in position with over 50 guns. The French started to bombard the town, and a lucky shot hit an ammunition store in the castle, resulting in a gigantic explosion that killed thousands. When the smoke cleared off, the castle had practically disappeared, and a great part of the city was damaged. On August 28, Almeida surrendered. The fortress that Wellington had hoped would buy him several months' time, fell after a siege of five weeks. Within a month, the Anglo-Portuguese allied army was in full retreat towards Lisbon. Wellington, on his victorious return from Torres Vedras, defeated the French on May 11, 1811, at Fuentes d'Onoro and subsequently retook the fortress of Almeida with no bloodshed.

Badajoz 1812

The siege of Badajoz in Spain lasted from March 16 to April 6, 1812. It opposed an attacking Anglo-Portuguese army to a French defending garrison. The siege was one of the bloodiest in the Napoleonic Wars and was considered a costly victory by the British, with some 3,000 Allied soldiers killed in a few short hours of intense fighting as the siege drew to an end. Badajoz, garrisoned by some 5,000 French soldiers, was well fortified with strong walls, bastions, explosives in countermines, and some areas around the enceinte flooded or mined with explosives. The allied army, some 25,000 strong, outnumbered

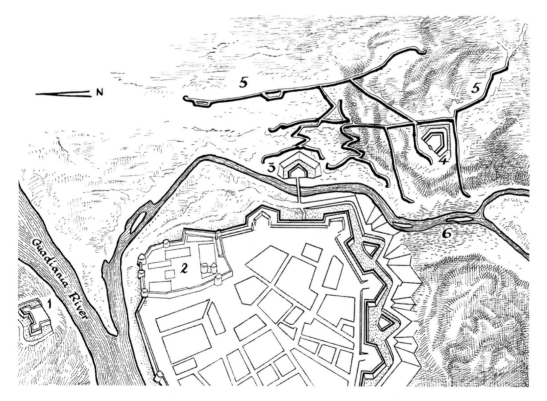

Siege of Badajoz 1812
1: Fort San Christobal; 2: Castle of Badajoz; 3: Fort San Roque; 4: Fort Picurina (taken on March 25, 1812); 5: British trenches and siege gun batteries; 6: inundation.

the French garrison by around five to one and, after encircling the town, began to lay siege by preparing trenches, parallels and earthworks to protect the heavy siege artillery. As the approach earthworks were prepared, the French made several sorties to try to destroy the lines advancing toward the wall, but were repeatedly repulsed. With the arrival of heavy artillery, the Anglo-Portuguese Allies began an intense bombardment of the town's defenses whilst one of the defensive bastions was attacked and soon seized by the British.

The capture of the detached fort Picurina on March 25 allowed the Allies to bring forward their siege artillery closer to the defenses. By April 5 two breaches were made in the rampart and the attackers readied themselves to storm Badajoz. In the meantime the garrison had mined the breaches in the walls and prepared for the imminent assault. The attack came on April 6. The defenders poured a lethal hail of musket fire, threw grenades and exploded their mines, causing enormous numbers of casualties (about 2,000) to the attackers. Despite the carnage the British redcoats continued to move forward in the breach and finally got a foothold on the rampart. Now the British and Portuguese soldiers were at an advantage from sheer numbers and began to drive the French back who — after hopeless resistance — were forced to surrender. The victors had, however, suffered a lot and the ranks were infuriated with anger and desire for revenge. The victory was fol-

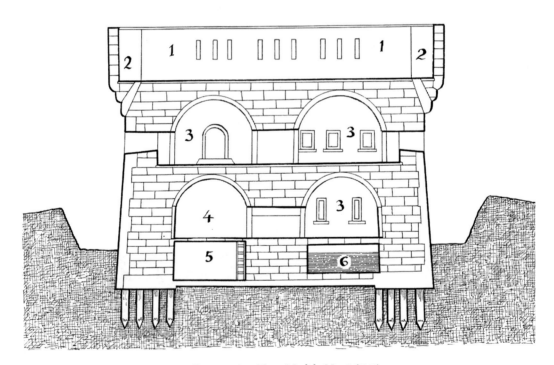

Cross-section Tour Modèle No. 1 (1811)
The upper open terrasse (1) was fitted with rifle loopholes, and four guns on Gribeauval fortress traversing mounts. It also included brattices with machicoulis (2) built on the faces of the wall; the brattice was a small projecting balcony fitted with openings permitting defenders to throw missiles down upon assailants. This medieval element was probably more decorative than suited for active defense. The first floor was divided into quarters (3) for the garrison. The ground floor included quarters (3) and an ammunition store (4). The basement housed a food store (5) and a cistern (6).

lowed by the atrocious looting of the town: homes were broken into, property vandalized or stolen, Spanish civilians of all ages killed, women raped, and even British officers were shot by their own men when they were trying to bring them to order.

Coastal Defense

REDOUBT AND TOUR MODÈLE

After the defeat of Trafalgar in 1805, the French lost any hope of supremacy at sea. Napoléon, a land commander but a poor naval strategist who knew very little of maritime warfare, was unable to reconstitute the French navy. To implement the Continental Blockade and suppress smuggling, and also to thwart British raids on the French-held shores, the Emperor was forced to rely upon coastal surveillance and defense. The Comité Central des Fortifications had to imagine new defensive dispositions and systems. For this purpose the Committee designed several standardized coastal works. It is generally believed that these standardized fortlets originate from a defense tower designed by engineer Mareschal in 1740 at Agde in southern France. Another source of inspiration seems to be fortified houses with square bastioned earthworks designed and built by Gaspard Joseph Chaussegros de Lévy in Canada in the 1750s. They also have similarities to Vauban's coastal forts built during Louis XIV's reign.

The *Redoute modèle 1811* was a small simple standardized fort. It was square or rectangular, and included a top terrace (serving both as an observation post and gun emplacement), riflemen's galleries, quarters for the garrison and the commanding officers, stores for food, water and ammunition, as well as a central yard. The redoubt was surrounded by a ditch, a covered way and a glacis, and featured counterscarp coffers — vaulted case-

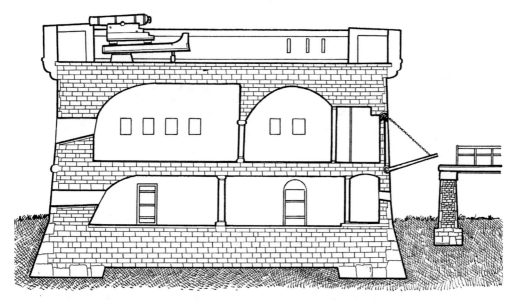

Cross-section Tour Modèle No. 1 (variant).

36-pdr. gun on traversing mount
The wheelless gun was mounted on a Gribeauval slide which served to check the recoil, and facilitated reloading and sliding back into firing position. The gun could thus be laid vertically onto the target, while training (or traversing) was accomplished owing to two small wheels swiveling on a rail fixed in the platform.

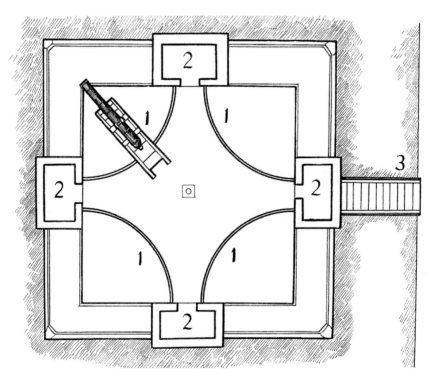

Plan platform of Tour Modèle No. 1
This example was built in 1812 at Fort Ruyter at Willemstadt in the Netherlands.
1: Rail for Gribeauval fortress artillery mount. 2: Projecting brattice with machicolation. 3: Access to tower via drawbridge across the ditch.

mates placed at the angles of the ditch for close-range defense. A variant existed with bastions at each of the four angles in the tradition of Vauban — Fort Liédot on Aix island being a good example.

A smaller standardized work, also designed by the Committee, was approved by Napoléon at the same time. Known as *Tour Modèle*, this coastal work was a masoned square tower which existed in several variants. Intended for both a surveillance and combat role, the tower could also serve as reduit for coastal batteries. It had a platform armed with four guns mounted on Gribeauval

Tour Modèle, Battery of Toulinguet at Crozon, Brest.

Tour Modèle, Fort at Point of Boyardville.
This variant had a caponier placed at the angles for short-range defense.

carriages, and pierced with loopholes for riflemen's fire. The bombproof vaulted story contained the garrison and store places. It was surrounded by a ditch crossed by a drawbridge, and was about 27 feet high, thus secured from escalade by an attacking party. Standardized redoubts and towers were, however, expensive to build and man. Originally some 160 units were planned but only a relative limited number (about 10) were built on the shores of the Napoleonic empire, namely on the French Atlantic coast, and in the Netherlands. A good preserved example still stands today at Fort de Hel, built by the Dutch in 1748 in Polder De Ruigehil near Willemstad. In 1812 Napoléon ordered the construction of a Tour Modèle in the fort. Standardized coastal towers continued to be used for many years, and in 1841 the Commission of Fortifications made further development including three classes; the first class were manned by 60 men and artillery; second class with 40 men without artillery; and third class coastal batteries with artillery.

BRITISH MARTELLO TOWERS

The French were not the only ones to make use of standardized coastal works. Martello towers (or simply Martellos) were small defensive forts built in several countries of the British Empire during the 19th century, from the time of the Napoleonic Wars onwards. Martello towers were inspired by a round fortress, part of a larger Genovese defense system, at Mortella Point in Corsica. Since the 15th century, similar towers had been built at strategic points around Corsica to protect coastal villages and shipping from North African pirates. They stood one or two stories high and typically measured 12–15 m (36–45 ft) in diameter, with a single doorway 5 m off the ground that could only be reached by climbing a removable ladder. The British were impressed by the effectiveness of these simple strongholds against their most modern warships and copied the design. However, they got the name wrong, misspelling "Mortella" as "Martello."

The typical British Martello tower stood up to 40 feet (12m) high (with two floors) and usually had a garrison of one officer and 15 to 25 men. Their round shape and thick walls of solid masonry made them reasonably resistant to smooth-bore cannon fire, while their height made them a good platform for a single heavy artillery piece, mounted on the flat roof and able to traverse a 360° arc. Some towers were fitted with riflemen's loopholes and surrounded by a moat for extra defense.

The first Martello towers were built in a hurry in 1803 when Napoléon threatened to

Martello tower.

Tower at Fort Frederic Kingston, Ontario, Canada.

invade Britain. They were later used throughout the 19th century, to guard the British coastline and strategic points in British colonial possessions around the world. Around 140 were built, mostly along the south coast of England and on the British Channel Islands. Others were constructed as far afield as Australia, Canada, Ireland, Minorca, South Africa and Sri Lanka. The construction of Martello towers abroad continued until as late as the 1850s but was discontinued after it became clear that they could

Martello tower at Magilligan Point Limavady.

not withstand the new generation of rifled artillery weapons, but many have survived to the present day, often being preserved as historic monuments.

Blockhouse

A blockhouse is a small, isolated fortified point often in the form of a single building. It is intended to serve as a defensive strongpoint against any enemy which does not possess siege equipment or, in modern times, artillery. If a fortification is intended to protect against such weapons as well, it is more likely to qualify as a castle or, in modern times, a fort. Originally blockhouses were often constructed as part of a large plan, to "block" access to vital points in the scheme, or for defense in frontier areas, or along a communication line, and less often as coastal surveillance posts.

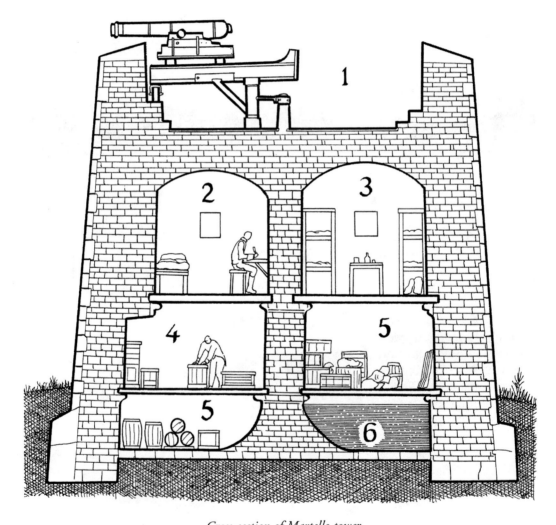

Cross-section of Martello tower.
1: Platform with gun on rotating mount; 2: officer's room; 3: crew chamber; 4: ammunition store; 5: food store; 6: cistern.

3. Imperial Fortifications

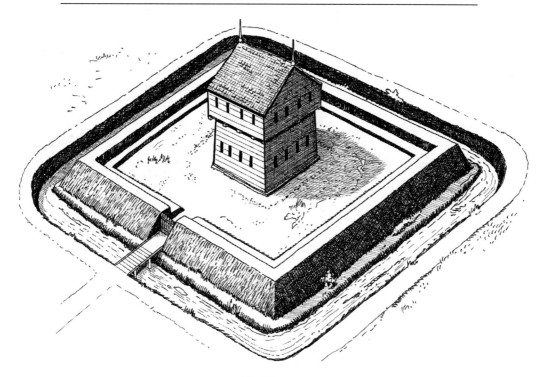

Blockhouse.

French blockhouse in Spain.

Blockhouses might be made of masonry where available, but were commonly made from very heavy timbers, sometimes even logs arranged in the manner of a log cabin, the very name deriving from the German *Block* (beam) and *Haus* (house). It is said that the concept of this temporary stronghold was developed by Austrian and Prussian engineers in the 1770s during the War of Succession of Bavaria. A blockhouse was usually two or even three floors high, with all stories being provided with embrasures or loopholes, and the uppermost story would be roofed. If the structure was of timber, usually the upper story would project outward from the lower so the upper story defenders could fire on enemy attacking the lower story. When the structure had only one story, its loopholes were often placed close to the ceiling, with a bench lining the walls inside for defenders to stand on, so that attackers could not easily reach the loopholes. Blockhouses were nor-

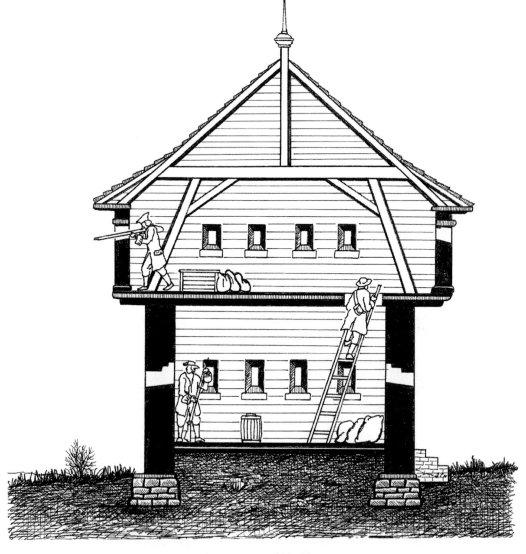

Cross-section of blockhouse.

mally entered via a sturdy, barred door at ground level. Most blockhouses were roughly square or rectangular in plan, but some of the more elaborate ones were hexagonal or octagonal, to provide better all-around fire. In some cases, blockhouses became the basis for a complete fort, by building a palisade or an earth wall with a ditch around the tower. A the time of Napoléon, many blockhouses were built by the French along the roads of Germany and Russia in order to have small protection detachments scattered along their communication lines. Blockhouses were particularly used by the French Napoleonic forces in Spain to counter the guerilla. Manned by *Gendarmes d'Espagne* (militarized policemen), the elaborate strongholds were intended to ensure the protection of the couriers and the supply convoys in the mountainous northern part of the country.

Cartography and Relief-Maps

Most evidently, the Napoleonic military authorities attached great importance to cartography for the design of their campaigns. In May 1795, the *Bureau Topographique de l'Armée* (Army Topographic Office) was created, and reorganized in 1809 as *Corps Impérial des Ingénieurs-Géographes* (Imperial Geographers Corps). As the name implies, it was composed of geographers charged to survey and make maps of the different parts of the Empire. During the Napoleonic era, cartography made significant advances by the general adoption (in 1801) of equidistant curved level lines. In cartography, a contour line (often just called a "contour") joins points of equal elevation (height) above a given level, such as mean sea level, clearly showing altitude, and standardized colors for other indications needed to have a precise view of a region. Data provided by accurate maps enabled Napoléon and his generals to have a detailed knowledge of their territories, and allowed them to make important decisions about planning a war or a campaign. Maps were top-secret state documents, and the very specialized cartographers were courted by rival sovereigns, as they carried with them visual knowledge of a land. A cartographer who changed employers could do significant harm to his former master by revealing strategic secrets.

In the domain of cartography, *relief-maps* occupy an important position. Relief-maps are architectural documents in the form of scale models giving three-dimensional volume, position and extension of fortifications. The collection was created in 1668 on War Minister Louvois's order. Most of the fortified places conquered, constructed or reshaped by Vauban and his collaborators were the basis of models with a scale of one foot for a hundred toises, which approximately corresponds to scale 1/600th (a toise, or fathom, was equal to six French feet, that is, 1.949 meters or 6.4 English feet). A spectator has the illusion of flying over the fortified place to an altitude about 400 or 500 meters. The collection was housed in a large room in the Louvre Palace in Paris. It was used by King Louis XIV and his headquarters as a strategical document for war-gaming or to follow an actual siege. Scale models also had the function of keeping the defenses of fortified places in memory; should one be captured by enemies, the King had a perfect knowledge of how to retake it. The scale models were remarkable visualizations of the art of fortification and also served an educational aim to engineers and other military personnel. They compensated for the lack of topographical maps and completed in three dimensions the ground-plans and drawings of a given fortification. The collection of scale models was Louis XIV's private property and kept secretly. The proud king was, however, pleased to show it as a warning or deterring object to ambassadors or important foreign visitors. Not only fortifications were represented but also, with an exceptional precision, houses, public buildings and the surrounding countryside within gun range. Every model, like a large jigsaw puzzle, consisted of several wooden plates assembled together by means of iron bars. Certain scale models are very large; some of them weigh up to 2,000 kilograms. The relief-map of Saint-Omer, for example, covers a surface of 50 square meters; that of Namur consists of fourteen plates, that of Strasburg is 10.86 m in length and 6.66 m in width. The fabrication of the relief-maps was very expensive and Vauban, at first, was opposed to Louvois's models, objecting that funds would be better used to build real fortifications. However he eventually recognized their educational worth.

Louvois's work was carried on and extended under the reigns of Louis XV and Napoléon. From 1870 on though, the progress of topographic maps and the introduction of photography rendered the scale models obsolete. They lost their military value and their fabrication was discontinued. During the past three centuries, the fragile and vulnerable collection has suffered a lot because of lack of maintenance, several removals, looting in 1815 and war destruction in 1940 and 1944. Since 1927, the exceptionally precious historical value of the collection has been recognized and it has been classed as a historic monument. Relief-maps enable to follow the evolution of fortification, they display the manners how cities were fortified, and they are a valuable source of information about the history of urban development and changing landscapes. Today about a hundred relief-maps are preserved and a selection is exhibited in the attic (fourth floor) of the Musée de l'Armée in the Hôtel des Invalides in Paris. Another part of the relief-map collection (including, for example, Lille, Calais, Ath, Maubeuge, Tournai, Charleroi, Bouchain, Bergues, Namur, and many others) is exhibited at Lille (northern France) in the Musée des Beaux-Arts, Place de la République.

Futuristic Weapons

The end of the 18th century and the reign of Napoléon saw the conception of futuristic projects most of which remained unfeasible due to the limited technology of the time.

STEAM AUTOMOBILE

The French engineer Nicolas-Joseph Cugnot (1725–1804) served in Germany, entered the service of Prince Charles in the Low Countries and came to Paris in 1763 to become a teacher in military arts. In 1769 Cugnot designed a three-wheeled, steam-powered automobile vehicle, which he proposed to the army for use as an artillery prime mover. During a test Cugnot's cumbersome and clumsy *fardier* (lorry) ran for twenty minutes, dangerously puffing along at a speed of 2.25 mph with four passengers. The vehicle was very unstable due to poor weight distribution, and its boiler performance was also particularly poor, even by the standards of the day, with the fire needing to be relit and steam raised again every quarter of an hour or so, considerably reducing overall speed. This project quickly fell into oblivion and automobile vehicles became a technical possibility only with the invention of the internal combustion engine in the 1880s. The experiment was

Cugnot's fardier.

Clermont.

judged interesting enough, though, for the *fardier* to be kept at the Arsenal until transferred to the Conservatoire National des Arts et Métiers in Paris in 1800, where it can still be seen today. It should be noted that Cugnot was trained as a military engineer. He also invented a musket and wrote a treatise titled *Théorie de la Fortification*, published in Paris in 1763, in which he advocated a rather curious fortified circular tracing without outworks.

Submarine and Steamboat

In 1801, the American engineer and inventor Robert Fulton (1765–1815) proposed to the French a new weapon of his invention: a submarine called *Nautilus* armed with a torpedo. An experimental mock attack took place at Camaret near Brest. The test was a failure and the submarine became a reality only by the end of the 19th century. A businessman in the first place, Fulton offered his service to Britain as well. He demonstrated the effectiveness of his weapon by sinking an old brig. The Royal Navy was not impressed, however, and the submarine was rejected. Fulton returned to the United States where he developed the *Clermont* in 1807, the first steam-powered craft to be economically employed in America, in active regular commercial service on the Hudson River between New York and Albany. The ship was 43.30 m (142 ft) long, 4.28 m (14 ft) in beam, flat-bottomed with a depth of 1.22 m (4 ft) and a displacement of 79 tons. Made of wood, she was equipped with an English steam engine made by Boulton, Watt and Co., developing some 20 hp, giving an amazing speed of five knots. The engine drove two side paddle wheels 4.60 m (15 ft) in diameter.

Balloon

The hot-air balloon is the oldest successful human-carrying flight technology. Hot-air balloons are based on a very basic scientific principle: warmer air rises in cooler air. Essentially, hot air is lighter than cool air, because it has less mass per unit of volume. A cubic foot of air weighs roughly 28 grams (about an ounce). If that air is heated by 100 degrees F, it weighs about 7 grams less. Therefore, each cubic foot of air contained in a hot-air balloon can lift about 7 grams. That is not much, and this is why hot-air balloons are so huge. For example, to lift 1,000 pounds, about 65,000 cubic feet of hot air are required. Lazare Carnot envisaged using lighter-than-air balloons for observation and artillery ranging. Carnot based his plan on balloons capable of carrying passengers using hot air to obtain buoyancy, which were built by the brothers Joseph and Etienne Montgolfier in Annonay, France. After experiments with unmanned balloons and flights with animals, the first balloon flight with humans on board took place in November 1783 with the physician Pilâtre de Rozier, the manufacture manager, Jean-Baptiste Réveillon and Giroud de Villette, at the Folie Titon in Paris. The first military use of aircraft took place during the French Revolutionary Wars, when the French used a tethered hydrogen balloon (still tied to the ground by ropes) to observe the movements of the Austrian army during the Battle of Fleurus (June 1794). A famous futuristic and visionary print from the Napoleonic time showed large balloons firing guns and carrying an army sky-high across the Channel and attacking Great Britain, while boats ferried other troops over the sea, and while another army was marching through a tunnel dug under the Channel.

Telegraph

The optical telegraph invented by the French engineer Claude Chappe (1763–1805) was a success. Tested in July 1793 between Ménilmontant Hill in Paris and Saint-Martin-du-Tertre (a distance of about 15 km), it was composed of a network of stations placed within sight of each other, generally on hills. Each post included a stone tower which was fitted with a room for an operator and equipped with a mast, on top of which articulated movable arms were fixed; these consisted of a rather large horizontal beam (called a regulator) and two smaller wing beams (called the indicators) whose position was coded. In only nine minutes the following text was transmitted: *Les habitants de cette belle contrée sont dignes de la liberté par leur amour pour elle et leur respect pour la Convention et ses lois* (the inhabitants of this beautiful region are worthy of freedom by the love for it and by their respect for the Convention and its laws). The optical telegraph was adopted, the National Assembly voted a 6,000-franc budget, and Claude Chappe was granted the title of telegraphic engineer and the rank of lieutenant in the military Génie. By 1804, lines were built radiating from Paris to 29 main French provincial cities, military arsenals, and important fortresses; there were 556 stations covering 3,000 miles, with stations placed approximately six miles apart, and employing over 1,000 people. By 1814, lines were extended to Italy, Germany and the Low Countries. Although slow and complicated to operate, and although useless at night and in bad weather, the Chappe system worked reasonably well. The optical telegraph was abandoned in 1854 when new techniques of communication were invented.

Chappe telegraph station.

4

Napoleonic Fortification Projects

Dismantlement of Obsolete Places

The establishment of a coherent defensive system often required not only the abandonment, but also the destruction of existing strongholds. Indeed, the maintenance of too many fortresses was always a drain on a state military budget; it unnecessarily scattered troops that could be deployed elsewhere, and useless and abandoned forts could be dangerous if taken by the enemy. The French Revolution, the Consulate and the Empire were periods of great changes, and France came to control larger territories than had been the case under the Ancien Régime. A reorganization of the defenses was thus necessary. As early as 1791, about twenty strongholds in France were declared obsolete and abandoned, while the rest were divided into three classes according to their strategical importance. However, the dismantlement of a fortified work was, and still is, a very costly business: it mobilized enormous manpower, the time was not always available, and the stones could not always be recycled or re-employed, particularly when explosives were used. The destructions that were deemed necessary could therefore not be carried out everywhere. So in the Netherlands, the French military authorities had decided the dismantlement of the fortifications of Hulst, Axel, and Saas-van-Gent; in Germany that of Coblence and Rheinfels. In the end, these projects were not carried out due to lack of funds, but the fortifications of Breslau in Upper Silesia (present-day Wroclaw in southwest Poland) were dismantled between 1806 and 1808. In Italy, important destructions took place between 1796 and 1801, including the forts of Bart, Demonte, Exilles and Fenestrelles (all of which controlled the strategically important Alpine passes), as well as the urban enceintes of Peschiera, Suza and Turin.

Napoleonic Arsenals

As imperial France's borders were largely extended to the north, east and southeast, the defensive system inherited from the Ancien Régime did not correspond any longer to the requirements of the new time. A redefinition was demanded concerning as much the spacial organization as the strategical conception. Abandoning the traditional monarchic policy of "Pré Carré," with its lines of passive fortresses placed along the previous borders, Napoléon set up a new aggressive scheme centering upon large military arsenals. The siting of these arsenals was of course of crucial importance. Some pre-existed in con-

4. Napoleonic Fortification Projects

Fort Exilles

The fort of Exilles, situated in the valley of the Suza River, originated from a stronghold built in the Middle Ages by the Count of Albon. Because of its strategical situation in the Alps in the province of Turin, it was hotly disputed between France and the Duchy of Savoy. It was often besieged, taken and reconquered by both parties. Between 1600 and 1610, under the reign of King Henri IV of France, it was reconstructed, and Vauban made a design to improve its defense in 1700. Given to Savoy after the Treaty of Utrecht in 1713, the fort of Exilles was totally destroyed by the French after the signature of the Treaty of Paris in May 1796. It was later rebuilt by order of the King of Sardinia between 1818 and 1829. It was disarmed in 1915 but stayed occupied by the Italian army until September 1943.

Right: *Fenestrelles, Italy (c. 1808). The fortifications were dismantled in the end of the 19th century.*

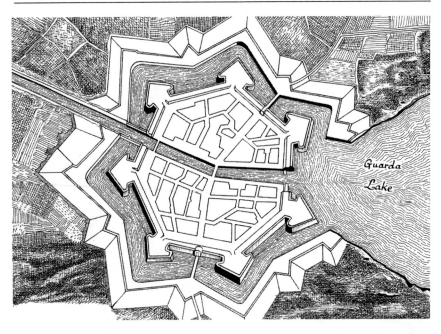

Peschiera, Italy
Situated in northern Italy at the mouth of River Mincio on the Lake of Garda, the castle (rocca) was built in the Middle Ages by Lord Mastino della Scalla. In 1439, the city of Peschiera became a part of the Venetian empire and bastioned fortifications were constructed in the late 1540s. These were dismantled during the French occupation from 1801 to 1813.

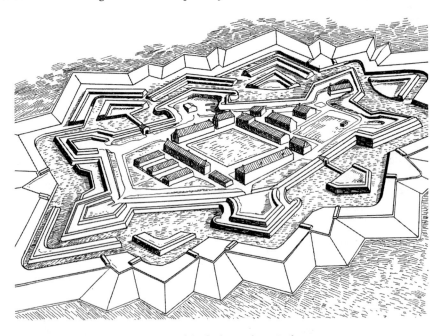

Citadel of Alessandria, Italy
Dominating the flat ground around it, the citadel lay at the key junction on the roads from Mantua and Genoa.

quered cities, others were created as military poles placed in strategical position. More than passive strongholds intended for a defensive role, these places were large military arsenals where troops were regrouped, where food and supplies were stored, and where weapons, ammunition and other military materials, including engineering equipment, were manufactured, maintained and stockpiled in order to launch offensive operations. All these arsenals were (or were to be, as many projects were not completed) heavily fortified with bastioned walls, outworks, and detached forts, and most of them included a citadel. A citadel was a fortress built within a fortified city. It was often placed on a dominating position inside the town and often overlapping the urban fortifications, which made it accessible independently from the city gates. In certain cases, the citadel was an ancient pre-existing castle or an enlarged and fortified nobleman's residence around which the city had developed. It might also be a newly-created fortress, but, whatever its origin, the citadel fulfilled three distinctive roles. The first function was logistical. The citadel contained everything needed in order to resist a long siege, such as living accommodations, food-, water- and foraging-stores, arsenal and workshops. It was also a supply point for armies in campaign, a winter troop quarters, as well as a military, fiscal and administrative center. Secondly, the citadel was a powerful military bulwark. Just like the keep in the medieval castle, it acted as a final fall-back position, a reduit from which to continue the defense even when the town was conquered. It was therefore strongly fortified

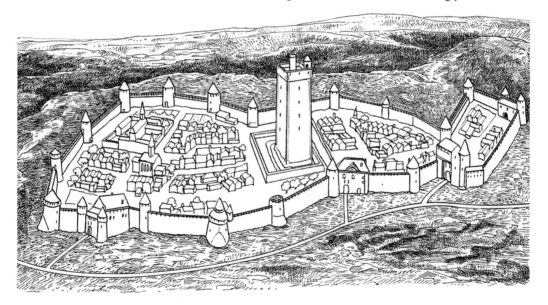

Château-Thierry

Situated on a 200-m-high hill dominating an important crossroad on the River Marne, between the provinces of Champagne and Ile-de-France, the castle of Château-Thierry originated from a Roman settlement (named Odomagus) which became a fortified residence in the 5th century. This was enlarged by the Counts of Vermendois in the 9th and 10th centuries, and by Count of Champagne, Thibaud II, in the 12th century. In 1285 the town was incorporated into the French realm and the defenses were reshaped by King Philippe le Bel. Château-Thierry was then a residence for the kings of France and their families, and a powerful stronghold that was several times enlarged, modernized, and adapted to new weapons. Greatly transformed in the 18th century, the castle was used by Napoléon as an arsenal in July 1814.

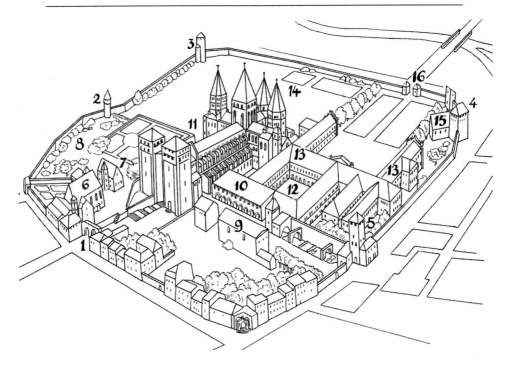

The Abbey of Cluny (before 1798)
The Benedictine Abbey of Cluny near Macon in Burgundy, founded in 910 by Abbot Bernon and Guillaume, Duke of Aquitaine, who provided land from an old hunting lodge, rapidly developed. Under the brilliant leadership of particularly remarkable abbots, it soon became one of the most important Christian monastic centers in the Middle Ages, with an international influence. As head house of the Order, Cluny controlled its "daughters" which it had created all through Europe. Cluny remained prosperous until the 18th century even though from the 13th century onwards its intellectual and political influence slowly declined. At the time of the French Revolution, this symbol of clerical opulence and power was pillaged, secularized and badly damaged. All monastic orders were disbanded (1790), the monks were forced to leave, the abbey was seized by the municipality of Cluny, and some of the conventual buildings (built between the 11th and 18th centuries) were demolished for the piercing of new streets and squares. The huge abbatial church (named by historians and archaeologist "Cluny III," built between 1088 and 1138), a remarkable masterpiece of medieval architecture, was 187 m (613 ft) long; the five sections of its nave opened onto a great transept which was topped by three bell towers. The chancel, itself endowed with a smaller transept and a tower, was surrounded by an ambulatory and five radiating chapels. The church was 90 percent demolished between 1798 and 1823 in order to sell the stones, and eventually a haras (horse-breeding studfarm) was established for Napoléon's cavalry.

Before the destruction of the end of the 18th century, the Abbey included the following features: An enclosed fortified wall with main entrance (1); Fabry Tower (2); Round Tower (3); Mill Tower (4); and Tower of Cheeses (5). The buildings outside the "enclosure" (part of the Abbey closed off to the laity) included the Palace of Abbot Jean de Bourbon from the 15th century (6); the Palace of Abbot Jacques d'Amboise from the 16th century (7); the abbatial garden (8); and Saint Hugues's Stables from the 11th century (9), which was used as a guest house. The buildings within the enclosure included Pope Gelase façade from the 13th century (10); the abbey church (11), today reduced to one bell tower named Clocher de l'Eau Bénite; the 18th century cloister (12); the 18th century conventual buildings (13); and the 18th century garden (14) replacing medieval buildings and today housing the ENSAM (École Nationale Supérieure des Arts et Métiers); the grain house from the 13th century (15); and the 18th century entrance (16).

with powerful defenses, fortified gatehouse with drawbridge, deep ditches, and an empty and bare esplanade isolating it from the rest of the city. This display of strength was meant to impress the population, and also intended to deter enemies from laying siege. The third and most important role was political. The fortress on its rocky height dominated the city and its approach, while the town, nestled below in its shadow, was perpetually reminded of its dependence. In conquered foreign lands, the citadel was intended to subjugate, control and overawe recently conquered populations with questionable loyalty or municipalities with rebellious propensity. The citadel was headed by a governor appointed by the Emperor, it was garrisoned with French civil servants collecting taxes and with officers who organized the conscription of the local male population, and it had its own garrison, loyal to the French Emperor and ready to repress unwillingness to serve, popular riots, insurrections, and revolts.

The Napoleonic policy of arsenals included two major axes: maritime arsenals for control of the sea, and land arsenals for domination of the European countries.

At sea, first to prepare the invasion of Great Britain and — after the disaster of Trafalgar in 1805 — to defend the European coasts from British attacks, the major maritime arsenals included: Cherbourg, Brest, and Rochefort (for the Atlantic and the Channel); Calais, Antwerp and Den Helder in the Netherlands (for the North Sea); Toulon and La Spezzia (Mediterranean Sea); and Zara and Corfu (Adriatic Sea). Most of these military ports pre-existed, and ambitious plans were made to enlarge, fortify, and equip them with all facilities, quarters, and workshops necessary for the building, maintenance and repair of ocean-going warships. Along this large scheme, many secondary ports were also militarized and equipped. At the same time, vulnerable coasts were fitted with watchtowers, redoubts, coastal forts and batteries intended to repulse enemy landings, to see to the application of the Continental System (blockade), and to repress smuggling.

In Europe, the arsenals of Lille, Metz and Strasbourg (in France), Alessandria (Italy), Wesel, Coblence, Cologne, and Juliers (Germany), Maastricht (Low Countries) and Luxembourg, as well as many secondary places, were developed to regroup and equip the Napoleonic armies. They served as rear bases for the preparation of offensives against Austria, Prussia and Russia. The militarization of these places meant more or less important transformations in their urban structures, including the creation or the widening of a central place-of-arms for ceremonies, parades and maneuvers, magazines for food, supply-stores, depots for equipment, artillery parks, ammunition and weapon dumps, gun foundries, powder manufactures, and stables and facilities for the cavalry, as well as barracks for the troops, quarters for officers, and military hospitals.

The facilities and fortifications of these foreign military cities were mainly pre-existent, but often obsolete, ill-maintained and often not adapted to the French machinery of war. As a result, numerous modernizations, adaptations, additions and enlargements were necessary.

Even older medieval fortresses were incorporated into the Napoleonic scheme, including the castle of Vincennes near Paris or the castle of Château-Thierry, for example. It should be noted that religious buildings were often secularized and militarized, the most spectacular examples in France being the abbey of Cluny in Burgundy, Mont Saint Michel in Normandy, and the Papal Palace at Avignon. Abbeys and churches were not the only targets of the angry populace during the early period of the French Revolution. All buildings connected with monarchic oppression and tyranny were targets as well: medieval cas-

Avignon Papal Palace

The Palais des Papes in Avignon, southern France, is one of the largest and most important medieval Gothic buildings in Europe. Avignon became the residence of the Popes in 1309, when the Gascon Bertrand de Goth, as Pope Clement V, unwilling to face the violent chaos of Rome after his election (1305), moved the Papal Curia to Avignon. His successor Pope John XXII set up a magnificent establishment there, but the construction of the palace was begun in earnest by Pope Benedict XII (1334–42) and continued by his successors to 1364. Under Popes Clement VI, Innocent VI and Urban V, the building was expanded to form what is now known as the Palais Neuf (New Palace). The popes departed Avignon in 1377, returning to Rome, but this prompted the Papal Schism, during which time the antipopes Clement VII and Benedict XIII made Avignon their home until 1408. Although the Palais remained under papal control (along with the surrounding city and the small Comtat Venaissin province) for over 350 years afterwards, it gradually deteriorated despite a restoration in 1516. When the French Revolution broke out in 1789, this symbol of papal power was already in a bad state when it was seized and sacked by revolutionary anticlerical forces. The Palais was subsequently taken over by the Napoleonic French state for use as a military barracks and prison. It was further damaged by the military occupation, especially under the anticlerical Third Republic, and was only vacated in 1906, when it became a historic monument and a national museum.

tles were attacked and sacked, medieval archives burned, royal citadels looted, and monarchic statues mutilated. It is significant that the first action of the Revolutionaries in 1789 was the destruction of the hated Saint-Antoine Bastille castle/prison in Paris.

France

Paris

Napoléon I had great ambitions for Paris, the capital of his Empire, which, in 1800, counted no fewer than 800,000 inhabitants, making it the most populous city in Europe. The Napoleonic area was, above all, the expression of a will to grandeur. Compared to Napoléon's great expectations and megalomaniac ambitions, time was short and the actual results may seem poor. Many of Napoléon's grandiose projects never got off the ground, but several monuments were created.

The principles of Napoleonic town planning were not new. It was the typical application of grandiose rectilineality, imposing uniformity and monumental perspective characterized by the rue de Rivoli, rue de Castiglione and rue de la Paix. In architectural style, attention was drawn to the desire to imprint the mark of antiquity, reviving imperial Rome mainly in the form of triumphal arches (the Étoile and the Carroussel), up-scaled Greek and Roman-styled temples (the Madeleine and the Palais Bourbon, for example), and commemorative columns like that of the Vendôme Square; this column has a spiral bronze relief recalling the glorious deeds of the French army. The column replaced an equestrian statue of Louis XIV which was destroyed in 1792 during the French Revolution. The present monument, 44m (144 ft) high, was erected by Napoléon in imitation of Trajan's Column in Rome. It is topped by a statue of Napoléon in the garb of a Roman emperor. In 1814 the original statue was melted down and the metal used for the statue of Henri IV on the Pont Neuf, to be replaced by a new one in 1833. In 1871, during the Paris Commune, the column was pulled down but was later re-erected with a copy of the statue of Napoléon. Other grandiose schemes for Paris included extravagant plans such as the creation of a huge *naumachy* (artificial lake); a roadstead in the plain of Grenelle; and a curious fountain on the Bastille Square (the prison/castle itself having been destroyed in 1790) which would have been built in the form of a giant 24-meter-high elephant made of bronze provided by cannons captured from enemies.

At the time of Napoléon, Paris was a defenseless open city. Fortifications had been razed in the 1670s during the reign of Louis XIV but the capital of France was surrounded by a large enceinte (23 km in length and about 4 m high) called Fermiers Généraux' Wall, built between 1784 and 1787. It was not a military defense, but a wall especially designed as a fiscal barrier furnished with 60 tollhouses (designed by the architect Claude-Nicolas Ledoux). In addition, the wall clearly showed the administrative limits of Paris; secondary advantages were that it offered a possibility for the police to control the accesses to the town, and an opportunity to give work to the jobless. The Enceinte of the Fermiers Généraux was a prosperous private business at the service of the authorities; it made huge profits by raising taxes, and of course it was very unpopular. By the time of the French Revolution, many demanded the abolition of taxes and the destruction of the hated Farmers' Wall. In 1789, breaches were made in the wall and several tollgates were set afire by the angry populace. In 1791 the tax-collecting company was abolished but as Napoléon badly needed the money raised at the gates of Paris, the highly unpopular taxes levied at the enceinte were re-established in 1798. The Wall continued to function until its demolition in 1860.

When the Allies were close to capturing Paris in 1814, military engineer Joseph Rogniat was commissioned by Napoléon to fortify the highly vulnerable capital of France. Hastily the enceinte of the *Fermiers Généraux* was militarized and reinforced with low earth-protected artillery combat emplacements. Field fortifications and temporary gun batteries — manned by Parisian volunteers — were placed in villages surrounding the capital. In spite of stubborn resistance by General Marmont at Romainville and General Mortier at Pantin, Paris was captured in March 1814. After Napoléon's return from the Island of Elba, and after Waterloo, Paris was once again put in state of defense, but the Parisians did not defend their town for fear of plunder and devastation. The Allies entered Napoléon's capital for the second time in July 1815 without any serious fight.

Calais

The proximity of England (only 38 km; by clear weather one can see the cliffs of Dover) foredoomed Calais to be an embarkment harbor between the British Islands and

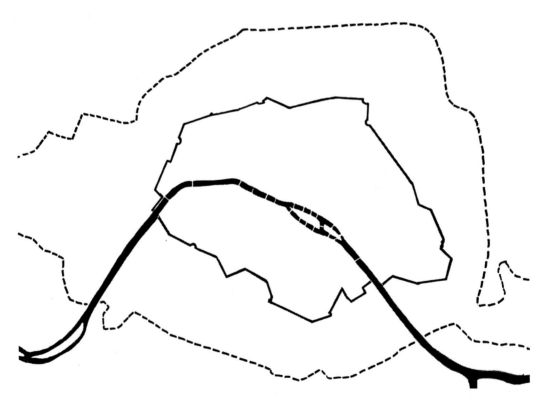

Fermiers Generaux's Wall in Paris
Built between 1784 and 1787, the highly unpopular fiscal wall was dismantled in 1860. The dotted line indicates the present-day administrative limit of Paris.

the European continent. The city started as a small fishing village, and became a port in the 12th century. For centuries, the possession of the port was eagerly contested. In 1228 Count Philippe Hurepel, the son of King Philippe Auguste, built a castle and ringed the town with a stone wall. After the victory of Crécy-en-Ponthieu on August 26, 1346, the King of England, Edward III, besieged and took Calais in 1347 (the sculptor Rodin later immortalized the "six burghers" in bronze). The port proved an important asset to establish a firm grip upon the occupied territory and enabled easy access to the Continent. For two hundred and eleven years the city was English and the occupiers made of Calais an administrative center, a foothold and a powerful fortress with fortified advanced posts at Sangatte, Marck, Oye, Fretun, Hames, Guines and Balinghem.

The medieval defenses were adapted to the increasing power of artillery with the construction of Italian-styled bastions in the 16th century. Calais was besieged, taken and given back to France by Duke François de Guise in 1558. Henri IV and then Richelieu carried out considerable works. The British fortifications were redesigned by the Italian engineer Castriotto in 1560 and a citadel was built by Jean Errard in 1564. The Dutch mathematician and military engineer Simon Stevin proposed to establish flooding in 1591 but his project was not carried out. In 1640, a fortress (called Fort Risban) was built to protect the entrance to the harbor. The fortifications of Calais were inspected and modified by Vauban in 1675, 1689 and 1694. He advocated the construction of a stronghold in the west of the town, Fort Nieulay, which was completed in 1679.

Project to enlarge the port of Calais by engineer Saint-Haouen in 1806
This ambitious project, which was never materialized, would have included the following. 1: The town of Calais. 2: Citadel. 3: Old port. 4: New port. 5: Arsenal, shipyards. 6: New bastioned enceinte with demi-lune and covered way.

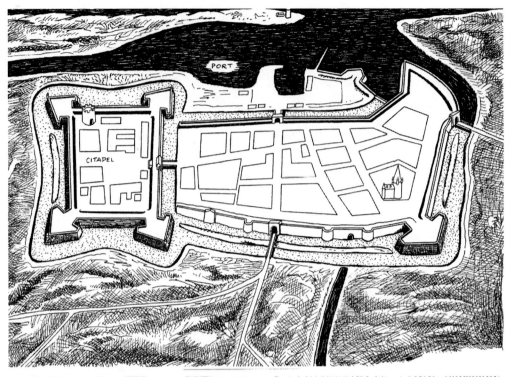
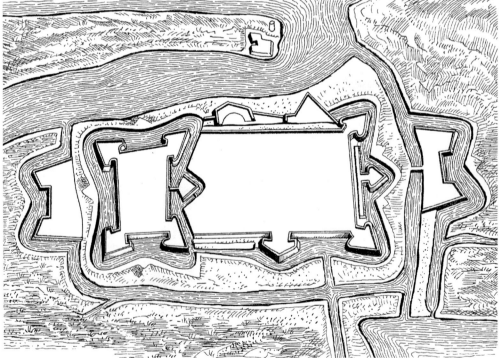

Calais
Top: *Calais in the 16th century.* Bottom: *Project by the Dutch engineer Simon Stevin in 1591.*

At the time of Napoléon, a vast and ambitious program was launched to increase the capacity of the port. The engineer Saint-Haouen designed a project including a large bastioned enceinte, a huge dike to protect the port and many facilities for a navy arsenal. The fall of Napoléon in 1815 thwarted the realization of this plan. Although its military role declined, Calais remained a key to France and a check against invasion. During the Second World War Calais suffered heavy bombardment in 1940 and 1944, and almost the whole of the old town was destroyed. Fortunately numerous vestiges of its defensive heritage remain, including sections of medieval walls, the citadel, the maritime fort, and Fort Nieulay, protecting the sluice-gate. Engineers of the Nazi building *Organisation Todt* have left behind a number of imposing bunkers and super-heavy batteries in the dunes around the city.

BOULOGNE

Boulogne-sur-Mer, a fortified seaport of northern France and chief town of an arrondissement in Pas-de-Calais, situated on the shore of the English Channel at the mouth of the River Liane, had always been an important ferry port between France and England. From there the Romans sailed (A.D. 43) to conquer Britain, and there again Napoléon assembled his Grande Armée and an invasion fleet (which never sailed) in 1803–5. On occasion of the projected invasion of England, Napoléon made great preparations. His plan included the construction of a large (Spartan) camp to house his army, made of huts of wood and daub and a system of perfectly straight paths built by the sol-

Fort de l'Heurt at Le Portel Situated 5 km south of Boulogne on a rocky promontory submerged at high tide, the fort was designed in 1803 by Lieutenant Colonel Dode de la Brunerie and built under the supervision of Captain Gouville of the French Engineering Corps. The fort, actually a large coastal artillery tower, was semicircular and arranged as a gun platform. It had a height of 13.5 m and a diameter of 15 m, and the parapet was 2 m thick. The entrance was only accessible by means of a ladder. The fort could house a garrison of 40 men and was intended to be armed with twelve 36-pound guns and three 12-inch mortars, all placed on the top terrasse. The tower included quarters for the gunners and officers, food, water and ammunition stores, and a furnace for firing red-hot shots. The tower was used by the Germans during World War II as a flak (antiaircraft) battery. Today the fort, badly damaged by time and sea erosion, stands in a precarious balance on a steep rock, and awaits a new destiny.

Fort Ambleteuse
Located between Montreuil-sur-Mer and Boulogne-sur-Mer at the mouth of river Slack facing England, Fort Ambleteuse was constructed between 1684 and 1690. Typical of Vauban's coastal defense, the fort included a tower topped with an artillery and observation platform, a low half circular gun battery facing the sea with the capacity to house 20 artillery pieces, a quarter for the gunner, a house for the officer and various service buildings. The fort was modernized in 1803 when Napoléon gathered a large force at Boulogne in order to invade England.

diers themselves. In the harbor a quay was built, a semicircular basin was excavated to accommodate the French fleet, and an inner harbor was developed to hold the rest of the fleet. In addition several coastal fortified points were built to protect the fleet, like the Fort of Heurt and Battery of Couppes (eventually rebuilt in 1886 by Séré de Rivières) at Le Portel, while Fort Ambleteuse (built by Vauban in 1682–1690) was reactivated and modernized. The Grand Army gathered at Boulogne caused panic in England; however, Napoléon's plans were halted by other European matters and the supremacy of the Royal Navy. Indeed, the British victory at Trafalgar (October 21, 1805) destroyed all French hope of dominating the sea.

Following the abandonment of the invasion plan, the port was completely neglected as a military establishment. Among the objects of interest in the neighborhood the most remarkable is the *Colonne de la Grande Armée*, erected at Wimille on the high ground above Boulogne. The Doric-order pillar, designed by the French sculptor François Joseph Bosio (1769–1845), is 50 m (166 ft.) high, and was surmounted by a statue of the emperor. The impressive column is the central point in a long monumental avenue which goes from the Boulogne countryside to the commemorating monument and on to the sea. The column was initially intended to commemorate the successful invasion of England, but it now commemorates the first distribution of the Imperial Légion d'Honneur at the camp of Boulogne by Napoleon to his soldiers. Though begun in 1804, the monument was not completed till 1841.

CHERBOURG

As already noted, Cherbourg by the end of the 17th century was only an insignificant little coastal town, and its actual development as an Atlantic military port came under the reign of Louis XVI. Napoléon manifested a great interest in Cherbourg, which he intended to transform into a large maritime arsenal against Britain. The construction of the port was continued by the completion of forts on the land and sea fronts (notably the ill-fated *batterie Napoléon*), the building of the large dike, and the establishment of the navy arsenal. When Napoléon's regime collapsed, Cherbourg was far from completion. Work stopped and was resumed in 1832 under the aegis of King Louis-Philippe. The port of Cherbourg was not opened until 1853, the naval base planned by Louis XVI and Napoléon I was eventually inaugurated by his nephew, Napoléon III, and the first transatlantic passenger ship — of the Hamburg Amerika Linie — did not berth there until 1869.

SAINT MARCOUF

Fort Saint Marcouf with its defensive tower is situated on the largest of two small rocky islets off Ravenonville-Plage (south of Saint-Vaast-La-Hougue) in the Cotentin Peninsula in Normandy. The strategical situation of the small islands, which control the

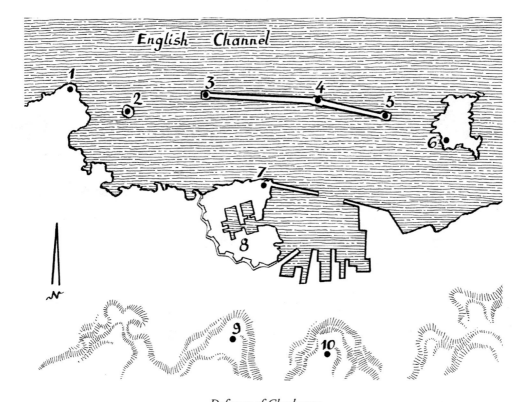

Defenses of Cherbourg
1: Fort of Querqueville; 2: Fort Chavagnac; 3: Fort Musoir West; 4: Dike Central Fort; 5: Fort Musoir East; 6: Fort of Pelée Island; 7: Fort of Homet; 8: bastioned enceinte around the Arsenal; 9: redoubt of Couplets; 10: Fort du Roule.

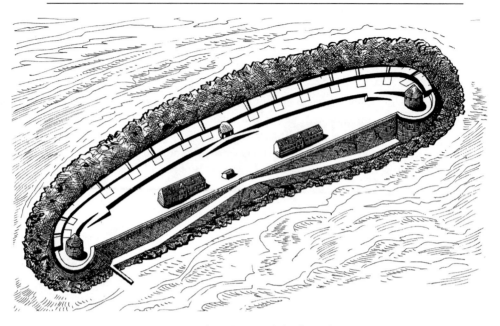

Napoléon Battery (Cherbourg)
Designed by engineer Cachin, the battery, situated in the middle of the Cherbourg roadstead, was completed in 1803. It was damaged beyond repair during a particularly ravaging storm in 1808.

Fort Central (Cherbourg)
After the destruction of the Battery Napoléon by a storm in 1808, it was decided in 1811 to replace it by a fort designed by engineer Cachin. Situated in the middle of the dike protecting the port of Cherbourg (whence its name of Fort Central), the fort was to include two levels of casemated gun batteries and an oval open-top gun platform. Work on Fort Central only started during the reign of Louis-Philippe and was completed in 1858.

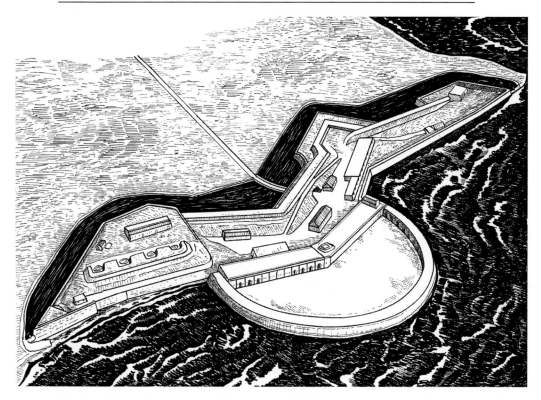

Fort of Querqueville
The coastal fort of Querqueville, situated west of Cherbourg, was built between 1787 and 1806 in order to defend the western access to the port. On the sea front, it included a large half-circular gun battery with fifty-three casemates, a large two-story barracks in the gorge, and two wide wings. The total length was 800 m. On the land front the work was defended by a vast, bare and flat glacis, a wet ditch, bastions and curtains. Two heavy-caliber batteries were established on the wings in 1879 and modernized in 1901. The fort was used by the French navy until 1976.

navigation along the east coast of the peninsula and the Bay of River Seine mouth, was recognized and various projects to fortify them were envisaged in 1706, 1756 and 1780, but none of them was undertaken. During the French Revolutionary Wars the islands were held for nearly seven years by the British Royal Navy as a strategic forward base. In July 1795 the islands were occupied by sailors from the Western Frigate Squadron under the command of Captain Sir Sidney Smith in HMS *Diamond*. He sacrificed two of his gun vessels, HMS *Badger* and HMS *Sandfly*, to provide materials and manpower for fortifying the islands and setting a temporary naval garrison. Further defenses were constructed by Royal Engineers, and Royal Marines and Royal Artillery detachments were established. The islands served as a forward base for the blockade of Le Havre, a launching point for intercepting coastal shipping, and as a transit point for French émigrés. A major attack by French troops was repelled in May 1798.

The islands were given to France by the Peace of Amiens in 1802. The British occupation spurred the First Consul Bonaparte to order the establishment of a stronghold on the islands. Inspired by the tower of Fort of Pelée Island near Cherbourg built in the period 1777–1784, and based on Montalembert's conception, Fort Saint Marcouf was designed

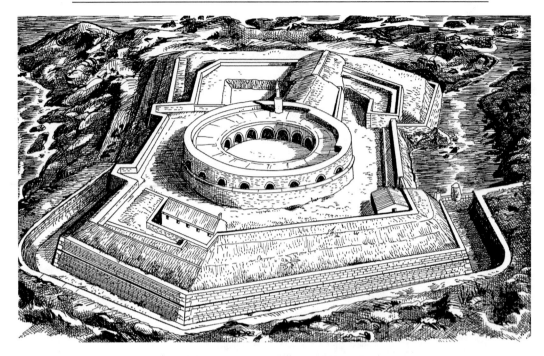

Fort Saint Marcouf
The view shows the fort as it is today.

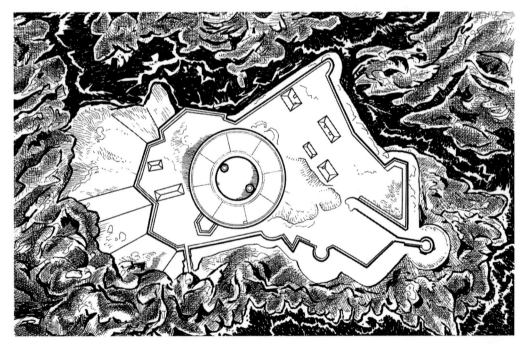

Plan of Fort Saint Marcouf
The plan displays the original design of the enceinte from 1802, which slightly differs from the actual fort.

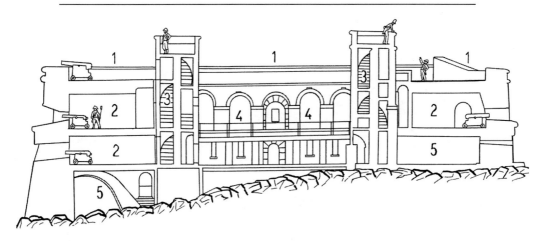

Cross-section of Saint Marcouf gun tower
1: Gun platform; 2: casemate; 3: staircase; 4: quarters; 5: supply store.

in the form of a large, circular, casemated gun tower. Due to lack of funds, the construction was slow. Worked started in 1802 under the supervision of Engineer Captain Bruno de Boyer, and by 1810 the fort was far from completion. Finally, owing to extra funds, it was combat ready in 1812. Still existing today, it is composed of two parts: a gun tower and an enceinte. The tower is a massive cylindrical two-story structure with a height of 10 m and a diameter of 53 m. In the middle there is a circular yard with two staircases enabling access to the floors which house food and ammunition stores, a cistern, quarters for the garrison, and 24 artillery casemates. The upper surface of the tower was arranged as a wide barbette artillery platform with 24 guns mounted on a fortress mount. The strongly masoned tower is protected by a simple low enceinte dug in the rock and filled with seawater. The islands were the first territory taken on D-Day by seaborne Allied forces. At 4:30 A.M. on June 6, 1944, soldiers of the 4th and 24th U.S. Cavalry landed on the unoccupied islands to secure the approaches to Utah Beach (landing sector between Les Dunes de Varreville and La Madeleine). Today the small Saint Marcouf islands are directly administered by the French government, and form a protected nature reserve with restricted access.

Belle-Ile

Belle-Ile, the "Beautiful Island," is situated in the Atlantic Ocean in front of the Quiberon Peninsula (southern shores of Brittany, called Morbihan). The most important village of Belle-Ile, Le Palais, was first fortified by some monks of Quimperlé in the 14th century, as it belonged to the Abbey of Sainte-Croix in Quimperlé. On a hill dominating the small town and its harbor, King Henri II ordered the construction of a fort in 1549. Work was continued by the family Gondi, lords of Belle-Ile, from 1574 to 1635. The ambitious and immensely wealthy Nicolas Fouquet, Viscount of Vaux and Louis XIV's finance superintendent, purchased the island in 1650 and carried out its fortification, wishing to make the island a safe retreat in case of misfortune. But the king's jealousy and Colbert's hatred brought about his disgrace in 1664. Fouquet was arrested by the famous d'Artagnan and died in prison in 1680. Belle-Ile had been attacked several times

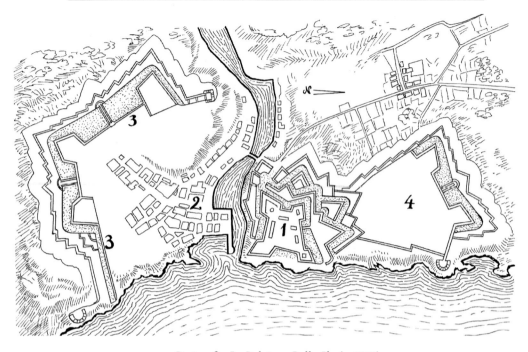

Project for Le Palais at Belle-Ile (c. 1810)
1: Citadel; 2: village of Le Palais; 3: southern enceinte completed in 1866; 4: northern enceinte never completed.

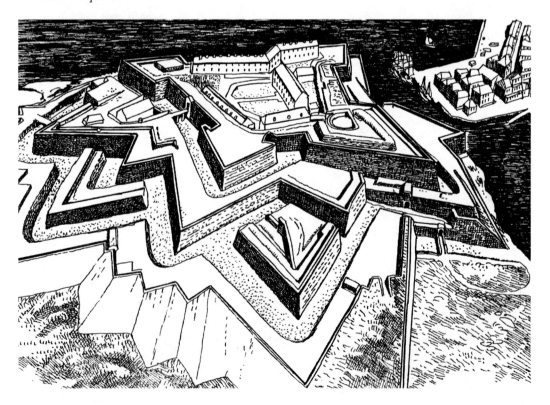

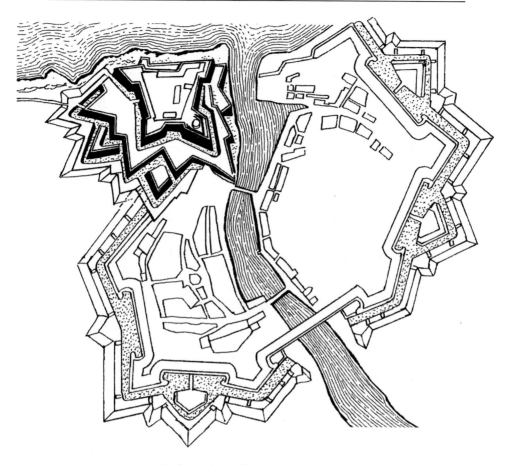

Vauban's design for Le Palais, Belle-Ile
This ambitious extension, designed in 1683, was intended to protect the port of Le Palais. The project was not accepted by King Louis XIV and thus never built.

by British and Dutch fleets; it had even been briefly occupied in 1672. Therefore Vauban wrote a project proposal in March 1683, including a large bastioned enceinte around the town, but this plan was not enacted. However, Vauban, assisted by fortifications director Jean-Anthenor Hue de Luc de Caligny and Guillaume Deshouillières, brought substantial modifications to Le Palais citadel in 1685 and established nineteen detached batteries on beaches where landings could occur. The garrison of Belle-Ile repulsed Brit-

Opposite: *Citadel, Belle-Ile. Vauban's exterior defenses included a covered way with places of arms, a ditch, a counterguard, a traversed demi-lune and an envelope. Henri II's citadel is a massive irregular square surrounded by a ditch. The main access is the Bourg gate situated west; la porte de Secours, or Rescue gate, situated north, leads to the second entrance, the Donjon gate. The citadel is composed of high and thick curtains, three bastions and a half-bastion; the most important one is fitted with a cavalier and a circular powder-house. The terre-plein is occupied by the officers' pavilion, the arsenal, the governor's house and three barracks. South of the fortress, steep slopes dominating the harbor are fortified by redans, and in the east, facing the sea, the rocky shore forms a natural obstacle.*

ish raids in 1696 and in 1703. The island was besieged, taken and again occupied by the British between 1761 and 1763, when Belle-Ile was exchanged for the Spanish island of Minorque. From 1763 to 1802, to thwart another foreign invasion, the citadel of Le Palais was reinforced by engineer-inspector Marescot, and Vauban's 1683 plan resurfaced. Designed by engineer Mutel, work started in 1810. The new fortifications included a bastioned enceinte, artillery casemates and riflemen emplacements. Working was stopped by the fall of the Empire, but eventually resumed. The enceinte was completed in 1866.

Brest

Situated in the mouth of River Penfeld, the site of Brest originated from a castellum built in Roman times. In the 13th century the dukes of Brittany built a castle which was several times enlarged, strengthened, and then adapted to firearms with a barbican and gun towers in the 15th century. Brest was chosen by Richelieu to become, with Le Havre and Brouage, one of the ports from which the French Navy would operate in the Atlantic Ocean. The military haven was further developed by Colbert, who completed Richelieu's task, by improving and enlarging the dockyards and mooring facilities. The Minister of the French navy also founded a school of gunnery, a college of marine guards, a school of hydrography, and a school for marine engineers. King's engineer Chevalier de Clerville improved the castle defenses and surrounded the city and its suburb Recou-

Brest Castle
The castle is the last remainder of the fortifications of Brest. The Penfeld gate has been fortified since Roman times, and the towers and wall were built between the 12th and the 17th centuries.

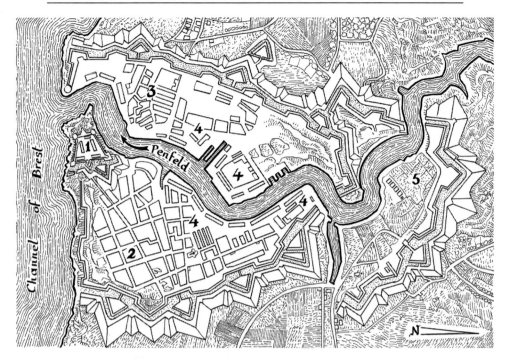

Top: *Brest (c. 1791)*. 1: Castle; 2: old town; 3: recouvrance suburb; 4: port and military arsenal; 5: Bouguen suburb. Bottom: *Fort of Minou, Brest (c. 1810)*. An advanced defensive position to Brest, the Fort of Minou was composed of a low battery from 1694, which was enlarged at the time of Napoléon and modernized in 1886 and 1887.

vrance, as well as the maritime arsenal and naval base, with a bastioned enceinte. Between 1682 and 1692, a new wall was built according to a design made by engineer Sainte-Colombe. Featuring bastions, demi-lunes, ditch, covered way and glacis, the fortifications were very large in order to put ships and harbor out of range of enemy artillery. The castle was reinforced by a huge bastion called Sourdéac. Vauban, helped by engineers Niquet, Garangeau and Robelin, completed the harbor installations and the urban layout. They also organized the defense of the *Goulet* (strait) of Brest on a large scale by establishing detached batteries: in the south Camaret-sur-Mer and Cornouailles, in the north Bertheaume and Léon. After the repulsed English invasion of 1694, Vauban reinforced the defensive network by placing new coastal batteries at Portzic, cape des Espagnols, Ile Longue and Plougastel. At the time of Napoléon, Brest remained a significant maritime arsenal, and tours-modèles and coastal batteries were added. During World War II, Brest, with its port, dockyard and roadsteads, formed an advanced base of first strategic importance to the Germans. The Nazi *Organisation Todt* (militarized building company) estab-

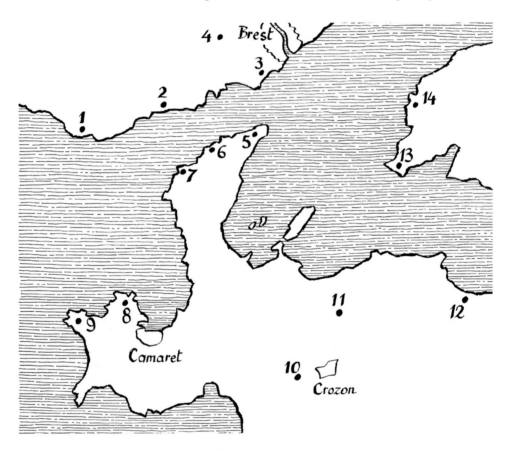

Defenses around Brest
The defenses around the roadstead of Brest included the fort of Toulbroc'h (1); fort of Mingant (2); Fort Portzig (3); Fort Montbarrey (4); fort and battery on the Pointe des Espagnols (5); battery of Robert (6); fort and battery of Cornouailles (7); battery of Petit Gouin (8); battery of Toulinguet (9); fort of Crozon (10); Fort Landaoudec (11); naval school (12); fort of Armorique (13); and fort of Corbeau (14).

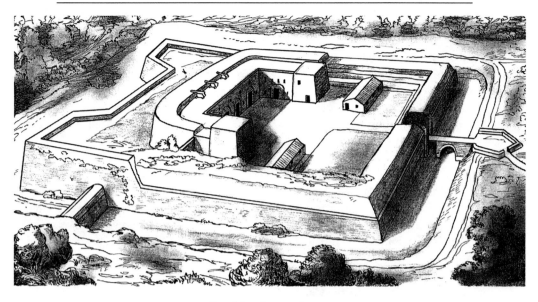

Fort Montbarrey, Brest
Intended for the defense of the land front west of Brest on the right bank of River Penfeld, Fort Montbarrey (originally named Fort Saint Pierre) was completed in 1784. The fort was a large hornwork closed at the gorge, and fitted with a high U-shaped central cavalier on top of which guns could cross their fire with those of the neighboring Fort Portzig. Under the cavalier there were an underground barracks for a garrison of 600, a bakery, a food store, an infirmary, and a powder store.

lished a formidable submarine base at Brest which became a considerable threat to Allied convoys in the Atlantic. The port was, therefore, heavily bombarded for four years.

Pontivy and La Roche-sur-Yon

The French Revolution of 1789 was also a cultural revolution with an attempt to reach two major aims: greater social equality and a secularization of the state. These aims were, however, not shared by the whole population, particularly in the deeply regionalist, Royalist and Roman Catholic-minded Brittany and Vendée. These western provinces revolted in March 1793 when smoldering discontent at religious repression, social interference and the worsening economic situation were fanned into flame by the threat of military conscription. An alliance of Royalist and Catholic counterrevolutionary forces (known as the "Whites" or Chouannerie) was formed. These rebellious irregular troops captured a number of towns, and atrocities against Republicans were commonplace. The government reacted and sent troops (the "Blue" Republican army) that regained the initiative and inflicted a series of crushing defeats on the rebellious Chouans at Cholet (October 1793) and Le Mans and Savenay (December 1793). The ensuing repression was extremely savage, leading to widespread, large-scale massacres perpetrated by Republican general Turreau's *colonnes infernales* (infernal columns), implementing a scorched-earth policy. In Nantes, the duty representative Jean Baptiste Carrier (1756–94) had almost 3,000 White prisoners drowned in the Loire River. For most of the next three years a bitter guerilla struggle was carried out by the White Chouans against the Blue Republicans.

Until 1804, there were flickers of resistance in the western provinces devastated and depopulated by the horrors of this civil war. In all, rebellion and repression produced some 400,000 victims — 220,000 Whites and 180,000 Blues.

Uprising in Britanny and Vendée was the cause of the development of two cities in the Napoleonic era: Pontivy and La Roche-sur-Yon.

The little town of Pontivy stands on the Blavet River in the department of Morbihan in Brittany. The local tradition says that it was created in the 7th century by the monk Saint Ivy from Lindisfarne in Scotland. The evangelist had a bridge (*pont* in French) built, whence the name of the city (Pont-Ivy). The city and its territory became a viscounty, eventually a duchy led by the family of Rohan since 1341. The castle, built by Jean II de Rohan in the 15th century, includes a façade flanked by two large towers with ramparts 20 m (64 ft) high surrounded by a dry ditch. The small prosperous town declared wholeheartedly for the Republic in 1790, and as a result was besieged by the Chouans in 1794. Napoléon, who was Consul at the time, knew the local feeling and was interested in the town's position in the center of the rebellious province. Moreover, during the wars of the First Empire, coastal navigation between Brest and Nantes was very dangerous because of British cruisers in the Channel. Napoléon, therefore, decided to build a canal between the two ports. As Pontivy was about halfway between them, he also decided to

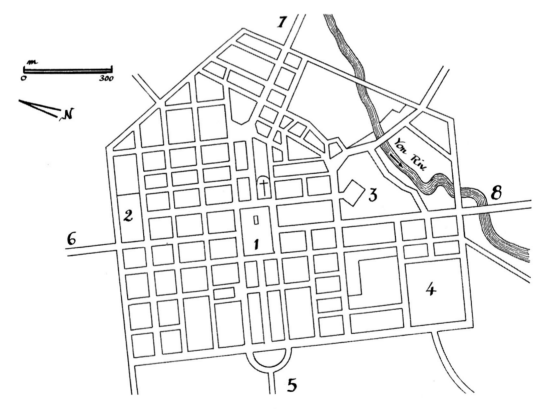

La Roche-sur-Yon
The plan shows the following: 1: Place Napoléon; 2: military hospital; 3: administrative city; 4: studfarm; 5: road to Les Sables d'Olonnes; 6: road to Saint-Nazaire and Nantes; 7: road to Angers and Cholet; 8: road to La Rochelle and Poitiers.

Chouan
It is said that the Chouans were named after their call imitating the hoot of an howl (chat-huant).

develop it into a military town that would become the strategic center of Britanny. From 1807, the Blavet was canalized, a large extension was planned with straight streets and avenues with a vast place-of-arms (present-day Place Aristide Briand), barracks, cavalry stables, a tribunal, a theatre, a new *mairie* (town-hall) and a *lycée* (grammar school). The new city — which took years to be completed — was named Napoléonville in 1804. After the fall of the Emperor it became Pontivy once more. The name was changed again under Napoléon III's Second Empire to Napoléonville, but in due course reverted again to Pontivy in 1871. Today, Pontivy is a unique witness of Napoleonic urbanism, and the narrow winding streets of the old town contrast with the geometrical town plan laid out by imperial urbanists.

The city of La Roche-sur-Yon, placed in the heart of the province of Vendée halfway between Nantes and La Rochelle, had existed since the 10th century as a small seigneurie belonging to various noble medieval families. In 1793, it was occupied by the Chouans, soon retaken and partly destroyed by the Republican army. In May 1804, Napoléon — who was anxious to have a military place from which to control and repress any further revolt by the rebellious Catholic and Royalist population of the province of Vendée — ordered its reconstruction. The plan of the town, designed by the military engineer Duvivier and originally named Napoléon, was a large pentagon with a geometric checkerboard street pattern and a large central place-of-arms. The city — which was not completed before 1829 — was fitted with barracks for the troops, a military hospital (today the Hôtel du Département), an administrative center, and an important *haras* (studfarm) destined to provide horses for the imperial cavalry. Like Pontivy, La Roche-sur-Yon was an artificial city mostly populated with military personnel and civil servants, and eventually it changed its name according to political regimes. The monarchic Restoration renamed it Bourbon-Vendée, the name La Roche-sur-Yon was used during the Second Republic, Napoléon-Vendée reappeared during the Second Empire, and after 1870, it changed again to La Roche-sur-Yon.

Defense of the Pertuis

Pertuis are straits between the French Atlantic islands off La Rochelle and Rochefort. The pertuis of Antioche is situated between the isles of Ré and Oléron, the pertuis Breton between Ré and the mainland of Vendée. The defense of these islands was already a necessity in François I's time because of insecurity caused by raiders and pirates of all nationalities, specially English and Dutch. The islands possessed great strategical importance because of their closeness to the continent and, if conquered and occupied by any enemy, formed a threat to this part of the French kingdom. During the Wars of Religion and Louis XIII's reign, the important harbor of La Rochelle was dominated by the Protestants and their Anglo-Dutch Allies. Besides, the rich haven of Brouage, owing its wealth to the exploitation of salt, had to be protected. Moreover, the military harbor and the maritime arsenal of Rochefort were created in 1666. All these reasons explain the particularly high number of fortifications in the region.

Aix Island

Aix is a small crescent-shaped island with an area of 133 ha, strategically situated in the middle of a narrow strait named Pertuis d'Antioche, between the northern point of

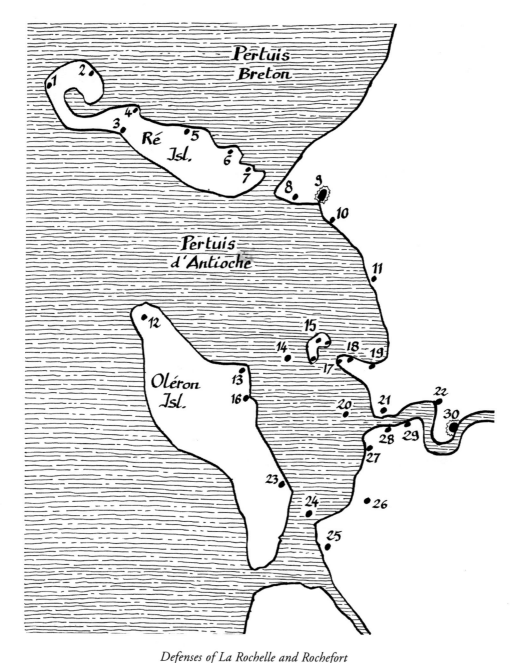

Defenses of La Rochelle and Rochefort
1: Lighthouse Les Baleines. 2: Redoubt of les Portes. 3: Redoubt of Martray. 4: Redoubt of Grouin. 5: Bastioned enceinte of village of Saint-Martin-de-Ré. 6: Fort La Prée. 7: Redoubt of Sablanceaux. 8: Redoubt of Chef-de-Baie. 9: Bastioned enceinte of port and city of La Rochelle. 10: Redoubt of les Minimes. 11: Redoubt of Châtelaillon. 12: Lighthouse of Chassiron. 13: Fort Saumonard. 14: Fort Boyard. 15: Aix Island, with fortified village of Le Bourg, Fort de la Rade, Fort Liédot and Battery of Coudepont. 16: Logistic base (later village) and battery of Boyardville. 17: Fort of Enet. 18: Redoubt of Aiguille. 19: Battery and castle of Fouras. 20: Fort Ile Madame. 21: Fort of La Pointe. 22: Battery Le Vergeroux. 23: Bastioned enceinte of city of Le Château d' Oléron. 24: Fort Chapus. 25: Village of Marennes (non-fortified). 26: Bastioned enceinte of village of Brouage. 27: Fort Chagnaud. 28: Fountain Saint-Lazarus. 29: Fort Lupin. 30: Bastioned enceinte of port, arsenal and city of Rochefort on the estuary of Charente River.

Oléron Island and Fouras on the mainland (Charente-Maritime). Together with other strongholds, its three fortified works (Fort de la Rade, Fort Liédot, and Battery of Condepont) formed an advanced point defending the approaches to the military port of Rochefort, created in 1666. The defenses had been inspected by Napoléon in 1808, then at the zenith of his glory. Aix Island also played an important symbolic role in the des-

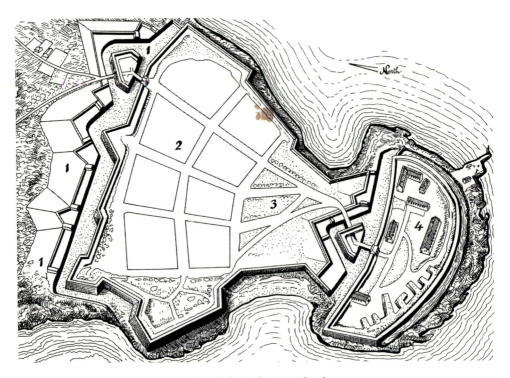

Fort de la Rade, Aix Island

At the southern cape of Aix Island, named Pointe Sainte-Catherine, a fort was erected in the 1690s after a design by Vauban. The work, named Fort de la Rade, comprised a large semicircular battery with 75 cannons facing the sea, and a wet ditch, a demi-lune and a tower turned toward the landfront. The tower, probably ill-constructed, collapsed. It was rebuilt in 1699. The fort was completed in 1703 and the nearby small village was fortified a year later by a wet ditch, and a bastioned wall with demi-lunes. During the Seven Years' War in 1757, the fort was bombarded by a British naval task force headed by Admiral Hawke, the island captured, the village looted and burnt, and the fortifications greatly damaged. After the departure of the raiders, the defensive works were temporarily repaired by a team of French engineers, one of whom was Choderlot de Laclos, the future author of Liaisons Dangereuses. In the 1770s, the Marquis of Montalembert suggested ambitious designs including a huge triangular fortress with large artillery towers. This design was rejected, but Montalembert built a temporary fort made of wood. In 1801, Napoléon ordered the re-establishment of defenses, and Marescot proposed and obtained the task of reconstructing the fort just like it was at the time of Louis XIV. Vauban's semicircular 75-cannon battery was rebuilt, and in addition a ditch (4 m deep, and 6 m wide) was dug in the rocks. The bastioned wall intended to protect the village was also reconstructed. The whole affair, completed in 1837, is still to be seen today and includes the following features: 1: Land front defending the village, composed of a glacis, a ditch, a wall with a redan, a bastion and a demi-lune. 2: Village, named Le Bourg, with Saint-Martin church. 3: Square of Austerlitz, previously an esplanade for military parade. 4: Fort de la Rade, with sea battery on the Sainte-Catherine Point.

tiny of Napoléon, as it was the last place on French soil where the deposed emperor briefly resided in 1815. In the evening of July 8, 1815, Napoléon sailed from Rochefort and Fouras on the frigate *La Saale* to the Fort of Enet with the intention of escaping to America. As a British fleet blockaded the Pertuis of Antioche, he was forced to land at Aix the next day. On July 9, the emperor, cheered by the villagers, held his last parade in France with the garrison of the island, 1,500 sailors from the 14th Marine Regiment. Re-embarking

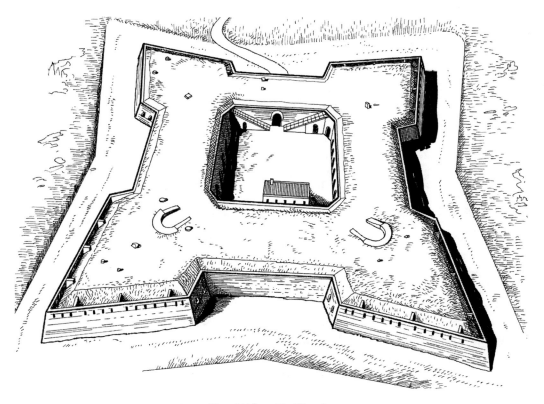

Fort Liédot, Aix Island
At the northern point of Aix (which commands the pertuis of Antioche) the establishment of a fort was ordered by Napoléon in 1808. Originally named Fort de la Sommité, the work still exists today. It was designed by engineer Thuillier, and its construction began in 1810. The fort is actually a large square redoute-modèle (90 m × 90 m) with four casemated bastions at each angle, surrounded with a ditch and a covered way. In the middle there is a large place-of-arms, and the artillery was placed on the ramparts. The scarp wall is 7 m high, and under the ramparts there were stores and quarters for a garrison of 500. The fort was renamed Fort Liédot in honor of Colonel Liédot, killed in 1812. The fort was completed in 1834, and eventually was used as a state penitentiary for political prisoners and PoWs: e.g., Communards in 1871, Germans in 1914–1918, and Algerian nationalists in the 1950s, like Ahmed Ben Bella, who later became president of the Algerian Republic from 1962 to 1965.

As for the battery of Coudepont, which constituted the third fortified position on Aix Island, it was built in 1810 at the instigation of General-Inspector Marescot. It was a simple semicircular epaulement (45 m in diameter) with a building in the gorge used as quarter for the garrison and store-place. The battery was refurbished and slightly enlarged in 1846 to house ten guns served by fifty artillerymen. Having lost all its military value in the 1880s, it was abandoned, and the ground was sold as private property.

aboard the frigate, whose captain refused to sail (having received order from Paris), Napoléon began to bargain with the British. On July 12, the emperor landed again on Aix Island, lodged at the commanding officer's place, and received his brother Joseph, who proposed to organize an escape during the night with a Danish schooner. After a dramatic scene, Napoléon decided to surrender and, on the next day, wrote a famous letter to the British Prince Regent: "Facing factions which divide my country, and hostility from the greatest European powers, I have decided to terminate my political career, and I come, like Themistocles, putting myself under the protection of the laws of your Royal Highness, the most powerful, the most constant and the most generous of my enemies." General Gourgaud was charged to carry the letter to London but was not allowed to land at Plymouth. On July 15, in the early morning, Napoléon donned his sober green uniform of Colonel of the Chasseurs de la Garde (the one he wore at the Battle of Austerlitz), embarked aboard the bark *Epervier*, and sailed in direction of Fort Boyard. There he was transferred by means of a rowboat to the British HMS *Bellerophon*, which took him away to his destiny in another small island in the Atlantic Ocean. Today Aix is a pleasant tourist destination. The house where Napoléon sojourned has, of course, become a museum (Musée Napoléon) with numerous art pieces, artifacts and historical documents. There is also an African ethnographic and zoologic museum established by Baron Gourgaud (a descendant of the General cited above) in ancient military buildings.

Fort Boyard

Due to the limited range of late-17th-century artillery, there was a gap in the defenses between Aix and Oléron Islands. After the foundation of the maritime arsenal of Rochefort in 1666, it was envisaged to build a fort in the middle of the sea between the two islands. A place was found, a rocky bank known as *longe de Banjaert* or *Boyard*, conveniently situated halfway between the Saumonards Point on Oléron and Sainte-Catherine Point on Aix. Engineer Descombes designed a project in 1692, but because of the cost that would be involved and the difficulties that would be encountered the project was canceled by Louis XIV. Vauban is said to have declared about the construction of this fort: "Your Majesty, it would be easier to seize the moon with your teeth than to attempt such an undertaking in such a place." The idea of a fort on the Boyard bank was thus abandoned but resurfaced after the disastrous British raid on Aix Island in 1757. A certain engineer Filley made a new design, but once again, due to the complexity of the task, nothing happened for nearly half a century. The ambitious project was finally reconsidered and relaunched by the First Consul Bonaparte in 1800.

Designed a year later by Vice-Admiral Rosilly and Génie engineers Ferregeau and Marescot, the new fort was to be a kind of motionless stone battleship, an elliptical-shaped ring in the middle of the sea, with a length of 80 m, a width of 40 m, and a height of 20 m. The fort would comprise a central arcaded yard with, around it on the ground floor, stores, magazines, officers' rooms, and the garrison's quarters. The first floor would house a series of gun casemates and quarters, and the top terrace was to be arranged as a large platform for coastal barbette guns and mortars. Work started in 1804, but first, on the northern point of Oléron Island, a port was created in order to bring materials to the site, and a village was built to lodge the numerous workers. The new settlement was named Boyardville. The first step was to bring, sink and pile up stones, rubble, rocks and other materials in order to establish a wide plateau (100 m × 50 m) on the rocky

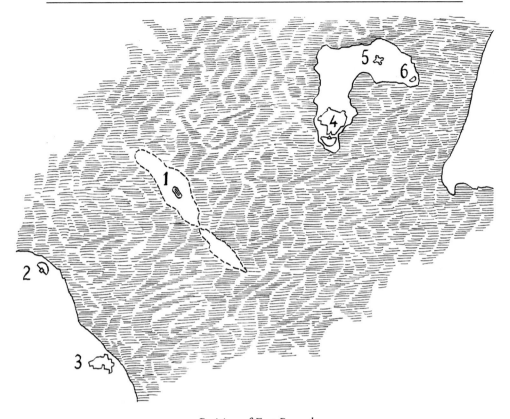

Position of Fort Boyard
Fort Boyard (1) was built on a rocky and sandy bank (submerged at high water) halfway between Aix and Oléron Islands. Together with the Saumonard battery (2) and Boyardville battery (3) both on Oléron Island, and Fort Saint-Catherine (4), Fort Liédot (5) and Coudepont Battery (6) on Aix Island, the fort was intended to form an advanced defense for the mouth of the Charente River and the military port of Rochefort.

Boyard bank, in order to form the foundations of the future fort. As can be imagined, that was a formidable undertaking and hard toil given the limited technology and transport capacity of the time. Besides, the transport could be effected only a few hours a day due to the tide and the current. In the winter of 1807–08, a series a enormously violent storms washed away the foundations that had been laboriously built over the past three years. This disaster, and the huge funds already invested for nothing, forced the designers to revise their ambitions. Napoléon came in person in August 1808 to see for himself the furtherance of the work. As it was, he decided to drastically reduce by half the size of the fort; length would now be only 40 m and width 20 m. Work was resumed on the foundations, but these collapsed and sunk into the bottom by their own weight. After having invested fortunes in materials and salaries for the manpower, the project was abandoned in May 1809. By that time Napoléon had other priorities.

The idea of Fort Boyard was reintroduced during the reign of King Louis-Philippe thirty years later. In 1839, Director of Maritime Works Mathieu and Génie-Chief Delaunay proposed to realize the 1801 plan. Besides, in 1840, tensions between France and Great Britain gave a new impetus to the protection of Rochefort. Under supervision of Engineer Garnier, the logistic base of Boyardville was reactivated and the complicated work started again. In 1846, due to violent storms, the construction of the foundations (entrusted to the navy) was slowed down again, and finally in 1848, the building of the fort proper (entrusted to the Génie) could begin. The hard Crazane stone was used for the external wall, the stone of Saint Savinien for the internal revetment and bricks for the embrasures. The new Fort Boyard had the same dimensions as planned in 1801: length was thus 80 m, width 40 m, height 20 m, and width of the wall at the base was 2.30 m. The fort was even higher than the 1801 design, as an additional floor of casemates was built in order to give the fort as much firepower as a three-deck battleship armed with 74 guns. The fort was to have a garrison of 250 who would have supplies, water and ammunition for

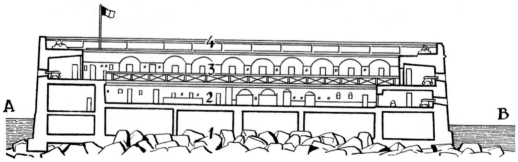

Fort Boyard.
Bottom: *Cross-section of Fort Boyard. This was the 1801 project with the foundations (1), the ground floor (2), the first floor with artillery casemates (3), and the top terrasse (4). AB shows the line of high tide.*

three months. In 1852 the first floor, housing the powder magazine, food store, kitchen and quarters, was completed. In 1857, the fort was completed with the construction of a high round watchtower which also served as lighthouse. In 1859, a strong breakwater was built in front of the fort to resist the violence of the Atlantic Ocean. At the same time the fort received its armament: 12 guns on the ground floor; 22 guns and howitzers on the first floor; idem on the second floor; and 18 guns and mortars on the top platform.

Fort Boyard, after two centuries of planning, and nearly sixty years of hard work, was finally ready. The designers could be proud of their formidable technical achievement: they had successfully challenged nature, they had vanquished the ocean, but alas, they were defeated by new metallurgy and technology provided by the Industrial Revolution. The French, indeed, had paid too little attention to the tremendous progress made by the artillery. The fort, which had engulfed enormous funds, was hardly completed before it was totally obsolete and useless. In the early 1860s, new guns appeared with rifled bores, breech loading, and sophisticated aiming devices, all of which increased accuracy and gave an enormous firepower and extra-long range. It was now possible to defend this portion of sea with batteries fitted with rifled guns placed on Aix and Oléron Islands. The gap between the two islands, the very *raison d'être* of Fort Boyard, no longer existed. The Fort Boyard dream was over; it was a marvelous example of Napoleonic design in Montalembert's fashion, but it was no longer adapted to the artillery of the days. The

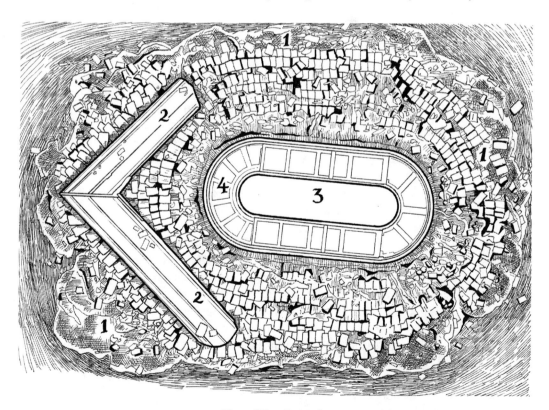

Plan of Fort Boyard
The sketch shows at low tide: the foundations (1), completed in 1848; the breakwater (2), completed in 1859; the inner yard (3) and the terrasse (4) of the fort.

fort was disarmed and transformed into a state prison — notably for the Communards of 1871. The French navy eventually established an observation and weather station. In 1913, the fort was declassed and abandoned until 1950, when it was added to the list of French Historical Monuments and sold to various owners. Today, the fort has started a new glamorous life. The department of Charente-Maritime has purchased and thoroughly repaired it. It is regularly leased to European television companies which use it as a site for an adventurous game known as *Fort Boyard*. The fort has also been used as set in two movies: *Le Repos du Guerrier* (1962) and *Les Aventuriers* (1967).

Cross-section of casemate, Fort Boyard (1801 project).

Fort of Enet

After the sacking of Aix by the British in 1757, surveys were undertaken to establish a fort near the right bank of the estuary of the River Charente. Lieutenant-General Filley made a design, but due to the high cost that would be involved, the idea was abandoned in 1773. In 1801 Director of Maritime Works Ferregeau revived the idea and presented a project, named Fort of Enet, situated on a rocky bank in the vicinity. Approved by Bonaparte, work started in 1802, and the fort was completed in late 1811. It included a wide semicircular battery (35 m in diameter) with five Haxo casemates for coastal guns and mortars turned toward the sea, an inner yard, and a powder house, store-places, and quarters for the garrison and the officers. The fort was linked to La Pointe de la Fumée on the mainland via a causeway submerged at high tide, and this was protected by a redan at the rear. In 1813 Napoléon ordered the construction of a Tour Modèle in the gorge of the fort for additional defense and quarters for 60 men. The fall of the Empire prevented this addition. Badly gnawed by sea, salt and wind, the masonry of the fort was repaired between 1825 and 1834. A year later, the roof of the work was arranged as a gun platform for seventeen additional cannons. Although having lost most of its military value, the fort was again repaired in the 1850s. In 1864, it was decommissioned and used as a target for testing armored plates. However, the military authorities changed their minds; apparently the fort still had a role to play in the defense of the port of Rochefort. Between 1883 and 1905, the Fort of Enet was modernized with long-range rifled breech-loading guns, protected behind parados, concrete layers, and armored plates. Eventually, right before the First World War, they changed their minds again. In spite of important sums of money invested, the fort was disarmed, declassed and sold to a private owner.

View of Fort of Enet.

Oléron Island

The island of Oléron (department of Charente-Maritime) is situated in the Atlantic Ocean off La Rochelle and the mouth of River Charente. The fortifications of Château d'Oléron, the main village on the island, were marked by misfortune and unskillfulness. In 1633, engineer Pierre de Conty d'Argencourt was entrusted by Cardinal Richelieu to edify a citadel. D'Argencourt designed a fort with two bastioned fronts on the landside and two casemated half-bastions facing the sea. In 1673, Louis Nicolas de Clerville, Vauban's rival, was appointed governor of Oléron and added a bastioned envelope to d'Argencourt's citadel. Vauban made two projects for Oléron in 1674 and in 1685. He modified certain bastions, constructed a hornwork in the surrounding marshes, and built another hornwork on the landfront, which brought with it the destruction of a part of the village and the forced departure of the population. Work was apparently conducted

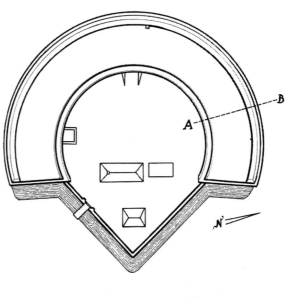

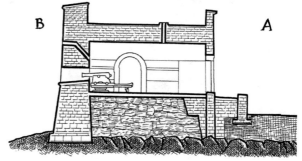

Fort of Enet.
Top: Plan; Bottom: Cross-section AB

hastily and disorderly. The marsh hornworks sank in the mud and a part of the ill-constructed citadel was damaged by a storm in 1689. One year later, Vauban conceived a bastioned enceinte, based on his "second system," to enclose the whole village with four bastioned towers and large counterguards. The expensive works began in 1699 but the construction was interrupted in 1704, resulting in unfinished fortifications.

The fortifications of Oléron Island were continued during the Napoleonic era. As already seen, the logistic base of Boyardville was founded in 1803 at the northern point of the island to shelter the installations required for the construction of the sea-fort Boyard. The point of Boyardville was fortified in 1810 by the installation of a gun battery and a standardized tour-modèle. Work started in 1812 and was completed in 1818. The fortifications of Boyardville were declassed at the beginning of the 20th century.

Another coastal work, called Fort des Saumonards, was established in 1810 on the northeastern shore of the island. It originally included a Napoleonic standardized tour-modèle and a half-circular gun platform for 20 cannons facing the sea. Work on the fort, incomplete at the time of Napoléon's fall, continued under the reign of King Louis-Philippe. Fort des Saumonards, redesigned and enlarged in 1848, was only completed in 1855.

Worthy of mention is Fort Chapus, also called Fort Louvois, situated on the continent on the Bourcefranc cape facing the village and the citadel of Château d'Oléron. The work was constructed by engineer François Ferry in 1691 and completed by engineer

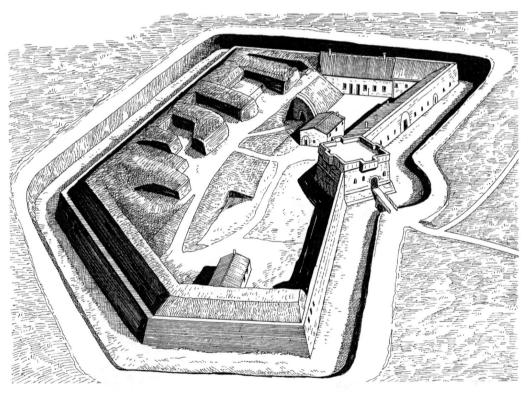

Fort des Saumonards, Oléron Island
The illustration shows the situation in 1855 with the Napoleonic tour-modèle on the right in the gorge and the gun battery with traverse on the left.

Henri-Albert Bouillet in 1694. Intended to defend the strait of Maumusson and the mouth of River Seudre, Fort Chapus is placed on a few rocks 400 meters into the sea and connected to the mainland by a passage which one can use only at low tide. It is composed of an oval low gun battery (78 m in diameter), a three-story tower in the gorge and various service buildings on its semicircular terre-plein. The fort, part of the defense of Rochefort, was rehabilitated in 1875. Although damage occurred as a result of combat in April 1945, Fort Chapus is well preserved, and today houses an oyster-farming museum.

Fort Les Rousses

The military importance of this site at the top of La Faucille Pass (altitude: 1,150 m) near Switzerland in the Jura Mountains was originally recognized by the First Consul Bonaparte in May 1800 when on his way to Italy right before his victory at Marengo. Eventually he decided to create a military road leading to Milan via the passes of Simplon and La Faucille. The junction of three important ways of communication between France, Switzerland and Italy in the Jura called for a stronghold to guard the crossroad, but it was only at the end of the Emperor's reign that — under pressure of invasion — things took shape. In May 1815, Colonel Christin was ordered to fortify the site of Les Rousses by building five redoubts, but due to lack of time, manpower and materials, only one entrenchment was made combat-ready. In July a small garrison of 420 led by Lieutenant Dreuther courageously tried to stop an Austrian invasion force of seven battalions.

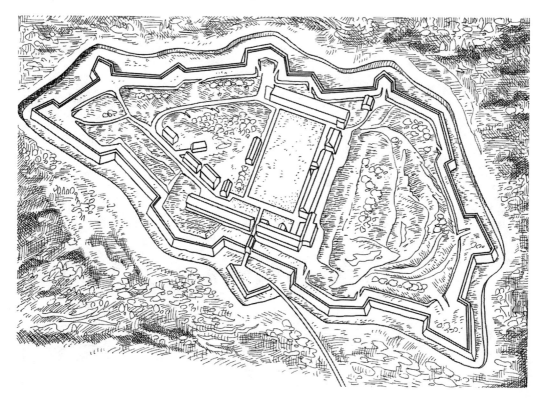

Fort Les Rousses.

A few years after the fall of Napoléon, in 1817, the construction of a strong permanent fortress near the village of Les Rousses was decided by General Haxo, but it was not before 1841 that work started on a nearby steep rocky ridge named Le Cernois. Work proceeded slowly, thwarted by the difficult access to the mountain, by accidents, bad weather and lack of funds and manpower. Finally the fort was ready to house its first garrison in 1863, but work continued until 1867. The fort had to be repaired in the late 1880s. When completed, the bastioned Fort Les Rousses was a vast entrenched camp with an area of 21 hectares, which could garrison between 2,500 and 3,000 men, and numerous artillery pieces. But it was totally outdated and obsolete because of the progress made by artillery by the second half of the 19th century. Moreover, an invasion from neutral Switzerland had become highly improbable, so the fort was never modernized. Instead it was used as base for custom-officers, and as a regional military depot during the mobilizations of 1870, 1914, and 1939. After World War II the fort was used as training ground for the French army until 1997, when it was sold to the municipality of Les Rousses. Today a cheese-producing company is established in the cool underground galleries, store-places and casemates.

Montdauphin

The fortress of Montdauphin is situated near Embrun in the Dauphiné in the Upper Alps. This vulnerable region was invaded in 1692 by Duke of Savoy Victor-Amédée, and

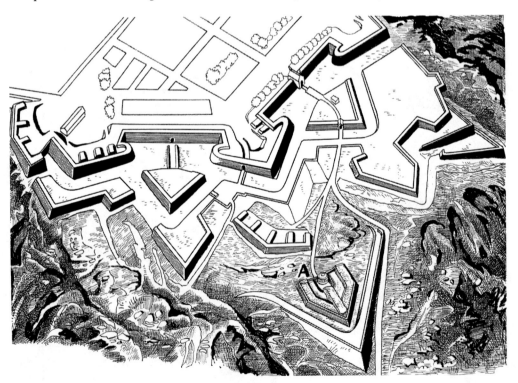

Montdauphin
A: The Arçon Lunet.

Vauban easily convinced Louis XIV to allow the creation of a fort near the village of Guillestre on a steep rocky ridge dominating the Guil torrent and the track leading to the Vars Pass. Work on Vauban's design started in 1693, and by 1700, the formidable fortress — named Montdauphin in honor of Louis XIV's son — was completed. Between 1765 and 1783, a casemated barrack (Caserne Rochambeau) was added, and during the Revolution, an advanced demi-lune was transformed into a powerful self-containing lunette d'Arçon. Montdauphin, originally designed to become both a village and a military place, failed to attract a civilian population, and the vast interior of the fortress is bare and empty. Montdauphin was eventually used as a prison, and today is perfectly preserved in a wild and breathtaking mountain landscape.

Strasbourg

Strasbourg is situated on several arms of River Ill near the Rhine. The site occupies an important strategic position (Straßburg in German means "castle on the road"). The town, called Argentoratum, founded by the Romans about 15 B.C., grew to a wealthy commercial center and a fortified stronghold facing barbaric German tribes. Devastated during 4th- and 5th-century invasions, Strasbourg grew again to a prosperous city belonging to the kingdom of Lotharingy and then to the German Empire (870). From 1201 on, Strasbourg was enlarged, was emancipated from German tutelage, and became a free town

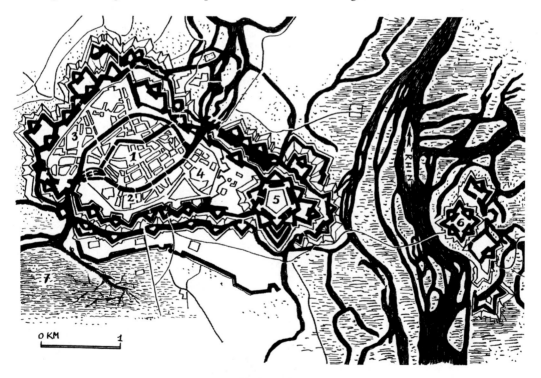

Strasbourg (1690)
1: Ancient city or Altstadt up to 1200. 2: Medieval extension between 1228 and 1344. 3: Second medieval extension from 1375 to 1390 on which Daniel Specklin built bastions 4: between 1577 and 1589. 5: Vauban's citadel. 6: Fort Kehl in Germany. 7: Floodings.

surrounded by stone walls, towers and gates. During the Wars of Religion, Strasbourg was an artistic, cultural and economical Protestant center. From 1577 to 1589, the Strasbourger military engineer Daniel Specklin established modern bastioned fortifications which were redesigned in 1633. Strasbourg was brutally annexed by Louis XIV in 1681. Vauban, assisted by engineer Jacques Tarade, undertook a vast program of modernization from 1682 to 1690, including new bastions, demi-lunes, hornworks, detached lunettes and flooding; gatehouses were particularly monumental and decorated to show the Germans Louis XIV's power, richness and magnificence. East of the town, dominating the Rhine and facing Germany, Vauban and Tarade built a powerful pentagonal citadel with two hornworks; on the right Rhine bank, they established a stronghold, named Fort Kehl, acting as a bridgehead.

At the time of Napoléon, Strasbourg became an important military land-arsenal used — together with Mayence, Jülich and Wesel — as a supply depot for the Emperor's campaigns against Prussia, Austria and the other German principalities.

Fort of Portalet

The construction of Fort Portalet, situated south of Pau in the department of Pyrénées Atlantiques, was ordered by Napoléon in 1811 to defend the Imperial Road 134 which linked Paris to Madrid via the Somport Pass. As with many other Napoleonic fortifications, the fall of the emperor prevented the completion of this plan. One had to wait some forty years to see this project realized. The fort, built between 1842 and 1858, was dug out the rock of a steep canyon. It includes terraced emplacements for artillery and riflemen, a powder house, a barracks for the garrison, quarters for officers, and various service underground premises. Eventually the fort was used as a prison, notably in 1941 when politicians and military leaders including Blum, Gamelin, Daladier, Raynaud and Mandel, held to be responsible for the defeat of June 1940, were imprisoned by the Vichy regime. The fort was declassed in 1945, and today is a historical monument.

Another Napoleonic fortified site existed in the region: The *Redoubt of Lindux*, now totally in ruins. This little-known work, situated about 30 km south of Saint-Jean-Pied-de-Port, at an altitude of 1221 m was intended to control the Val-

Entrance of the Fort of Portalet.

ley of Valcarlos between France and Spain. Nearby is another famous historical site: the Pass of Ronceval, where Emperor Charlemagne suffered a defeat in August 778, which was popularized in the epic poem known as *Song of Roland*.

Toulon

Neither the Greeks nor the Romans paid attention to the exceptional site of Toulon, but today France's chief naval port lies behind its anchorage, one of the safest and most beautiful harbors of the Mediterranean, surrounded as it is by sunny slopes and high hills crowned by forts. In the Middle Ages, Toulon remained a modest fishing village. The annexion of Provence by France in 1481 marked the beginning of a new destiny. Toulon grew to a military and commercial harbor used during the Italian Wars. In 1514, under Louis XII's reign, a circular gun tower was set up to defend the eastern entrance to the harbor. The enormous Royale Tower (known also as the Grosse Tour de la Mitre), with a diameter of 55 m, and walls 7 m thick, was completed ten years later under François I's reign. The Tower proved its efficiency by repulsing two Spanish attacks in 1524 and in 1536. The fortune of Toulon came from the naval arsenal created by King Henri IV. From 1589 onwards, on orders of the Duke of Epernon, Governor of Provence, the harbor and the town were enlarged and surrounded by an enceinte with five Italian-styled bastions whose design was attributed to the Piedmontese architect Ercole Negro. About 1600, the fortifications were reshaped by King Henri IV's engineer Raymond de Bonnefons. In 1635,

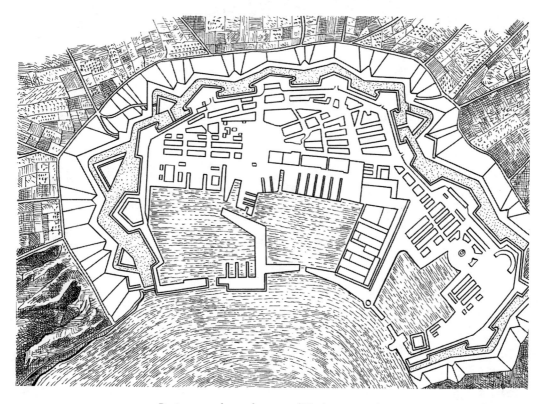

Project to enlarge the port of Toulon in 1794

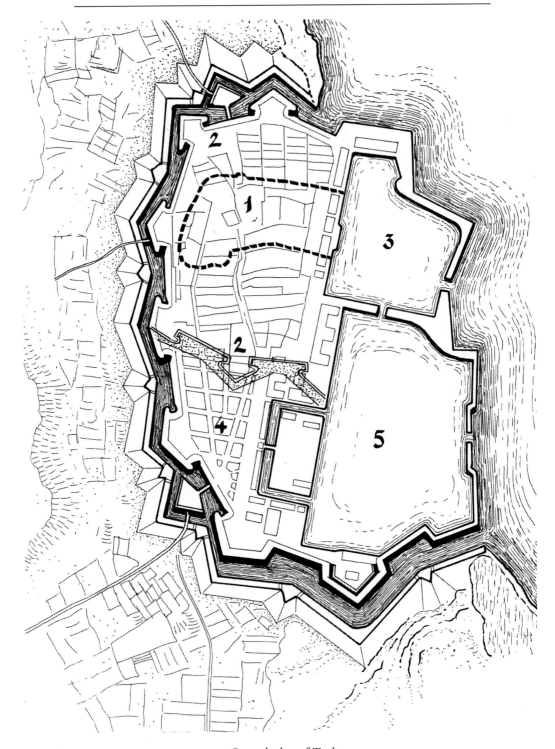

Ground-plan of Toulon
1: Medieval village; 2: fortifications about 1600; 3: old harbor; 4: city and arsenal extension at Louis XIV's time; 5: new harbor.

4. Napoleonic Fortification Projects

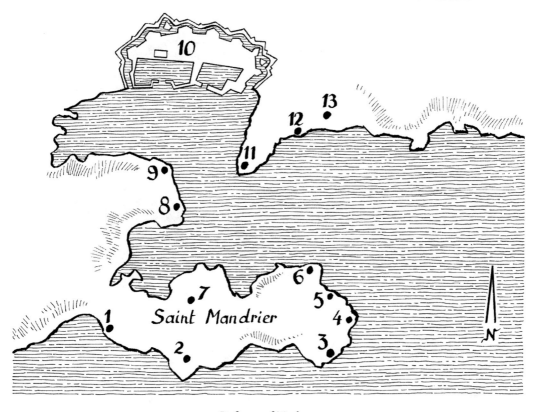

Defenses of Toulon
1: Fort and battery Saint-Elmo. 2: Fortlet of Gros Bau. 3: Fort Cepet. 4: Battery of Maud'huy. 5: Fort Croix des Signaux. 6: Battery of La Carraque. 7: Battery of Lazaret Haut. 8: Fort Balaguier. 9: Fort of Aiguillette. 10: Bastioned enceinte of Toulon arsenal. 11: Royal Tower. 12: Fort Saint-Louis. 13: Fort Lamalgue.

Richelieu created a military arsenal to build and repair warships, making Toulon the strategical center of the French Mediterranean (mostly galley) fleet. The western harbor defenses were completed by the construction of the Balaguier Tower facing the Royale Tower. In 1680, Colbert decided upon the reinforcement of the important military city. The harbor was widened; shipyards, a new wet dock and an enlarged arsenal were built. Around the arsenal and the town, Vauban built a strong bastioned enceinte and two detached bastioned works: Fort des Pommets and Fort Saint-Louis. In 1707 an entrenched camp was built (Camp Sainte-Anne). Between 1760 and 1780, the engineer Millet de Montville added new reinforcements by establishing detached forts including Forts Lamalgue, Sainte-Catherine, Artigues and Vieux-Pommets as well as redoubts Saint-Antoine, Faron and Malbousquet. In 1793, a Royalist revolt enabled the British to capture the port. Toulon was besieged and retaken by the army of the Convention, in which a young artillery captain named Napoléon Bonaparte distinguished himself. During the Consulate and the Empire, standardized tours modèles were built at Croix des Signaux and La Seyne, and several plans were launched aiming to increase the naval infrastructures and enlarge the capacities of the port. The archipelago of Hyères (Porquerolles, Port-Cros and the Levant Islands), south off Toulon, was also fortified with several coastal towers and forts.

Entrance to Fort Croix des Signaux, Toulon
The fort, situated south of Toulon on the peninsula of Saint-Mandrier, originated from a tour modele No. 1, built in 1812 on Napoléon's order. Between 1849 and 1853, the tower was enclosed by a pentagonal defensive wall, and a barracks for the garrison was added. The position was reinforced in 1877 by several coastal batteries, and an ammunition store was dug out in the rock in 1891. In the 1920s and 1930s, the fort was enlarged and the batteries updated with modern artillery. Used by the Germans during the occupation of 1940–1944, today the fort is the property of the French navy.

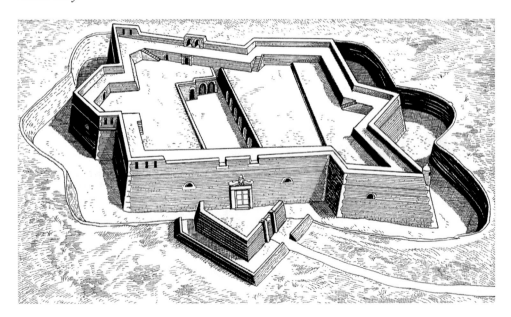

Fort des Pommets
Situated north-west of Toulon, the fort was built between 1748 and 1755.

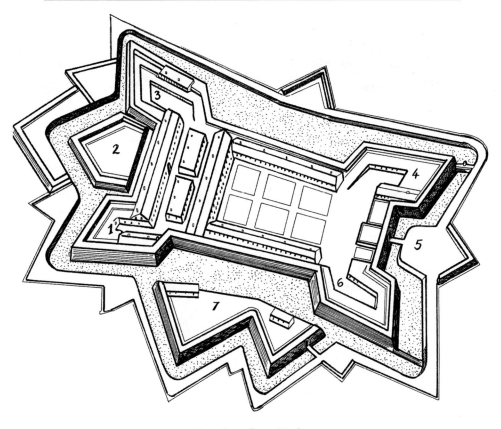

Fort Lamalgue, Toulon
Built between 1764 and 1792, Fort Lamalgue had a garrison of 500 men and could be armed with 200 artillery pieces. 1: Bastion du Roi. 2: Demi-lune. 3: Bastion de la Reine. 4: Bastion du Dauphin. 5: Main entrance. 6: Bastion de Normandie. 7: Double demi-lune.

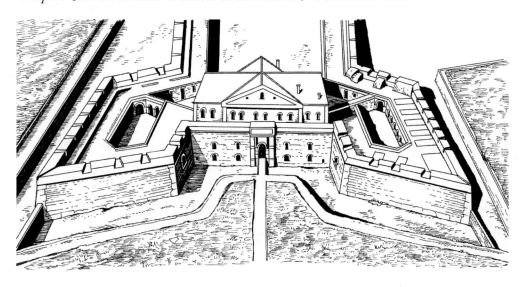

Entrance to Fort Lamalgue, Toulon.

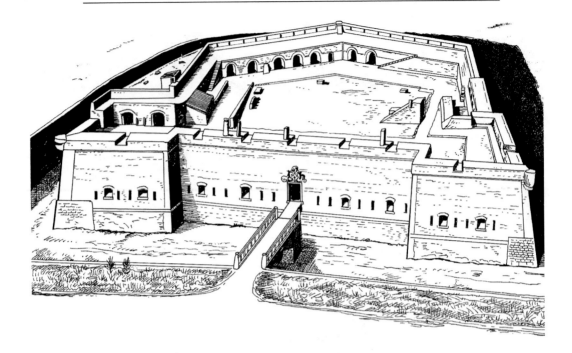

Fort d'Artigues, Toulon.

Fortin de la Vigie Port-Cros Island (c. 1813).

Today, of Toulon's fortifications, there still exist the Royal Tower, three bastions arranged as a public park with the Salle Omega Zenith (Concert Hall) and the Espace Culturel des Lices (Culture Hall). Another bastion still exists near the ancient Porte d'Italie (Italy Gate). Several detached forts built in the 18th and 19th centuries (e.g., Fort Sainte-Catherine), as well as French concrete coastal batteries established in the 1930s and German World War II bunkers, make of Toulon an open museum of the history of fortification. Fort Lamalgue at Mourillon and the Fort de Peyras at La Seyne-sur-Mer are still occupied by the French Navy.

The Netherlands

From 1795 to 1814 the Netherlands were ruled by the French, a period known in Dutch history as the *Franse Tijd* (French Era). The occupation of the Low Countries, with their rich hard-working trading citizens, their good fleet, and the important ports of Amsterdam, Rotterdam, Vlissingen, and Antwerp (in Belgium), allowed the French to control an important part of the North Sea, a significant and major asset for the war and the blockade aiming to starve England. From 1795 to 1806, the Pays-Bas (Netherlands) were submitted to France as a satellite state known as the *République Batave*. In 1806, the Low Countries were instituted as the *Royaume de Hollande* (Realm of Holland) with Louis-Napoléon (Napoléon's youngest brother) as king. In 1810, Napoléon was extremely irritated by his brother's attitude: he preferred to serve the interests of his subjects rather than the demands of France. The affable and generous Koning Lodewijk (King Louis in Dutch) refused to impose conscription, relying instead on Hessian mercenaries. He also tried to introduce a mild version of the Continental System. Louis, who had come to enjoy his new position and perhaps to love the Dutch more than the French, was fired by his exasperated brother. The Netherlands were simply and purely annexed to France, and divided into administrative departments. Napoléon had then realized a very old French ambition: domination of the Rhine delta, and thus of much of the commercial contacts between the North Sea and Central Europe.

Being a part of France was, however, an ordeal for the Dutch. The continental blockade imposed by the Emperor ruined the economy of the Low Countries, traditionally based on trading with Europe and England. Moreover, the conscription and the heavy casualties resulting from Napoléon's ceaseless wars added to the resentment of the population. Some 15,000 Dutch draftees were forced to accompany Napoléon on his ill-fated Russian campaign in 1812, and few of them survived this terrible and foolish experience. In 1813, as anti–French feeling ran high, the Dutch entered into rebellion against the French yoke and joined the anti–French European coalition. Gradually the French troops of occupation were harassed and forced to withdraw. In December 1815, the Dutch recovered their freedom, and the Prince of Orange became King of the Netherlands.

French Napoleonic fortifications in the Netherlands were mainly focused on the protection of the important ports and arsenals of Antwerp, Amsterdam and Den Helder. In early 1805 tensions grew between France and Prussia, and there arose the possibility of a war in which the small Batave Republic would be involved. Prime-Minister Schimmelpenninck then gave orders to the Minister of War, C.R.T. Baron of Krayenhoff, and Colonel-Director Croiset of the Dutch engineering corps, to plan and envisage some kind of protection against the dangerous and threatening neighbor. This policy was continued by King of Holland Louis-Napoléon Bonaparte, and existing fortified points were modernized and several others created at the border between the Netherlands and Germany.

Antwerp

Napoléon's main preoccupation in the Pays-Bas was the protection of the access to the port of Antwerp. This city appeared in the 3rd century A.D. and developed in the

Map of the Low Countries (c. 1810)
The Netherlands, as integral part of France, were divided into départements (administrative regions).

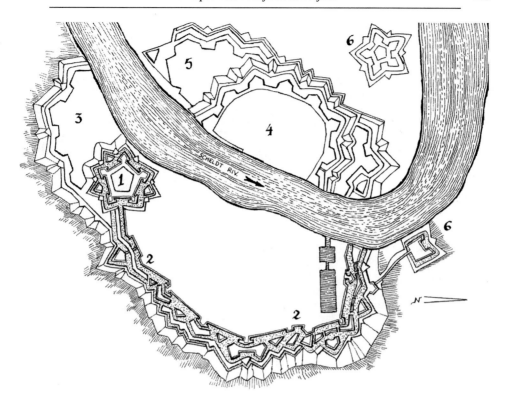

Project for Antwerp (1810)
The French Napoleonic scheme included the modernization of the citadel (1) and the old Spanish enceinte (2), as well as the creation of an entrenched camp (3) south of the citadel, and a city extension (4) on the left bank of the Scheldt, with another entrenched camp (5) and detached forts (6).

Fort Lillo, Antwerp (c. 1810)
Fort Lillo was built between 1579 and 1582 by order of stadhouder William of Orange on the right bank of River Scheldt north of Antwerp. Together with Fort Liefkenshoek (placed on the left bank), they were intended to defend the access to the port of Antwerp. After the British attack of 1809, Napoléon gave orders to refurbish the fort. A new powder house was built, a gun battery and two fortified shelters were established, as well as a covered way "en crémaillère" (sawtooth-shaped). Fort Liefkenshoek on the opposite bank 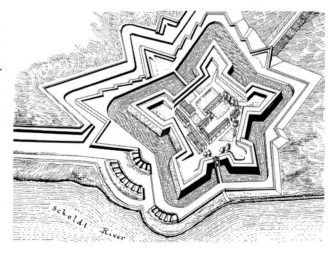 was also modernized by the French occupiers. Declassed as a military place in 1894, Fort Lillo still exists today and has formed a green oasis, an island of calm and nature in the heavily industrialized suburbs of Antwerp.

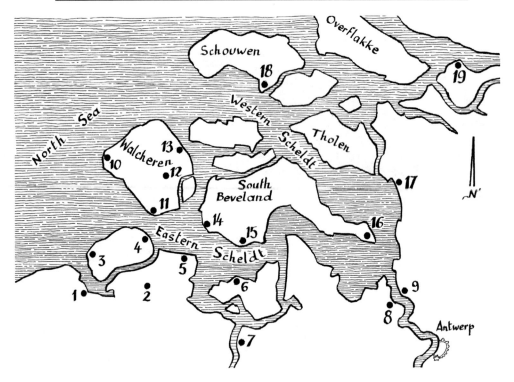

Defenses of Antwerp
Following the British attack of 1809, the defenses of the port and arsenal of Antwerp were reinforced and enlarged by order of Napoléon. They involved the whole province of Zeeland and included the fortified cities, strongholds and forts of l'Ecluse or Sluis (1), Ysendijk (2), Cadzand (3), Breskens (4), Hoogplaat (5), Terneuzen (6), Sas-de-Gand (7), Fort Liefkenshoek (8), Fort Lillo (9), Westkapelle (10), Flessingue (11), Middelburg (12), Veere (13), Borselen (14), Ellenwoutswijk (15), Batz (16), Bergen-op-Zoom (17), Zierickzee (18) and Willemstadt (19).

Middle Ages as an important commercial port, notably with England. Medieval fortifications were modernized by the Italian Donato Buoni di Pellezuoli in the 1540s. A citadel, designed by Francesco Pacciotto and Bartholomeo Scampi, was built in 1567. From 1794, Belgium was annexed by France and divided into nine administrative departments. In 1803 the First Consul Bonaparte decided to make of Antwerp (Anvers in French) a strong navy arsenal, a "pistol loaded and aiming at England," in his own words. Soon work started for the construction of a large military port and shipyard on the right bank of the Scheldt river. In 1809 a sudden and brutal British raid clearly showed the weakness of the defenses: the raiders occupied the port and town of Vlissingen and inflicted heavy damage before withdrawing. After this disastrous attack, it was decided to increase the defenses (notably of the access to Antwerp), and plans were made to transform the city into a formidable fortress with bastioned enceintes and detached forts. Paciotto's citadel was reinforced by a continuous envelope, demi-lunes, counterguards and a covered way en crémaillère. The much-neglected Spanish bastioned enceinte from 1540 was modernized by the addition of various outworks. The huge undertaking was, however, not completed at the time of Napoléon's fall. In 1815 Belgium was incorporated in the newly created Kingdom of the Netherlands.

4. Napoleonic Fortification Projects

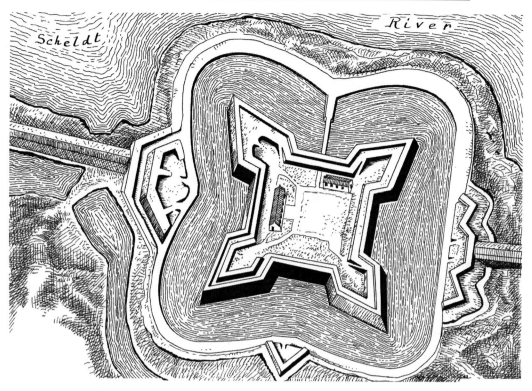

Fort Liefkenshoek, Antwerp (c. 1810)
Smaller sister fort on the left bank, Fort Liefkenshoek was constructed and declassed at the same time as Fort Lillo on the right bank of the Scheldt River.

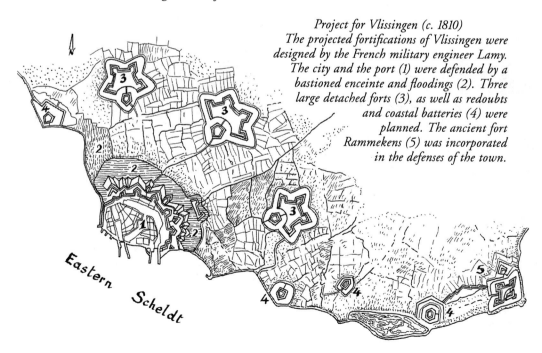

Project for Vlissingen (c. 1810)
The projected fortifications of Vlissingen were designed by the French military engineer Lamy. The city and the port (1) were defended by a bastioned enceinte and floodings (2). Three large detached forts (3), as well as redoubts and coastal batteries (4) were planned. The ancient fort Rammekens (5) was incorporated in the defenses of the town.

Vlissingen and Breskens

The port of Vlissingen (*Flessingue* in French, *Flushing* in English) is situated on the southern part of Walcheren Island in the Dutch province of Zeeland. Because of its excellent strategic situation on the north side of the Eastern Scheldt mouth, the French authorities decided to make of Vlissingen a sort of dependence of the port of Antwerp. From 1796 to the end of the Napoleonic Empire, Vlissingen was the object of numerous projects including enlargement and modernization of its maritime installations: shipyards, dry docks, arsenal, quays, sluices, magazines and stores, workshops and barracks. After the devastating British raid of 1809, Napoléon ordered the reinforcement of the fortifications. The old Dutch bastioned urban enceinte from the 17th century, as well as the old Renaissance Fort Rammekens, were modernized, while a belt of detached forts and coastal batteries were planned both on the land and sea fronts of Vlissingen.

Vlissingen Duin Gate (c. 1812)
This sketch shows how ancient fortifications could be modernized. 1: City wet ditch. 2: Duin Gate with drawbridge. 3: Bastion No. 2 (Dutch-built, 17th century). 4: Bastion No. 1 (Dutch-built, 17th century). 5: Hollow West-Beer (Western batardeau), connecting to counterscarp and separating the waters of the city ditch from the Eastern Scheldt. 6: Counterscarp with French-built riflemen's gallery and underground countermine gallery enabling the defenders — if need be — to blow up the Platte dike, thereby forming a defensive inundation. 7: Curtain (Dutch-built, 17th century), reinforced by the French as traversed gun battery facing the Eastern Scheldt. 8: Beach, named Klein Zandje (Small Sand). 9: Two-story French-built bombproof barracks. 10: Bastion No. 13 (Dutch-built, 17th century). 11: Eastern Scheldt River.

Fort Rammekens (1547)

Situated east of Vlissingen, Fort Rammekens was built in 1547 by order of Mary of Hungary (sister of King of Spain Charles V, then governess of the Low Countries). Designed by the Italian engineer Donato de Boni and constructed by the Dutch master-builder Peter Fransz, the fort includes a diamond-shaped enceinte, one casemated bastion turned towards the Scheldt and two flanking half-bastions turned towards the rear.

Fort Rammekens, Vlissingen

At the time of the French domination, Fort Rammekens (1) was incorporated in the defenses of Vlissingen, modernized, and reinforced with a large crownwork (2) and a line en crémaillère (3) on the land front.

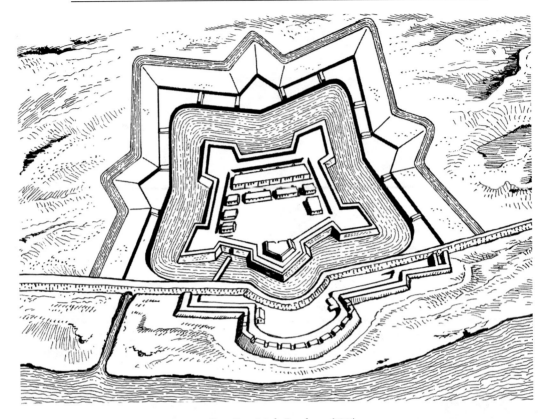

Fort Impérial, Breskens (1811)
Situated on the left bank of the Eastern Scheldt, Fort Impérial was built in 1811. It is a classical bastioned pentagon with wet ditch, covered way, glacis and additional outer wet ditch. The fort also included a gun battery placed on the opposite side of the dike; this was armed with twelve 36-pound guns, twelve 24-pound guns, six 16-pound guns and twelve 12-inch mortars. After the French withdrawal in 1814, the fort was renamed Fort Frederik-Hendrik by the Dutch.

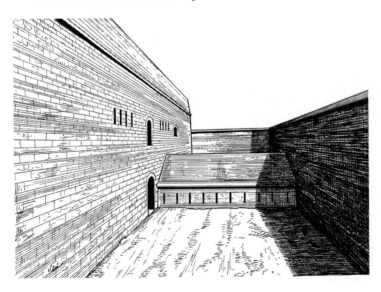

For the defense of the southern bank of the Eastern Scheldt estuary, the French planned a series of fortified positions at Cadzand, Breskens, Hoogplaat, and Terneuzen. At Breskens, for example, they built in 1811 Fort Napoléon, Fort du Centre, Fort Impérial and the lunette Caffarelli. It was also

Caponier at Fort Napoléon, Oostende.

planned to establish an entrenched camp around the village of Breskens, including a bastioned wall and a pentagonal fort, as well as a canal connecting to Brugge, but the fall of the Empire prevented these works from being carried out.

Amsterdam

As a satellite of France, the puppet République Batave was unwillingly involved in the Napoleonic Wars. On August 26, 1799, an Anglo-Russian task force landed in the north of the province of Holland and marched in the direction of Amsterdam. The Franco–Batave forces, after a series of bloody battles at Bergen, Alkmaar and Castricum, managed to force the raiders to re-embark and leave. The incursion, however, had clearly demonstrated the vulnerability of the defensive system around the important city and port of Amsterdam. To palliate this weakness, the so-called Line of Bewerwijk was created at the instigation of General Guillaume Brune (1763–1815). It was designed by Lieutenant-Colonel C. Gillet of the French Engineer Corps, and by his Dutch colleague

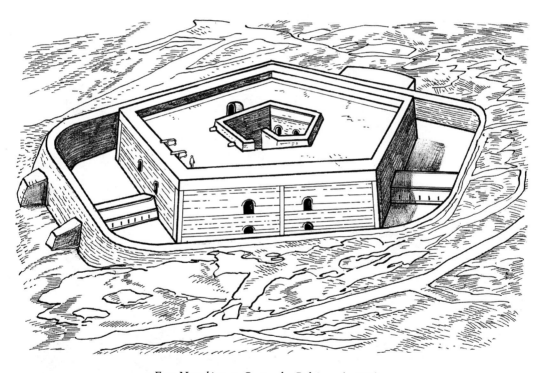

Fort Napoléon at Oostende, Belgium (c. 1811)
The construction of this fort was ordered to protect the port of Oostende from a British attack. That never came, and the fort was completed only upon the fall of the Emperor in 1814. The fort, quite modern for its time, showed some of Montalembert's influence. It is a massive casemated pentagon with a gun battery on its open top terrace, and its deep dry ditches were defended by caponiers. During the two World Wars, the fort was used by the Germans. After the war, it fell into disrepair. Since 1995 it has been managed and restored by the Flanders Heritage Association. Today Fort Napoléon has withstood the test of time, and houses a museum and a restaurant. Worthy of mention is the German coastal battery (MKB Hundius) that stands close to Fort Napoléon and which gives a typical example of what the defenses of the Atlantic Wall actually were like.

Lieutenant-Colonel Krayenhoff. Both designers were influenced by the theoretical book *Tracé d'un système de lunettes disposées en lignes* written by a certain Gay de Vernon, a teacher in fortification at the Polytechnique School of Paris. Established between February and July 1800, the line was composed of 26 detached *lunettes* (fortlets) spaced out in two rows in the dunes west of Amsterdam and spreading from Wijk-aan-Zee in the West near the coast to Beverwijk landwards in the East. Each lunette was independent, most were triangular in plan (a few were pentagonal), defended by a glacis, a ditch, and fitted with a thick earth breastwork protecting infantry and artillery. No attack ever occurred again, and after the departure of the French in 1814, the provisory and perishable lunettes were neglected, and abandoned. Soon the grounds were sold to private owners and the works were progressively swallowed up in the landscape. Today only two small earth mounts in the flat North-Holland countryside indicate the remnants of lunettes No. XI and No. XIV.

Den Helder

Den Helder, situated in a marshy peninsula in the Dutch province of North Holland, originated from a simple fishers' village named Huisduinen in the Middle Ages. After centuries of hard toil the region north of Amsterdam was protected by dikes and lands reclaimed from the sea by polderization. In the 15th century Den Helder became a port, and redoubts were built in the 1580s. When the United Provinces were set free by Spain in 1648, Den Helder, which with the island of Texel controlled the passage to the port of Amsterdam via the then open Zuiderzee, was fitted with coastal batteries. The port and the Dutch fleet were taken in January 1795 by 400 hussars led by Major Lahure, a part of General Pichegru's army. This episode has become famous as the horsemen attacked

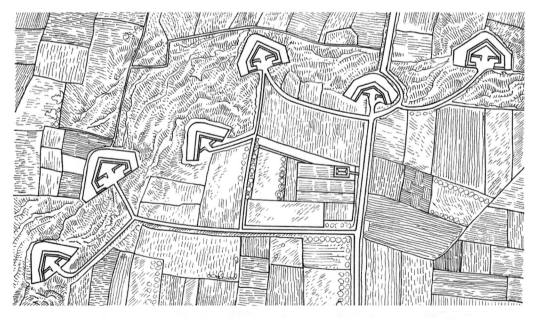

Beverwijk Line, Amsterdam
This section of the Beverwijk Line shows some of the Dutch-French lunettes established in 1800.

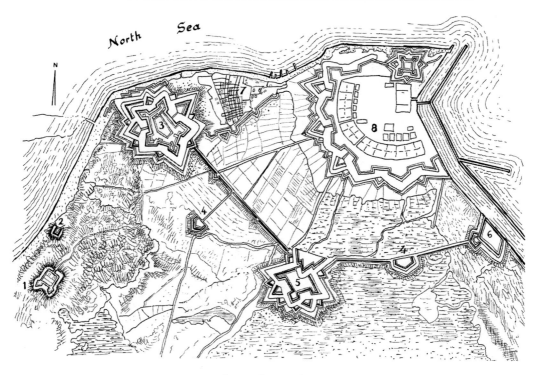

Defenses of Den Helder
The Napoleonic fortifications of Den Helder included: the coastal Fort Morland, renamed Fort Kijkduin by the Dutch after the fall of Napoléon in 1814 (1); the coastal battery de la Fraternité (2); Fort Lasalle, later renamed Fort Erfprins (3); two redoubts (4) formed an advanced position on a continuous earth wall joining Fort Lasalle to Fort l'Ecluse, later renamed Fort Dirk Admiraal (5); the wall continued to Fort Dugommier, later renamed Fort Oost-Oever (6). The project to fortify the village of Den Helder (7), the naval base and the arsenal (8) was never completed. Several additional coastal batteries were temporarily established between Fort Lasalle and the arsenal, including Batterie de la Révolution, Batterie du Roi de Rome, Batterie Le Réparateur, Batterie de l'Indivisibilité, and Batterie de l'Union.

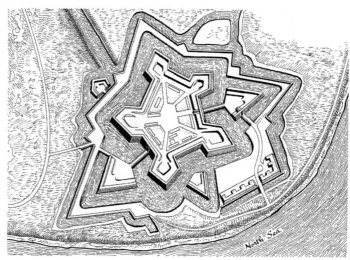

Fort Lasalle Den helder
Fort Lasalle (today named Fort Erfprins) was one of the three main forts built by the French to protect Den Helder. The fort was a classical bastioned pentagon with outworks, envelope, two wet ditches and a traversed gun battery facing the North Sea.

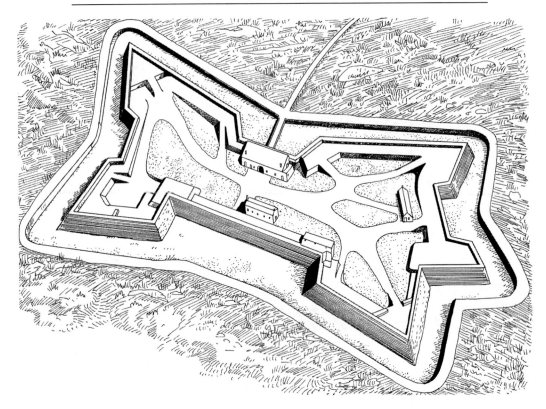

Fort Dufalga, Den Helder (1810 project)
The construction of Fort Dufalga started in 1781 as a battery in the dunes south of Den Helder at a place known as Kleine Keeten. The fort was eventually renamed after Louis Marie Joseph Maximillien de Caffarelli Dufalga (1756–1799), a French military engineer who was killed during the campaign of Egypt at the Battle of Saint John of Accre in 1799. The fort was to be made of earth and designed according to the bastioned system. It would have had a length of 380 m, and was intended to house twenty-two 36-pound guns and sixteen mortars. Plans called for a "Tour Modèle" for the garrison to be built in the gorge of the work. However, in 1812 the fort was not yet completed, only including a bastioned front facing the sea, a palisade defending the rear, and a temporary barracks made of wood. The fort, which was never completed, was abandoned in February 1814. Today it has vanished in the dunes and nothing remains of it.

the ships by charging onto the ice of the frozen port. Den Helder was attacked and held for a while by the British in August 1799. Den Helder was radically transformed by Napoléon in 1811 to constitute an important arsenal and a military port for the French navy. The project for Den Helder was quite ambitious. On the land front the arsenal was to be defended by a citadel and a bastioned enceinte; neither of these works was ever built, but three large forts (named Forts Lasalle, l'Ecluse and Dugommier), linked together with continuous walls reinforced by redans and lunettes, were actually constructed. In addition the marshy grounds south of the arsenal could be flooded, thus making of Den Helder a formidable camp retranché. On the sea front several forts were planned (Morland and Dufalga), as well as a number of coastal batteries. In 1814, all works were taken over by the Dutch and given Dutch names, and the installations were completed in the 19th century. Den Helder remained until the end of the 20th century an important Dutch navy base.

Fort De Schans, Texel island
Strategically situated north of Den Helder on the island of Texel, the Fort De Oude Schans ("the old sconce") was designed by the Dutch military engineers Jan Crab and Adriaan Dooren in 1572 to defend the passage leading to the then still open Zuiderzee and Amsterdam. Completed about 1574, the fort was constantly improved and enlarged, notably in 1665 during the Second Anglo-Dutch War (1665–1667). During the War of American Independence (1775–1783), the fort was used as a hospital for sick and wounded British sailors who had been captured by the American Captain John Paul Jones. The Fort Oude Schans (renamed Fort Central by the French), occupied by some 300 men, both French and Dutch, was attacked in 1799 by a strong party of Anglo-Russians who had landed at Callandsoog. The fort was taken for a short while by the raiders. During his visit in 1811 Napoléon, anxious to protect the waterway leading to Amsterdam, ordered the construction of a demi-lune and the reinforcement of the covered way, which was transformed into an envelope with large places-of-arms and a second outer wet ditch. Two detached works known as Redoute and Lunette were also built about 700 m west of the fort as additional defenses. These digging works were carried out by Spanish prisoners. The fort, which was also used as a prison for British prisoners of war, was occupied by the French until November 1813. Fort Oude Schans on Texel Island, several times modified and adapted to modern artillery, was used by the Dutch as observation post and coastal battery until 1922. In 1931, due to the reinforcement of the dike protecting the island against sea and storm, the fort was partly destroyed. Today about half of the work has been restored and forms a cultural historical object in the wild nature of the island.

Northern Netherlands

The French also built or reactivated a number of strong points in the north of the Netherlands in the provinces of Drenthe and Groningen (then designated *Département de l'Ems Occidental* and *Département des Bouches de l'Yssel*). These were generally small works intended for surveillance roles, namely repression of smuggling between Germany and the Netherlands.

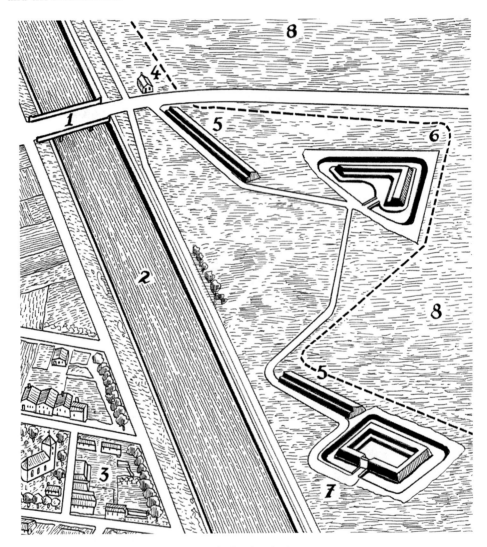

De Leethe border check point
Near the village of Bellingwolde at the frontier with Germany at border markstone No. 188, the French occcupiers buit a defensive post in 1797. This included a flèche, a redoubt and two infantry positions. The post was also intended to thwart smuggling, which had always been a fruitful activity between Germany and the Netherlands. The Leethe control post was abandoned in 1828. Today both works have been restored as tourist sites. The sketch shows the following. 1: Wijmer Bridge; 2: B.J. Tijdens Canal; 3: village of Bellingwolde; 4: border post; 5: infantry breastworks; 6: flèche or arrow; 7: redoubt; 8: Germany.

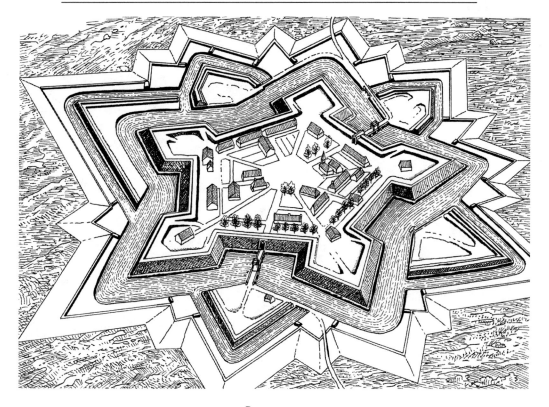

Bourtange
Fort Bourtange is situated in the Dutch northern province of Groningen. The fort, controlling a small passage in large impassable marshes that marked the natural frontier with Germany, was built in the 1590s by order of Prince William of Orange. Fort Bourtange, originally intended as a simple temporary bastioned pentagonal sconce made of earth, was later incorporated in the defense of the Dutch United Provinces. The fort was enlarged in 1607 and 1645 by the addition of outworks, wet ditches, and crownwork. Fort Bourtange lost its military value in the 19th century. It was dismantled and the grounds sold to local peasants in the 1850s. Fortunately, in the 1960s, the municipality decided to revive the old fort: it was completely and exactly rebuilt as it was in 1742. The fort is now a tourist attraction where the past is cleverly and skillfully re-enacted.

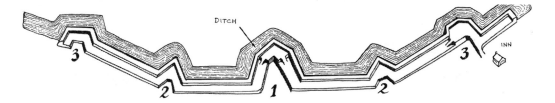

Line of Abeltjeshuis at Fort Bourtange
By the time of the "French Era," the strategically important passage between Bourtange and Germany was reinforced by the occupiers. Between what today are border poles 181 and 182, they established a line, named Abeltjeshuis Linie (named after a small inn "the House of Little Abel"), composed of a central bastion (1), two redans (2) and two batteries (3) linked together by an earth wall defended by a wet ditch.

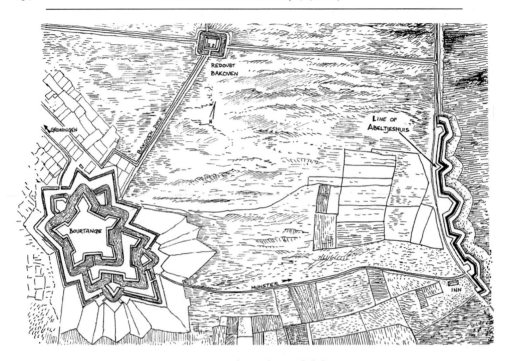

Bourtange and its advanced defenses
The line of Abeljeshuis, the redoubt Bakoven and Fort Bourtange defended the only passage between Germany and the northern Netherlands in a vast and impassable marsh.

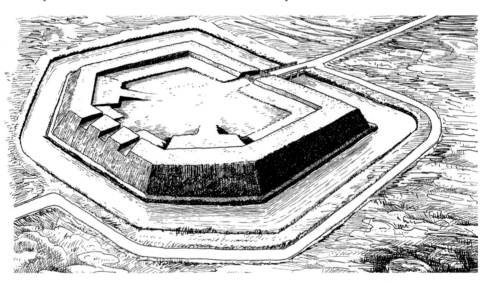

Emmerschans
The Emmerschans (Sconce of Emmen) was built by the French in 1800. It was a simple redoubt made of earth, surrounded by a wet ditch, with a front length of about 60 m and a width of about 45 m. Together with the Katshaarschans, it was intended to defend the eastern border of the province of Drenthe against an attack from Germany. The Katshaarschans and the Emmerschans remained a part of the Dutch defenses until 1851. Since 1935 both redoubts have been owned by the association Stichting Oude Drenthe and still stand today in the flat green landscape.

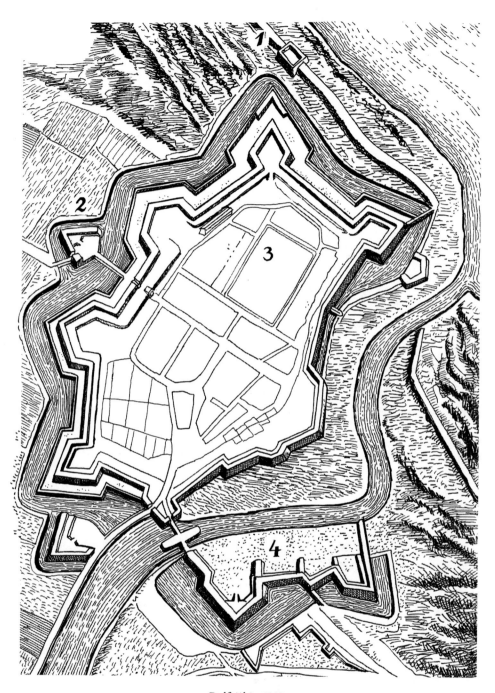

Delfzijl in 1812
The village of Delfzijl was probably established in 1272 by monks who built a zijl (sluice) on the river Delf. By 1500, Delfzijl had developed into a port which played a role in the Eighty Years' War (1568–1648) between the Dutch Protestant Spain. The city was fortified during that period in Old Dutch Bastioned System. During the Napoleonic occupation, the French established a coastal battery facing the sea (Batterie du Nord, 1 on the plan); added a demi-lune (2) in front of the Land Gate; arranged a vast place-of-arms (3); and refurbished the old Kostverloren hornwork (4) protecting the southern Farmsum Gate. The garrison (about 1,400) was besieged by the Cossacks and capitulated on May 23, 1814. Delfzijl remained a part of the Dutch defenses until 1874.

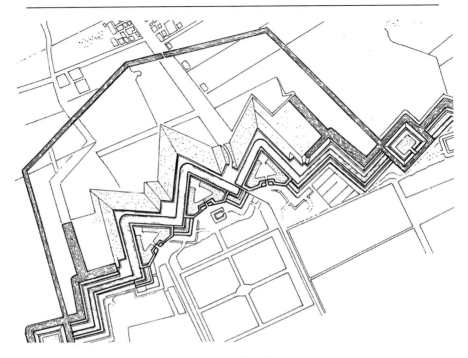

Helperdiep canal at Groningen
During the Franse Tijd in 1806, the French reactivated the defense of the capital of the Northern Netherlands, Groningen. A number of barracks were built in the town, the tenailled Line of Helpman (built in 1700 by the Dutch engineer Menno van Coehoorn) was refurbished, and a military defensive canal, named Helperdiep, was excavated ahead of the line.

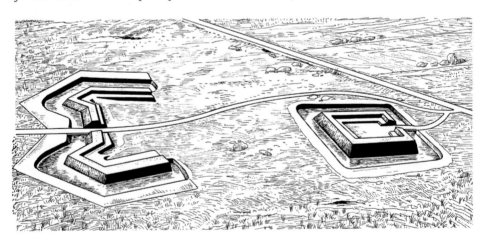

Katshaarschans
The Katshaarschans ("Sconce of the cat's hair") was built by the Dutch in 1672, during Louis XIV's invasion of the Low Countries. It was a simple rectangular earthen redoubt intended to control the Katshaar Pass, a narrow passage between Dalerveen and Vlieghuis in the marshes east of the town of Coevorden in the province of Drenthe. In 1797 the neglected redoubt was reactivated by the French, and a new advanced fortified point in the form of a sort of hornwork was added. This had a front length of about 150 m. The redoubt and the advanced work formed what was called the Post of Katshaar.

Germany

It is interesting to note that the French Revolutionaries and Napoléon resumed Louis XIV's policy of national expansion: overthrowing the dominion of the Hapsburgs, gaining possession of the left bank of the Rhine, and subjecting the German states to French supremacy. The right bank of the Rhine had been occupied and annexed by France during the early Revolutionary Wars in 1795. In 1806 the secular Holy Roman German Reich (founded in A.D. 962) was abolished and replaced by the so-called *Confédération du Rhin* (or *Rheinbund* in German), placed under the leadership and protectorship of France. The Confederacy of the Rhine, inspired and supervised by Napoléon, marked the final triumph of all the aims of French imperialism: the empire and crown of Charlemagne had been restored and usurped by the Corsican conqueror. The Confederacy included sixteen German minor states whose leaders decided more or less willingly to throw their nations' futures in with Napoléon Bonaparte and ally themselves with France. A further nineteen joined later. The more than 15 million people living within the Confederacy provided both a physical barrier against enemies on France's eastern borders and also sent large contingents of troops to join its armies. The members of the Confederacy included large kingdoms and duchies, together with smaller principalities and city states. The key ones were Bavaria (3.5 million subjects), Saxony (2 million), Westphalia (2 million), Wurttemburg (1.5 million), Baden (1 million), and the Duchy of Warsaw in Poland (4 million). The others were Cleve-Berg, Hesse-Darmstadt, Anhalt-Bernburg, Anhalt-Dessau, Anhalt-Kothen, Hohenzollern-Hechingen, Hohenzollen-Sigmaringen, Isenburg, Leyen, Leichtenstein, Mecklinburg-Schwerin, Mecklenburg-Strelitz, Ebersdorf, Gera, Gtreiz, Lobenstein, Schleiz, Saxe-Coburg-Saalfield, Saxe-Gotha-Altenburg, Saxe-Hildburghausen, Saxe-Meningen, Saxe-Weimar, Schaumburg-Lippe, Schwarzburg-Rudolstadt, Schwarzburg-Sonderhausen, Waldeck, Wurzburg, Erfurt and Frankfurt. The French domination was dictated by the principle *divide et impera* (divide and rule). By sowing the seeds of discord between South and North, between Catholics and Protestants, and by making capital of the venality of some of the German princes, this policy gave rise to a growing anti–French feeling. From 1809 onwards, it was Prussia which took the lead in the *Befreiungskrieg* (war of liberation). Disaffection within the group over continued support for France increased after Napoléon Bonaparte's invasion of and retreat from Russia. After the Allied victory at Leipzig (October 1813), many members of the Confederacy switched sides to help the Allies bring down Napoléon. As agreed at the first Treaty of Paris in 1814, a Congress of the great powers of Europe met at Vienna from November 1814 to June 1815 to settle the future boundaries of the continent. Almost every state in Europe was represented, including defeated France.

The Congress adopted a fair policy of no great rewards and no great punishments. It gave a balanced settlement which ensured no major conflict for forty years (the Crimean War, 1854–1856) and then until 1914. It was still generous to defeated France, in order to prevent French feelings of vengefulness, and the Capetian-Bourbon monarchy was restored. The Congress, however, ignored popular demands for greater democracy and nationalism; this led to the majority of conflicts in the 19th century, between and within countries. Germany remained parceled out, a conglomerate of duchies, kingdoms, principalities, free states, independent towns and free bishoprics, until unification by Bismarck in 1870.

French Napoleonic fortifications in the Confederacy of the Rhine were principally marked by the establishment of large military arsenals in existing fortified cities such as Wesel, Mayence, and Jülich for example.

WESEL

The city of Wesel, situated in the province of Rhineland at the joining of Rivers Lippe and Rhine, was created by the Romans as a military camp belonging to their fortified

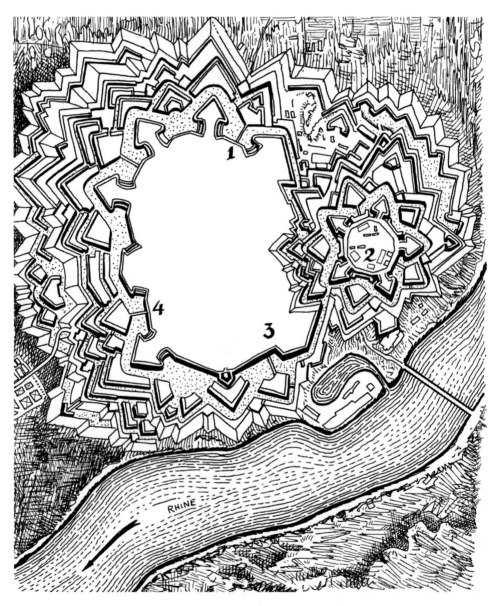

Wesel (c. 1757)
1: Berlin Gate. 2: Citadel. 3: Rhine Gate. 4: Cleves Gate.

border called limes. In the Middle Ages, the city became one of the numerous independent free cities of the Germanic Hansa and was fortified. In the 16th century the Italian military engineer, Giovanni Pasqualini, designed a bastioned enceinte which was successively enlarged and modernized in 1614, 1629 and 1681. The pentagonal citadel was built in the late 1680s. At the end of the 17th century Wesel became a part of Prussia, and again its fortifications were modernized in 1690 by engineer J. de Corbin. From 1806 to 1814, Wesel was occupied by France, and Napoléon decided to transform the city into a powerful arsenal to be used as logistic base against Prussia and Austria. For this purpose ambitious projects were made including magazines, stores, an arsenal, barracks, a second citadel and a wide extension on the opposite bank of the Rhine. The fall of the French Empire prevented the completion of this work, and in 1815 the Congress of Vienna gave Wesel back to Prussia. The fortifications were refurbished in Montalembert/Neo-Prussian style in the 1850s, including a belt of detached forts. The fortifications were officially declared obsolete in 1886 and dismantled. Wesel was also badly damaged during the Second World War. Today the town has kept some vestiges from its former defenses, notably a bastioned front from the ancient citadel, the Berlin Gate from 1720, several military buildings and the réduit/keep of Fort Fustenberg from 1885.

Mayence

The city of Mayence (Mainz in German) is situated at the joining of Rivers Rhine and Main in the province of Palatinate-Rhineland. Originating from a Roman border

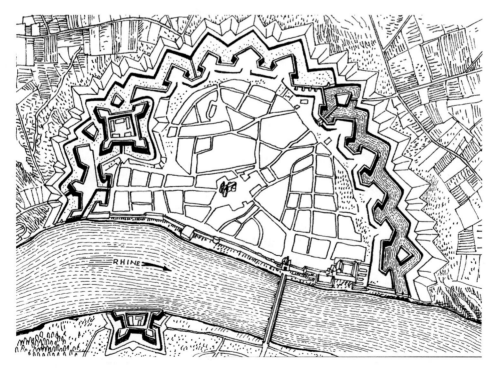

Mayence
The plan shows the fortifications of Mayence in the 17th century.

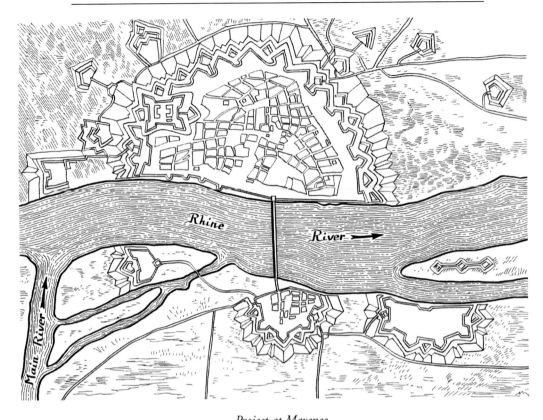

Project at Mayence
This project for new fortifications included the extension of the defense on the southern part of the city by the addition of outworks and detached works. On the right bank of the Rhine, it was planned to add a large bridgehead, and several secondary forts and detached works.

camp named *Moguntianum*, Mayence was chosen by the evangelist Bonifacius (675–754) to be the see of a bishopric. In the Middle Ages, Mayence became an important and wealthy free city led by a Prince-Elector (who participated in the election of the Emperor of Germany). The city, which spread on the left bank of the Rhine, was defended by stone walls, towers and gatehouses. These were adapted to the use of firearms in the 16th century, and modernized with a bastioned enceinte, demi-lunes, wet ditches, and a citadel in the 17th century. At the time of Napoléon, the Palatinate was occupied by France, and Mayence became an important border town that was used as a large logistic base and arsenal for the campaigns against Austria and Prussia. Napoléon had great ambitions regarding this city, which was also intended to remind the Germans of the glorious French presence — as it were, a shop window displaying his grandeur and might. In the period 1804–1807, the bulk of the work concerning the modernization of Mayence was entrusted to the French urbanist and architect Eustache de Saint-Far (1746–1822). The city was connected to the network of communication by an Imperial Road (today parallel to the Bundesautobahn 63). New streets were pierced and squares created or widened. The medieval Castle of the Elector was enlarged and used as French custom service. A hospital, named Hospice Joséphine (in honor of Napoléon's wife) was built, as well as a civilian cemetery independent of the religious authorities. The old castle of Martinsburg was

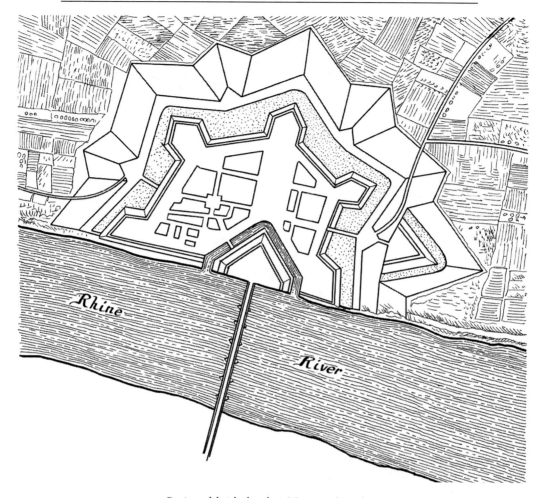

Projected bridgehead at Mayence (1807).
This was a part of the fortifications planned by the French on the right bank of river Rhine. The suburb, named Cassel, was linked to the city of Mayence on the opposite bank by a bridge designed by engineer Saint-Far.

destroyed and its stones used to make a new quay. The architect François-Auguste Cheussey designed and built a new church, Saint Achatius of Zahlbach. The existing fortifications were reinforced, detached works were built, and a wide extension with bridgehead and forts were planned on the opposite river bank. To connect these elements, Saint-Far designed a bridge named *Pont des Victoires* (Bridge of Victories) with imposing and magnificent gatehouses in Empire style. Like many other Napoleonic schemes, the ambitious new urbanization and fortifications of Mayence were not completed.

Jülich

The city of Jülich (Juliers in French) on the Ruhr River is situated west of Cologne in the federal province of North Rhine-Westphalia. Founded by the Romans (Juliacum), the city was taken over by the Franks, and became the capital of a small duchy during

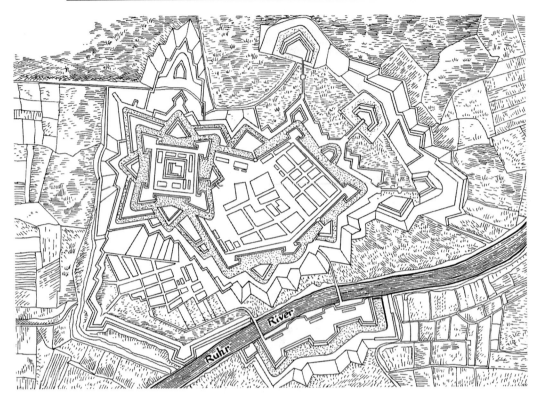

Jülich (Germany)

the Middle Ages. In 1547, Jülich was destroyed by fire, and was shortly after reconstructed according to a plan by the Italian military engineer, architect and urbanist Alessandro Pasqualini (1493–1559). Pasqualini designed a bastioned enceinte around the city and a square citadel with four bastions with ears around the castle of the Grand Duke William V of Jülich, Kleve and Berg. The citadel was eventually visited and inspected by Vauban, who rated it exemplary. Jülich was annexed by France in 1795, and renamed Juliers. The fortifications were modernized on Napoléon's order. A crownwork was built on the opposite bank of the river, and several defensive works and lines were established. By the Treaty of Vienna in 1815, Jülich became a part of the Kingdom of Prussia. A large part of the fortifications of the town were dismantled in 1860. Although greatly damaged during the Second World War, notably by an air raid in November 1944 and by bitter street fighting in February 1945, Jülich has kept a part of its former fortifications, notably the imposing medieval Hexenturm (Witches' Gate) and the bastioned citadel.

Italy

The history of Italy in the Early Modern period was characterized by foreign domination. Following the Italian Wars (1494 to 1559), Italy saw a long period of relative peace, first under Hapsburg Spain (1559 to 1713) and then under Hapsburg Austria (1713 to 1796). During the Napoleonic era, Italy was a client of the French state. As early as 1792, Rev-

4. Napoleonic Fortification Projects 247

Map of Italy and Illyria (c. 1810)

olutionary France annexed the Duchy of Savoy and the city of Nice. Under the Directoire, General Bonaparte's victories resulted in the creation of satellite states: the Cisalpine Republic in the north; the Ligurian Republic around Genoa; the Roman Republic around Rome; and the Napolitan Republic at Naples. During the Second Coalition in 1799, these states were lost, but after the victory of Marengo in June 1800, Napoléon created realms for his marshals and members of his family in 1804. The French then controlled the Papal States, and occupied Venice and the Dalmatian coasts. From 1813, the French domination collapsed under the attacks of Austria and Great Britain, and definitively came to an end in October 1815 by the deposition and execution of the King of Naples, Joachim Murat. The Congress of Vienna (1814) restored the situation of the late 18th century, which was, however, quickly overturned by the incipient movement of Italian unification.

In Italy, in the domain of military architecture, the Napoleonic achievements were characterized by the dismantling of places in the Alps, the enlargement and modernization of ports (La Spezzia, Genoa, Savone), the construction of roads crossing the Alpine passes, and the establishment of forts and arsenals like the Rocca of Anfo, and Alessandria.

Rocca of Anfo

The Rocca of Anfo, situated near Brescia (Lombardia), was a particularly interesting French imperial realization designed and built by engineers Haxo, Liédot, and Chas-

Tower at Rocca of Anfo, Italy.

Rocca of Anfo (c. 1803)
The drawing shows the entrance in the form of an arch of triumph; fortified barracks (1, 2 and 3) for the garrison of 400; artillery redoubts and batteries (4, 5 and 6); a lunet (7) and a two-story circular tower (8).

seloup-Laubat. The construction of this impressive fortified complex started in 1801 after the signing of the Treaty of Luneville. The large mountain fort was composed of eight interconnected terraced units, some partly dug out of the steep Mount Censo at various heights dominating the road between Trento and Brescia over Lake Idro in the Italian province of Brescia. The role of this fortress was to prevent Austrian forces taking French troops, deployed in the Po Valley, from the rear, as had happened in 1796 and 1799. The fortress of Rocca d'Anfo is also interesting as it marks the abandonment of fortified towns in favor of isolated works controlling communication routes. However, the fall of the Empire interrupted the works.

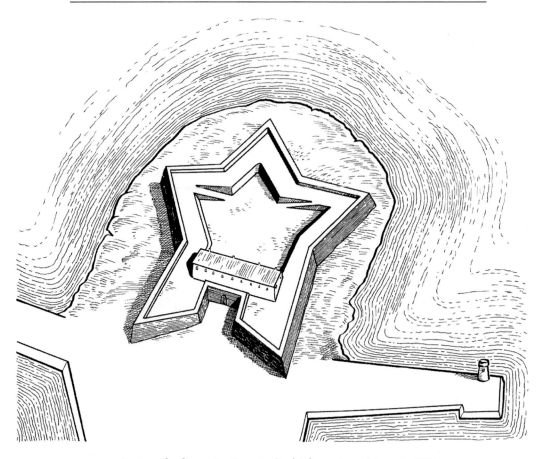

Project of a fort at La Spezzia (Italy) by engineer Viotte in 1810.

La Spezzia

In order to have a maritime base operating in the Mediterranean Sea, together with Toulon and Genoa, Napoléon decided upon the creation of an important arsenal at La Spezzia on the coast of Liguria. In 1808, the French engineer Viotte designed a vast project including the construction of the Saint-Marie coastal fort, six ship-building stocks, two dry docks, workshops, stores and magazines, barracks and administrative buildings. The defense of the port and its arsenal was to be done by the establishment of detached forts placed on the dominating hills and capes in the vicinity. Because of technical problems and financial difficulties, this grandiose scheme was not completed by the French, but after the collapse of the Napoleonic Empire, the Italians carried it out. La Spezzia became one of Italy's most important maritime bases, a trading port, and an important industrial and commercial center in the 19th and 20th centuries.

Alessandria

The city of Alessandria is situated on river Tanaro, southwest of Milan. Founded in 1163, and named by Pope Alexander III, it was an important stronghold, communication

4. Napoleonic Fortification Projects

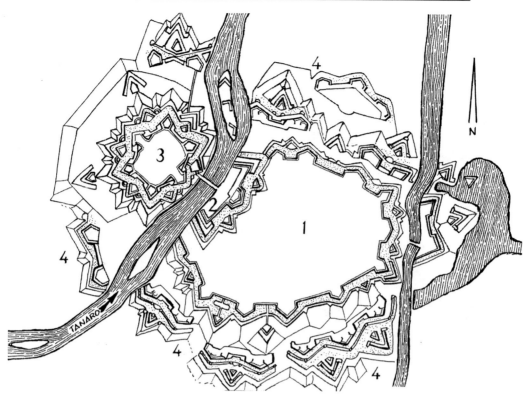

Alexandria, Italy (1808)
1: Military city; 2: bridgehead; 3: citadel; 4: Chasseloup-Laubat's detached fronts.

center and agricultural market. Three miles southeast, the city of Marengo is famous for Napoléon's victory over the Austrians thanks to General Desaix in June 1800. When Piemonte was annexed by France in 1802, Napoléon decided to transform the city into a powerful military arsenal to be used as a rear logistic base against future campaigns against Austria. Work started at once and included the creation of ammunition stores, an arsenal, powder houses, and four military hospitals, while the town was transformed into a vast barracks complex. The existing citadel was modernized, the urban enceinte reinforced and doubled with detached fronts (known as "fronts d'Alexandrie" in French) designed by engineer Chasseloup-Laubat. In 1811, a sluice-bridge was built on the Tanaro River, enabling large floodings around the city. In 1815, Austria demanded and obtained the dismantling of the French fortifications, with the exception of the citadel.

Palmanova

Palmanova is a city entirely new created by the Venetians near Udine in the Po Valley. The city, designed in 1593 by the engineers Vicenzo Scamozzi and Guilio Savorgnano, is remarkable not only for its regular fortifications (nine bastions, ditch, covered way, and two cavaliers on each curtain) but also for the layout of the urban space (with streets radiating outwards from a central square). It represents a splendid example of a realization of the "ideal city" as defined by 16th century Italian engineers and urbanists. In 1806, the

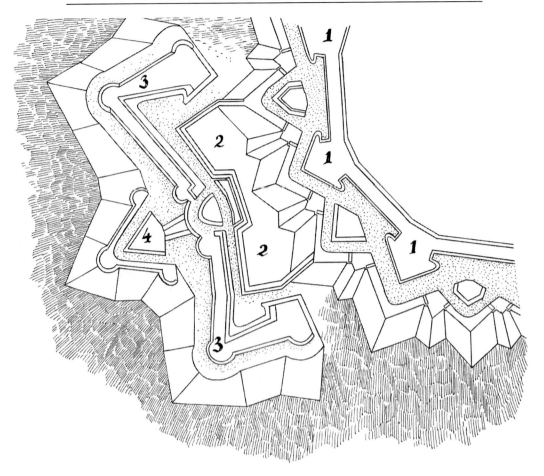

"Alessandria Front" at Palmanova, Italy, by Chasseloup-Laubat (1806)
In the glacis ahead of the classical 16th century Italian bastioned front (1), Chasseloup-Laubat planned to build a wide hornwork (2) which was to be protected by two large casemated counterguards (3) and a demi-lune (4).

inspector of fortifications in Italy, Chasseloup-Laubat, proposed to update the defenses with the addition of three "fronts d'Alexandrie," but this project never reached completion.

Illyrian Provinces

The so-called French *Provinces illyriennes* were territories and islands on the north and east coasts of the Adriatic Sea. The Illyrian Provinces as a political entity were founded by the Treaty of Schönbrunn in 1809 when the Austrian Empire was forced to yield the territories of Carinthia, Carniola, Croatia southwest of the river Sava, Gorizia and Gradisca, and Trieste to the French Empire after the defeat of Wagram. These territories, technically part of France, were integrated with Dalmatia into the Illyrian Provinces, the capital of which was established at Ljubljana (Laibach) in modern Slovenia. The terri-

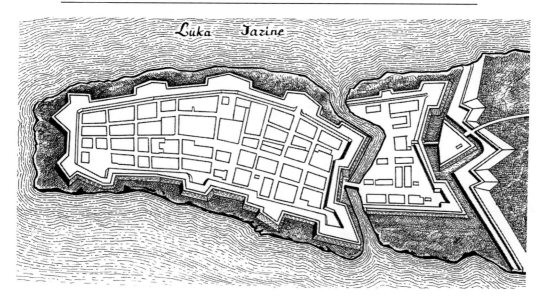

Zara, Dalmatia
Zara (or Zadar in ancient time), capital of Dalmatia, originated from a Roman colony. The city was attacked both by the Venetians and by the armies of the 4th Crusade in 1201. In 1409 it fell under Venetian rule, and was fortified during the Turkish wars in the 16th and 17th centuries. Zara was given to Austria after the fall of Venice in 1797 and the Treaty of Campo Formio. In 1806, the city was a part of Napoléon's Kingdom of Italy until 1809, when it became a part of the Illyrian Provinces. In 1813 it was given back to Austria. The sketch shows the Venetian fortifications built in the 16th century.

tory of the Republic of Ragusa (present day Dubrovnic), which was annexed to France in 1808, was also integrated into the Illyrian Provinces. The French administration introduced civil law (Code civil) across the provinces which were ruled by governor-generals appointed by Napoléon: August de Marmont from October 1809 to January 1811; Henri-Gratien Bertrand from April 1811 until February 1812; Jean-Andoche Junot from February 1811 to July 1813; and Joseph Fouché, who held this post for only one month in August 1813. Since the Treaty of Tilsit from July 1807, the British Navy imposed a blockade of the Adriatic Sea, which brought commerce and shipping to a standstill, a measure most seriously affecting the economy of the Dalmatian ports and cities. In August 1813, Austria declared war on France. Austrian troops invaded the Illyrian Provinces, and Zadar surrendered to Austrian forces after a 34-day siege in December 1813. At Dubrovnik an insurrection expelled the French and a provisional Ragusan administration was established, hoping for the restoration of the free Republic. It was occupied by Austrian troops in September 1813. The British withdrew from the occupied Dalmatian islands in July 1815, following the Battle of Waterloo.

Corfu

Facing the ancient province of Epire (present day Albania), Corfu (also known as Corcyre or Kirkira in Greek), with a length of about 60 km, is one of the largest of the

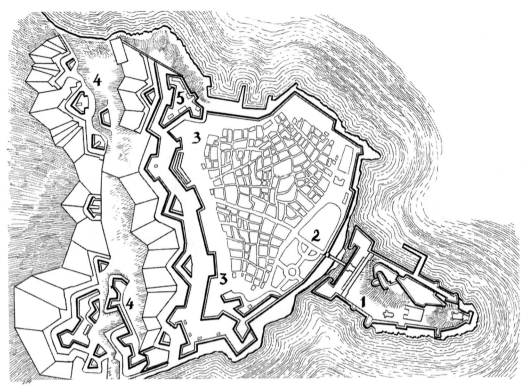

Fortifications of Corfu (c. 1814)
The fortifications of Corfu included the ancient citadel Paleo Frourio (1), the primitive site of the city; it was a cape with two hills crowned by a medieval castle, itself built on an ancient Greek acropolis. In the 16th century a port (Mandraki) for the galleys was established, and the cape was isolated from the mainland by the Venetians, who dug a ditch and built two bastions in the 1550s. The Spianada or esplanade (2), originally a vast empty and flat space used as a glacis, and as a place-of-arms for military training and parades, has now become a large promenade with trees bordered by cafes, restaurants, the palace, administrative buildings and monuments. The city was defended by bastions and walls (3) built by the Venetians after the Turkish attack of 1571, and eventually outer detached works (4) constructed by the French and the British. Both the urban enceinte and the outer works were dismantled after 1864 when Corfu was united with Greece. Today only the Paleo Fourio and the northern citadel, known as Neo Fourio or Fort San-Marco (5), are still preserved.

Ionian Islands with Cephalonia and Zakynthos. It is mentioned in Homer's legendary epic *The Odyssey* as the island of Scheria, the kingdom of the Phaeacians headed by King Alkinous and his daughter, "the white-armed" Nausicaa. The island — referred to as Drepani — also played a role as refuge for Jason and Medea in Apollonius of Rhodes's *The Voyage of the Argonauts*. Corfu was inhabited in the Old Stone Age (about 70,000–40,000 B.C.). Corfu City was founded by Greek Corinthian colonists in the 8th century B.C., and its possession was the cause of the Peloponnesian War in 431 B.C. The island was occupied by the Romans from 229 B.C. to A.D. 336, and by the Byzantines between A.D. 337 and A.D. 1204. After a short Venetian occupation from 1207 to 1214, it was ruled by the Despot of Epirus (1214–1267), by the French House of Anjou (1267–1386), and again by Venice for four centuries, from 1386 until 1797. Because of its strategic position, the island

4. Napoleonic Fortification Projects

Corfu's Old Venetian Fortress

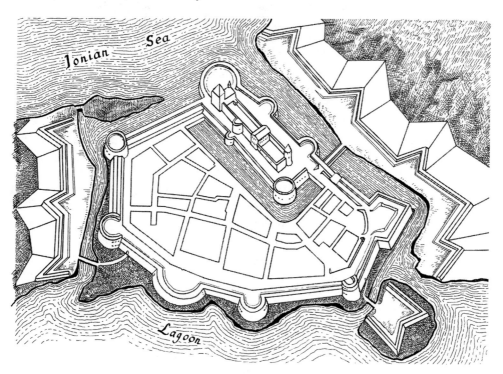

Lefkada, Greece
Originally named Santa Maura, the island of Lefkada is situated south of Corfu off the coast of Cephalonia. The fortifications of the capital of the island, named Lefkada, originated from a castle (Aghia Mavra) built about 1300 by Giovanni Orsini. The island was occupied by the Turks between 1479 and 1684, after which it passed under Venetian domination. After 1797, the island was ruled by the French between 1797 and 1798 and between 1807 and 1809.

was strongly fortified by the Byzantines in the 15th century. Venetian Corfu was the object of several attacks by the Turks in 1431, 1537, 1571 and 1716. After the attack of 1571, the fortifications were modernized, and were constantly improved in the following centuries. In June 1797, after the French had occupied Venice, they shipped a force of about 1,500 headed by the Corsican General Gentil and conquered the island. The first French occupation of Corfu lasted for two years, then they were expelled by a Russo-Turkish army, and a Republic of the Seven Islands was set up. In 1807, however, the Treaty of Tilsit gave Corfu back to France again. During seven years, French domination under the leadership of General Donzelot was marked by the improvement of the fortifications, the embellishment of the city, and the development of agriculture. After Napoléon's fall, according to the Treaty of Paris, the island was administrated by Great Britain from 1814 to 1864, when it became a part of Greece.

The French also dominated for a few years several former Venetian-held islands in the Ionian Sea such as Lefkada.

Malta

Strategically situated in the Mediterranean Sea between southern Italy and Tunisia, the islands of Gozo and Malta were successively occupied by the Phoenicians, Carthaginians, and Romans in ancient times, and in the Middle Ages by the Arabs, Normans, Germans, Angevins, Spaniards, and by the Knights of Saint John of the Hospital of Jerusalem. The origin of the Order of the Knights of Saint John dates back to about 900 years ago in Jerusalem. In those days the trade between Europe and the Middle East was dominated by Italian merchants. The tradesmen of the Italian town of Amalfi obtained permission to erect a chapel and a hospital in Jerusalem, dedicated to Saint John the Baptist and intended for the spiritual and physical needs of merchants and pilgrims. When the Crusades started, the Order of the Hospital of Saint John benefitted greatly. The Hospitallers received newly conquered territories, which had to be defended. Thus the military task of the Order was developed. In 1113 the Order was recognized by the Pope and it became an official military monastic order.

The Order of Saint John of the Hospital was driven away by the Arabs, and later on by the Turks, and had to retreat in the direction of Europe. In 1187 they settled in Acre, in 1291 they were driven to Cyprus, and from there to Rhodes in 1306. Also Rhodes fell into the hands of the Turks in 1522. Eight years later Charles V offered them Malta, Gozo and Tripoli, for the symbolic price of one falcon a year. From then on, the Hospitallers were often referred to as the Order of Malta. After they had resisted a dramatic siege from May to September 1565, the knights transformed their island into a formidable fortress. The new capital, Valletta, was built as a military, well-defendable city, strategically situated on the Sceberras Peninsula between the Grand Harbor and the Marsamxett Harbor. However, the knights lost their popularity amongst the Maltese population in the course of the 17th and 18th centuries.

When Napoléon's fleet (on its way to Egypt) appeared in June 1798 off the harbor of Valletta, initially the Maltese regarded the French as their liberators. Also because a large contingent of the knights was of French origin and did not intend to fight against their compatriots, Napoléon's troops captured Malta without a single blow, and French

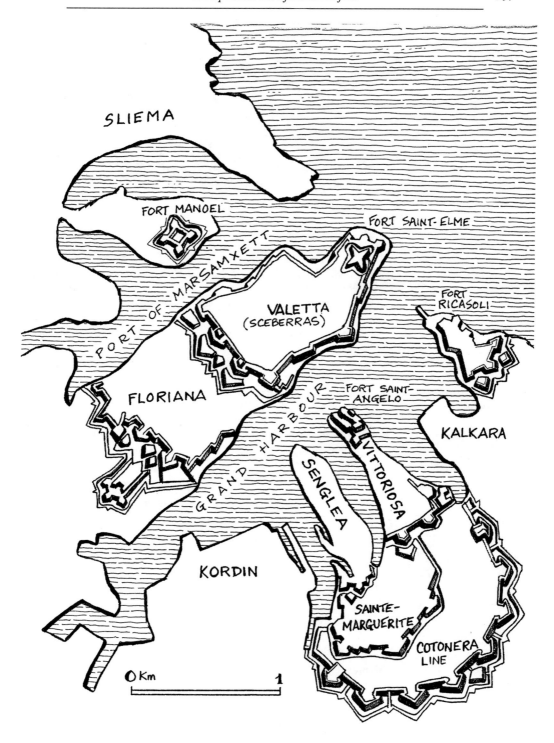

Fortifications of Valetta, Malta
In spite of their formidable fortifications, the Knights Hospitallers of Saint John surrendered the island of Malta without a serious fight in June 1798.

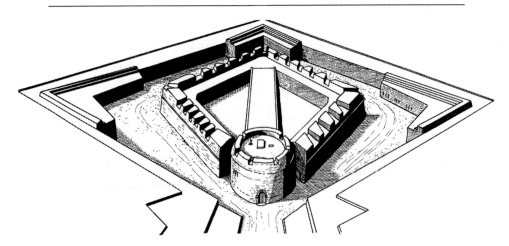

Fort Tigné, Malta (1792)
Built in 1792 by order of the Knights Hospitallers, Fort Tigné is located on the extremity of the Dragut Point in Sliema. Designed by engineer Stephen de Toussard, the fort includes many of Le Michaud d'Arçon's lunettes. It is composed of a round tower in the gorge serving as a bombproof quarter and a lozenge-shaped gun battery, hemmed with a ditch and reverse-fire casemates. The fort proved to be among the only one of the Knights' many redoubts and fortifications to attempt some kind of resistance against Napoleon's forces in 1798; ironically, it was also one of the first strongholds to fall to the local partisan militia during the subsequent insurrection. Garrisoned by British forces from 1805 until their departure in 1979, the fort was consistently armed, refitted and altered to maintain its function as a machine of war. Today, after years of neglect, only the tower, counterscarp and ditch remain visible.

troops occupied the Maltese islands. Already within a couple of days most knights had left Malta, leaving most of their belongings behind. All possessions of the knights' Order were confiscated by the French. Notwithstanding the French promises not to interfere with the church, convents were closed and church treasures were seized. The opposition to the French grew, and already in early September 1798 the first popular Maltese uprising took place. The French withdrew, barricading themselves in Valletta, but totally lost their control over the Maltese countryside. The Maltese rebels could not oust the French on their own and asked the British for support. The first British squadron reached Malta in October 1798. Lord Nelson, the British admiral, decided to force the French to surrender by means of a total blockade. In the meantime the Maltese resistance attempted to take the strongly fortified Valletta, but they did not succeed. The blockade lasted until September 1800, when the weakened French garrison surrendered. At the Treaty of Amiens in 1802 it was decided that the island was to be restored to the Knights of the Hospital of Saint John and Malta, but the Maltese population were not very keen on that. They requested the British to stay in Malta, and so it happened. Malta was to be ruled as a British crown colony until total independence was granted in 1974.

Military Roads and Canals

The conquests of the Revolution, Consulate and Empire required new infrastructures adapted to a continental scale. Napoléon, like the ancient Roman emperors, was

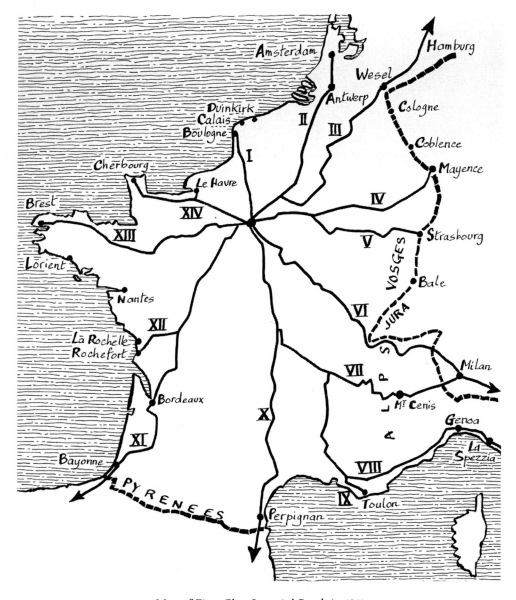

Map of First-Class Imperial Roads in 1811

Road No. I went from Paris to Boulogne, Calais and Dunkirk. Road No. II connected Paris to Amsterdam via Brussels and Antwerp. Road No. III went to Hamburg via Liège, Wezel, Munster and Bremen. Road No. IV linked Paris to Mayence and continued to Prussia and Berlin. Road No. V went from Paris to Strasbourg and continued into central Germany. Road No. VI went from Paris to Milan via the Simplon Pass. Road No. VII connected Paris to Milan and Turin via the Mont-Cenis Pass and continued in northern Italy. Road No. VIII went from Paris to Rome passing by Marseille, Nice, Genoa, La Spezzia and Florence. The sub-branch No. IX connected Toulon to Marseille. The Eastern Road, No. X went to Spain, Barcelone passing by Perpignan. The Western Road, No. XI linked Paris to Spain passing by Bayonne. The sub-branch No. XII connected to the military port of Rochefort and La Rochelle. Road No. XIII went to Brest, and Road No. XIV to Cherbourg. To these fourteen First-Class roads were added many other secondary roads serving towns and fortresses of lesser importance, such as Road 20 and Road 21 going to Cologne and Coblence in Germany, or Routes 18 and 27 leading respectively to Ostende (Belgium) and Lorient (Britanny).

well aware that swift communication was a factor of unification for his imperial territories. He therefore paid a great deal of attention to the development of a road network, necessary for the quick transmission of dispatches and orders, for the rapid deployment of his armies in campaign, and for the development of economic and commercial activities. This important task was entrusted to civilian engineers from the administration of *Ponts et Chaussées* (Bridges and Roads) such as Chaptal, Cretet, Montalivet and Molé. The Emperor took many measures to develop and facilitate the construction, maintenance, repair, security, markings and circulation on the French roads. Important highways, divided into three classes, radiated from Paris in the directions of the great cities, ports and arsenals as much in France as in the foreign conquered territories. The most spectacular realizations were the roads in the Alps, which were created in order to enable the passage of armies with horse-drawn wagons and artillery. For example, the Simplon

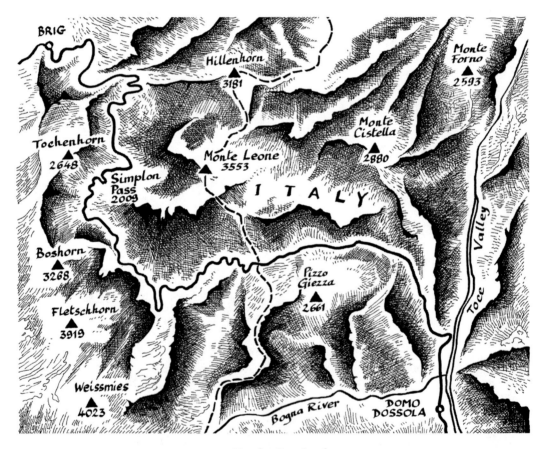

Simplon Pass Road
This road between Brig and Domo d'Ossola (the mountainous part of the strategic highway No. VI connecting Paris to Milan via the Swiss canton of Valais) was built between 1800 and 1807 by Chief-Engineer Nicolas Céard. The connection between France and Italy was so important to Napoléon that he had forced the neutral Swiss to yield their canton of Valais to France. The Simplon Pass Road, a great technical achievement, was about 8 m wide, had a slope of maximum 10 per cent, and included six tunnels pierced in the rocks, several bridges, and two fortified strongholds placed at Brig and Sion.

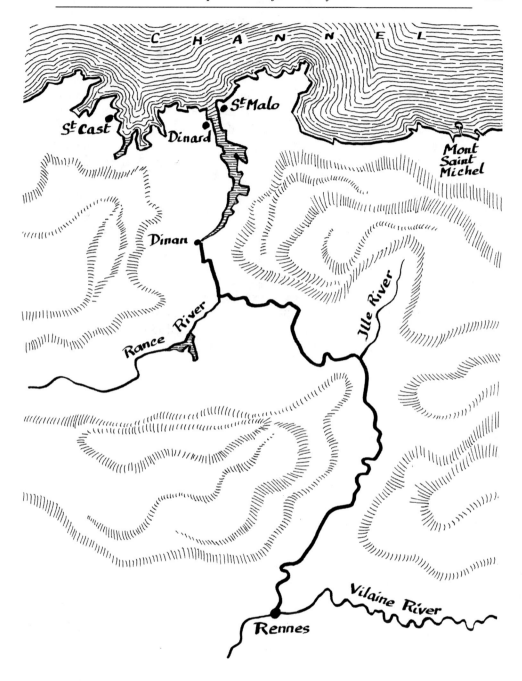

Ille and Rance Canal
This canal, dug in Britanny from the Vilaine River in Rennes to the Rance estuary near Dinan, was planned in October 1784. Work, spurred by the British threat in the Channel, started in February 1804. Completed by the end 1832, it connected Saint-Malo (on the English Channel) to Rennes, and from there to La Roche-Bernard (on the Atlantic Ocean) via River Vilaine. It had a length of about 85 km, and included 48 locks and 260 bridges. The traffic enabled the economic development of the province.

Pass Road, which went from Paris to Milan via the Swiss canton of Valais, was built from 1800 to 1807. The Mont-Cenis Road was established in 1803 and completed in 1806 by engineer Dausse. The Corniche Road along the Côte d'Azur (French Riviera) was completed in 1811. The road between Grenoble and Briançon, that of the Mont-Genèvre, and that of the Cabre Pass are other spectacular highways created or improved during the Napoleonic time.

Because the British fleets made the seas unsafe and blocked the French ports many cities could be supplied only by inland waterways. For this purpose, Napoléon launched a grandiose program of canals for inland navigation. However because of lack of budget caused by the wars, only 204 km were open for traffic between 1800 and 1814.

In Britanny the English Channel was linked to the Atlantic Ocean by a north-south strategic canal running via the Rivers Rance, Ille and Vilaine. Another strategic canal, dug between 1811 and 1842, crossed Britanny from Nantes in the east to Brest in the west. This made use of several small canalized rivers like the Erdre, Isac, Oust, Blavet, Hyère and Aulne. It was 360 kilometers long and had 237 locks. In eastern France, the canal Napoléon connected River Rhône to the Rhine via River Doubs. The canal of Saint-Quentin — with an underground section of 5 km — permitted to connect Paris to Anwerp. In 1809 work started on the Canal de Bourgogne, which was eventually to link Paris to the Mediterranean Sea. Many other ambitious projects planned and launched by Napoléon were only carried out and completed later in the 19th century. Inland navigation remained an important means of military and economic communication, but it drastically declined when the railroad was developed in the 1860s.

The Heritage of the Empire

Humanly speaking, the casualties caused by ten years of almost continuous wars are estimated to about one million dead. This figure is often contested but it is true that the demographical curve decreased after the Napoleonic period. Socially, the fall of Napoléon and the monarchic restoration after 1815 did not prevent the ascension of the bourgeoisie, the principal beneficiary of the French Révolution. Politically, France lost all the territories conquered by Napoléon, notably the left bank of the Rhine, but the most severe consequence of the imperial fall was the fact that France was, for decades, isolated, weakened and held in profound suspicion by the rest of Europe as a factor of trouble and a source of danger for the whole continent.

On the matter of fortification, the collapse of 1815 did not give time to the French engineers to complete the numerous projects designed by the Revolution, the Consulate and the Empire. However, many plans were carried out during the 19th century, as much in France as abroad. Certain ambitious Napoleonic projects were completed by some of the European nations (e.g., Den Helder in the Netherlands and La Spezzia in the Italian Piemonte). In France, as we have seen, several Napoleonic plans were carried out by the Restoration, the Monarchy of July, the Second Republic and the Second Empire. The great dike of Cherbourg was completed in 1853, and the forts intended to defend the port terminated by 1858. The construction of fortifications and maritime facilities were continued until the inauguration of the port of Cherbourg in 1858 by Napoléon III. Fort Boyard was finished about 1859, the enceinte of Le Palais on Belle-Isle in 1870. The occu-

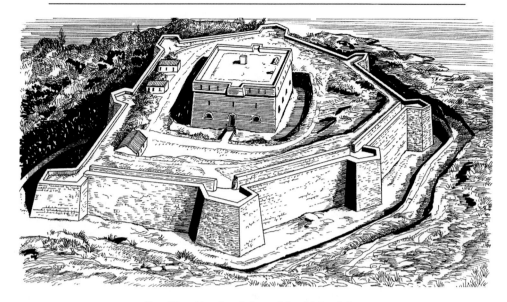

Fort Napoléon Les Saintes Island Martinique
Fort Napoléon was constructed in place of a previous 17th century work (then named Fort Louis) that was destroyed during a British attack in 1809. Planned under the reign of Napoléon I, the fort was built between 1844 and 1867 on the small Les Saintes Island between Martinique and Guadeloupe. It carries the name of the Emperor's nephew, Napoleon III. Situated on top of a 109 m high hill dominating a convenient enchorage and a beautiful bay, it is composed of a rectangular tour modèle barracks hemmed by a ditch, a bastioned enceinte and a dry outer ditch. The fort could accommodate a garrison of about 200 soldiers. At the beginning of the 20th century the fort was used as a prison. Restored in 1973, it houses today a museum and an exotic garden open to the public.

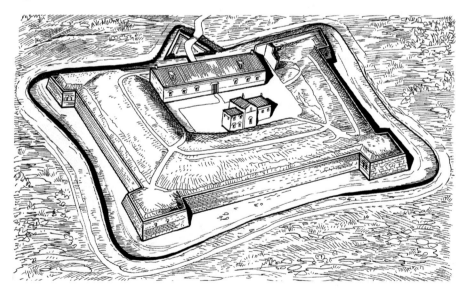

Fort Hoëdic Island, Morbihan
Situated between Belle-Ile and the continent, a fort on the small island of Hoëdic was planned by Napoléon I. As with many other projects, this was later carried out.

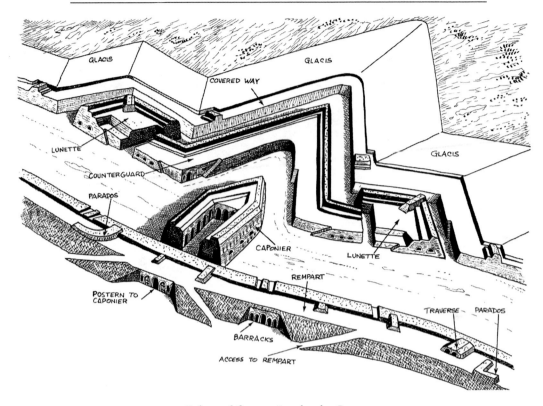

*Polygonal front at Ingolstadt, Germany
The influence of Montalembert is clear.*

pation of Paris in 1814 and 1815 by the Allies had been felt as a humiliation, and the idea of fortifying the capital of France (deprived of defense since the reign of Louis XIV), was reactivated, resulting in the construction of a large bastioned wall (known as *Enceinte de Thiers*) and a belt of detached forts built in the 1840s.

Compared to the huge number of 17th century fortresses left behind by Vauban and Louis XIV, Napoléon's legacy is very limited, but the Emperor and his engineers

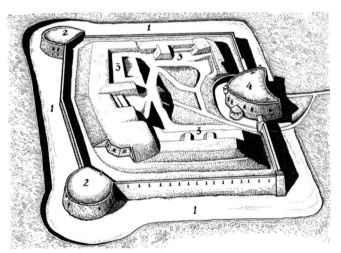

*Fort Oberer Kuhberg, Ulm
Fort Oberer Kuhberg was built from 1842 to 1857 to protect the city of Ulm. A typical German 19th-century polygonal fortress, it included a ditch (1), caponiers at the front (2), open batteries (3), and a réduit (4) in the gorge. From November 1933 until July 1935 it was used by the Nazis as a concentration camp for a total of 800 male political prisoners.*

were short of time, and only a small part of the military budget was allotted to fortifications. In spite of this, the impact of Napoleonic fortification, particularly its innovative aspect, was felt all over Europe in the 19th century. French Napoleonic methods influenced European nations wishing to protect their frontiers with modern defenses, and German engineers developed new systems owing much to Montalembert's theories with the addition of other novelties based on Arçon's lunet, Carnot's scarp profile and Haxo casemates, for example.

Appendix

French Republican Calendar

The French Republican Calendar or French Revolutionary Calendar was a calendar proposed during the French Revolution; it was used by the French government for about 12 years from late 1793 to 1805, and for 18 days in 1871 in Paris.

Years appeared in writing as Roman numerals, starting on September 22, 1792, the beginning of the Republican Era—the day the French First Republic was proclaimed, one day after the Convention abolished the monarchy. As a result, Roman Numeral I indicates the first year of the republic; that is, the year before the calendar actually came into use. The first day of each year was that of the autumnal equinox. The Republican Revolutionary year had twelve months, each divided into three ten-day weeks called *décades*. The tenth day, named *décadi*, replaced Sunday as the day of rest and festivity. The five or six extra days needed to approximate the actual year were placed after the months at the end of each year. Each day was divided into ten hours, each hour into 100 decimal minutes and each decimal minute had 100 decimal seconds. Clocks were manufactured to display this decimal time. As can be expected, the Revolutionary Calendar did not catch on and mandatory use was officially suspended on April 7, 1795, although some cities continued to use decimal time as late as 1801. Napoléon finally abolished the calendar with effect from January 1, 1806 (the day after 10 Nivôse Year XIV), a little over twelve years after its introduction. The Calendar was used again during the brief Paris Commune, May 6–23, 1871 (16 Floréal–3 Prairial An LXXIX) to mark the continuity of the spirit of the 1789 Revolution.

The Revolutionary Year, divided into four seasons, started in autumn and each month was given a poetic name based on nature as follows.

Autumn

Vendémiaire (from Latin vindemia, "grape harvest") started on September 22, 23 or 24.

Brumaire (from French brume, "fog") started on October 22, 23 or 24.

Frimaire (From French frimas, "frost") started on November 21, 22 or 23.

Winter

Nivôse (from Latin nivosus, "snowy") started on December 21, 22 or 23.
Pluviôse (from Latin pluvius, "rainy") started on January 20, 21 or 22.
Ventôse (from Latin ventosus, "windy") started on February 19, 20 or 21.

Spring

Germinal (from Latin germen, "germination") started on March 20 or 21.
Floréal (from Latin flos, "flower") started on April 20 or 21.
Prairial (from French prairie, "pasture" or "meadow") started on May 20 or 21.

Summer

Messidor (from Latin messis, "harvest") started on June 19 or 20.
Thermidor (from Greek thermon, "summer heat") started on July 19 or 20.
Fructidor (from Latin fructus, "fruit") started on August 18 or 19.

Bibliography

Association des Amis de la Maison Vauban. *Vauban, sa vie, son œuvre*. Saint-Léger-Vauban, 1984.
Bainville, Jacques. *Histoire de France*, Vol. 2: *1789–1919*. Paris: Editions Plon, 1933.
_____. *Napoléon*. Paris: Fayard Editions, 1931.
Barde, Yves. *Histoire de la Fortification en France*. Paris: Presses Universitaires de France (PUF), 1996.
Blanchard, Anne. *Vauban*. Paris: Editions Fayard, 1996.
Bonaparte, Napoléon. *Notes sur la fortification dictées à Sainte-Hélène*. Paris: Editions Berger-Levrault, 1897.
Bornecque, Robert. *La France de Vauban*. Arthaud, 1984.
Calvet, Henri. *Napoléon*. Paris: Presses Universitaires de France (PUF), 1960.
Camon, Hubert. *La Fortification dans la Guerre Napoléonienne*. Paris: Editions Berger-Levrault, 1914.
Un Canal, des Canaux. Paris: Caisse Nationale des Monuments Historiques, 1986.
Carpentier, Jean, and François Lebrun. *Histoire de France*. Paris: Editions du Seuil, 1987.
Casado, Antonio. *Castillos y Fortaleza*. Junta de Comunidades de Castilla-La Mancha, 1989.
Chandler, David. *The Campaigns of Napoléon*. London: Weidenfeld & Nicolson, 1967.
Chazette, Alain, Nicolas Faucherre, and Philippe Prost. *Les Fortifications du Littoral La Bretagne Sud*. Chauray: Editions Patrimoines et Médias, 1998.
Choury, M. *Les Grognards de Napoléon*. Paris: Editions Perrin, 1968.
Colin, J. *L'Education Militaire de Napoléon*. Paris: Chapelot Editions, 1901.
Desquesnes, Rémy, René Faille, Nicolas Faucherre, and Philippe Prost. *Les Fortifications du Littoral La Charente Maritime*. Chauray: Editions Patrimoines et Médias, 1993.
Dropsy, Christian. *Les Fortifications de Metz et de Thionville*. Metz: Published by the author, 1995.
Faucherre, Nicolas. *Places fortes, bastion du pouvoir*. Paris: Editions Rempart, 1986.
Foucart, Bruno. *La France à l'époque Napoléonienne* (38 essays). Paris: Armand Colin, 1970.
Fourcroy de Ramecourt, M., Nyon, aîné, Clousier. *Mémoires sur la Fortification Perpendiculaire par plusieurs officiers du corps royal du Génie*. Paris, 1786.
Funcken, Liliane, and Fred Funcken. *Historische Uniformen Napoleonische Zeit, 18. Und 19. Jahrhundert*. Munich: Orbis Verlag, 1997.
Gille, Bertrand. *Les Ingénieurs de la Renaissance*. Paris: Editions Hermann, 1964.
Gils, Robert. *Bevestigd Verleden*. Uitgeverij De Krijger (place and date unknown).
Hamlyn, Paul. *The Life and Time of Napoleon*. Feltham, UK: Hamlyn Pub. Group, 1968.
Head, Michael. *French Napoleonic Artillery*. London: Almark Publishing, 1970.
Kober, Pascal, and Patrick Gendey. *Citadelles d'Altitude*. Grenoble: Editions Didier Richard, 1995.
Lefebvre, Georges. *Napoléon*. Paris: Presses Universitaires de France, 1941.
Le Halle, Guy. *Précis de Fortification*. Paris: PVC Editions, 1983.
Lendy, August Frederick. *Treatise on Fortifications or Lectures delivered to Officers reading for the Staff*. London: W. Mitchell Stationer, Printer, Engraver and Bookbinder, 1862.
Lepage, Jean-Denis. *Vestingen en Schansen in Groningen*. Utrecht: Uitgeverij Matrijs, 1994.
Lombaerde, Piet, et al. *Antwerpen tijdens het Franse Keizerrijk 1804–1814*. Antwerp: Simon Stevinstichting, 1989.
Lucas-Debreton, J. *Soldats de Napoléon*. Paris: Editions Tallendier, 1977.
Méthivier, Henri. *Louis XIV*. Paris: Presse Universitaire de France, 1950.
Ministère de la Défense/SGA. *Sentinelles de Pierre, Forts et Citadelles sur les frontières de France*. Paris: Editions d'Art Somogy, 1996.

Minola, Mauro, and Beppe Ronco. *Fortificazioni di montagna Dal Gran S. Bernardo al Tonale.* Varese: Edizioni Macchione, 1999.
Miquel, Pierre. *Histoire de la France.* Paris: Editions Arthème Fayart, 1976.
Mohr, A.H. *Vestingbouwkundige Termen.* Zutphen: Stichting Menno van Coehoorn, 1983.
Montalembert, Marc-René. *La fortification perpendiculaire, ou Essai sur plusieurs manières de fortifier la ligne droite, le triangle, le quarré, et tous les polygones, de quelqu'étendue qu'en soient les côtés, en donnant à leur défense une direction perpendiculaire.* 10 vols. Paris, 1776–1795.
Musée des plans-reliefs. *Forts du littoral.* Paris: Published by Musée des plans-reliefs, 1989.
Neumann, Hartwig. *Festungsbaukunst und Festungsbautechnik.* Bonn: Bernard & Graefe Verlag, 1988.
North, René. *Military Uniforms 1686–1918.* New York: Grosser & Dunlap, 1970.
Parent, Michel, and Jacques Verroust. *Vauban.* Paris: Editions Jacques Fréal, 1971.
Pommier, Pascal. *Pierres de mer.* Paris: Editions Addim, 1996.
Poppema, Simon, and Jean-Denis Lepage. *Historische verdedigingswerken.* Amsterdam: Stichting Open Monumentendag, 1995.
Prost, Philippe. *Les Forteresses de l'Empire.* Paris: Edition du Moniteur, 1991.
Quimby, R.S. *The Background of Napoleonic Warfare.* Seelay Service, 1977.
Reverdy, Georges. *Histoire des Routes en France.* Paris: Presses Universitaires de France, 1995.
Robinet de Clery, Adrien. *Histoire de France 1789–1963.* Munich: Max Hueber Verlag, 1965.
Rocolle, Pierre. *2000 Ans de Fortification Francaise.* 2 vols. Paris: Editions Charles Lavauzelle, 1989.
Sailhan, Pierre. *La Fortification, Histoire et Dictionnaire.* Paris: Editions Tallandier, 1991.
Six, Georges. *Les Généraux de la Révolution et de l'Empire.* Paris: Editions Payot, 1947.
Standvastige Monumenten Europese Kastelen en Forten vanuit de lucht. Rijswijk: Uitgeverij Elmar BV, 2003.
Stichting, Menno van Coehoorn. *Terminologie Verdedigingswerken.* Utrecht, 1999.
Tarlé, Eugène. *La Campagne de Russie.* Paris: Editions de la Nouvelle Revue Française, 1940.
Taton, René. *L'Ecole Royale du Génie de Mézières.* Paris: Editions Hermann, 1964.
Treu, Herman, and Jaap Sneep. *Vesting Vier Eeuwen Vestingbow in Nederland.* Zutphen: Stichting Menno van Coehoorn/Walburg Press, 1982.
Truttmann, Philippe. *Fortification, architecture et urbanisme aux XVIIème et XVIIIème siècles.* Thionville: Service Culturel de la Ville de Thionville, 1976.
Traité de Fortifications. Unpublished handwritten anonymous manuscript, probably by 19th century military teacher.
Tulard, Jean. *Le Mythe de Napoléon.* Paris: Editions Armand Colin, 1971.
———. *Napoléon ou le Mythe du Sauveur.* Paris: Editions Fayard, 1977.
Viollet-le-Duc, Eugène. *Histoire d'une Forteresse.* Paris: Editions Berger-Levrault, 1874.
Wright, G.D. *Napoleon and Europe.* Harlow, UK: Longman Group, 1984.

Index

Abeltjeshuis, line of 245, 246
Acadia 98, 101
Aërostiere Company 140
Age of Enlightenment 14, 127
Aix Island 73, 76, 77, 165, 202, 205
Alessandria 148, 150, 181, 250; citadel of 178; front 252
Alexander, fort 78
Alexander I of Russia 26, 31, 39, 46
Almeida, siege of 159, 160
Ambleteuse 188
American War of Independence 7
Ammunitions 120, 125, 129
Amsterdam 231, 232
Antwerp 224, 225, 226
Arc de Triomphe 27
Arsenals 176–183
Artigues, fort of 222
Artillery 117–130; emplacements 130–135; trajectories 121
Asfeld, bridge of 89, 91
Austerlitz, battle of 26, 27, 30, 127
Avignon Papal Palace 182

Baboeuf, Gracchus 16
Babouvism 16
Badajoz, siege of 161
Balloon 140, 174
Banque de France 32
Barbette 130, 131
Barras, Paul 16, 19
Bastille 15, 16, 183
Bastion 46; fortification 46–48; front 47
Battle of the Nations 40
Bayonets 51
Beauharnais, Eugène de 32

Beauharnais, Joséphine de 20, 31
Beauséjour, fort 100
Belidor, Bernard 57, 119
Belle-Isle 193, 194, 195, 262
Beresina River 47, 149
Berg op Zoom 83
Bertrand, Henri 142
Beverwijk, line of 239
Biens Nationaux 9, 25, 43
Biloxi 97
Bitche 86, 87
Blockhouse 168, 169, 170
Bomb 125
Bonaparte, Carlo 17
Bonaparte, Caroline 32
Bonaparte, Elisa 32
Bonaparte, Jerome 32
Bonaparte, Joseph 17, 28
Bonaparte, Louis-Napoléon 223, 224
Bonaparte, Lucien 17, 21
Bonaparte, Napoléon: ambition in America 24; artilleryman 17, 19; character and personality 17, 18, 19, 20; coronation 24, 25; early aging 42; exile and death 44; interests 19; last days in France 205; reformist 23, 24, 33, 34; relationship with armies 19, 34, 35; relationship with France 18, 32; and religion 23; tomb in Invalides 45; at Toulon 14, 19, 158; view on Revolution 18; wives and mistresses 31
Borodino, battle of 39
Boulogne 25, 26, 187, 188
Bourbon, fort 110
Bourtange 237, 238
Bousmard, Henri Jean 142, 143, 151

Boyard, fort 206–210, 262
Brest 196, 197, 198
Briançon 88–94
Brienne, Artillery School of 25
Brumaire 21
Buchotte, Nicolas 55, 190
Buonaparte, Nabulione see Bonaparte, Napoleon

Cachin, Francois 143
Cadoudal, Georges 25
Caffarelli-Dufalga, Louis 143
Cajuns 98
Calais 184, 185, 186
Cambaceres, Jean-Jacques 24
Camp retranché 72, 85, 234
Campo Formio, treaty of 20, 253
Canals 258, 250, 260
Caponier 48, 67, 70, 71
Carbines 125
Carillon, fort 109
Carnot, Lazare 13, 61, 75, 143, 144–149; 146, 147, 265
Carronade 129
Casemate 69, 132, 134
Catholic Church 17
Cavalier 46
Cavalryman 37
Cavendish, fort 117
Central, fort 190
Chappe, Claude 175
Charles VIII 46
Charles X 8, 45, 75
Chartres, fort of 108
Chasseloup-Laubat, François de 148–151, 251, 252
Château-Thierry 179
Cherbourg 69, 95, 96, 97, 189, 262
Chiaramonti, Niccolo 31
Chouans 14, 199, 200, 201

271

Circular system 74
Circumvallation 82
Citadel 179, 180
Citoyen Louis Capet 11
Clermont 173, 174
Cluny, abbey of 180
Code Civil 24
Coehoorn, Baron Menno van 62, 64, 85, 240
Colbert, Jean-Baptiste 106, 201, 204, 227
Colle Noire, fort of the 81
Colonial fortifications 97–112
Colonne de la Grande Armée 188
Comité Central des Fortifications 138, 158
Committee of Public Safety 12, 75, 144
Communication Y 89
Concordat of 1801 23
Confederation of the Rhine 26, 241
Consulat 21–25
Continental System 26, 28
Corday, Charlotte 13
Corfu 253, 254
Cormontaigne, Louis 56, 57, 58, 59
Corneille, Pierre 18
Corvette 27
Counterguard 48
Countermine 163, 169, 236
Countervallation 82
Covered way 47
Croix des Signaux, fort of the 219, 220
Crownwork 48
Cugnot, Nicolas 55, 63, 173, 174
Cult of Reason 14

Danton, Georges, Jacques 11
Danzig, siege of 143, 159
Dauphin, fort 97, 100
David, Louis 114
Declaration of the Rights of Man and of the Citizen 9
Decree of Berlin 26
Decree of Milan 26
De Leethe, post of 236
Delfzijl 239
Delgrès, Louis 120
Demi-lune 47
Den Helder 232–234, 262
De Schans, fort 235
Directoire 16

Dode de la Brunerie, Guillaume 151
Dos de Mayo 37
Dufalga, fort 234
Dugommier, fort 233
Duke of Enghien 25
Duke of Reichstadt 31, 45
Dumouriez, Charles 11, 12
Duquesnes, fort 107

Eblé, Jean-Baptiste 151
Echauguette 49
Ecole de Mézières 54, 55, 138
Ecole des Ponts et Chaussées 141
Ecole Militaire 25
Ecole Normale Supérieure 23
Ecole Polytechnique 58, 141
Edict of Nantes, revokation of 51
Egypt, campaign of 20
Elba Island 42, 142
Embrasure 130, 131
Emigrés 8, 9, 23, 25
Emmerschans 238
Enet, fort of 210, 211
Engineer Corps 135–141
Entrenched camp 84, 85
Equals' Conspiracy 16
Equipment 126
Execution of Louis XVI 11
Exilles, fort of 177
Eylau, battle of 127

Farewell of Fontainebleau 42
Fenestrelles, fort of 177
Fermiers Généraux' Wall 191, 192
First Republic 11
Five Monkeys 17
Flanking 69
Flèche 48
Fleury, André, Hercule, Cardinal of 13
Fontainebleau, treaty of 42
Fontenoy, battle of 13
Fortress carriages 128, 129
Fouché, Joseph 24, 25, 40, 261
Fouquet, Nicolas 193
Franc Germinal 31
Francis II of Austria 39
Frederick II of Prussia 5, 13
French Napoleonic Army 34–38
Fulton, Robert 182
Fusil modèle 1777 Corrigé An IX 35, 126

Garde Nationale 8, 10
Génie 135–141
Géricault, Théodore 114
Girondists 12
Givet 92, 157
Glacis 47
Goya y Lucientes, Francisco de 29
Grande Peur 8
Great Fear 8
Gribeauval, Jean-Baptiste 119–126
Gribeauval artillery system 115, 119–126
Grognards 37
Groningen 240
Gros, Antoine 114
Grumblers 37
Guibert, Jacques-Antoine 59, 60, 61
Guillotin, Joseph 12
Guillotine 12
Gun carriage 115
Gun crew 116
Gun-port 130

Haiti 97
Haxo, François-Benoit 135, 152, 153
Haxo Casemate 133, 134, 135, 265
Hoche, Lazare 14
Hoëdic Island 263
Hohenlinden, battle of 22
Hot shot 129, 130
Howitzer 120
Hundred Days 43, 44

Ille and Rance canal 261
Imperial court 32
Imperial fort 230
Imperial guard 36
Imperial roads 259
Imperial style 114
Industrial Revolution 7
Ingres, Jean-Auguste 32
Inundation 49

Jacobin 25
Jemmapes, battle of 11
Jena, battle of 26
Jourdan, Jean-Baptiste 14
Jülich 245, 246
Julienne de Belair, Pierre-Alexandre 153
Juliers 245, 246
July 14, 1789 7

Index

Katshaarschans 240
Kellerman, François 11, 15
Krakow 80
Kufstein, castle of 68

Lafayette, Gilbert le Motier Marquis of 8
Lamalgue, fort 221
La Roche-sur-Yon 199, 200, 201
Lasalle, fort 233
La Spezzia 250, 262
Law, John 5
Ledoux, Claude-Nicolas 183
Lefkada 255
Légion d'Honneur 24
Le Havre 94, 95
Leipzig, battle of 40
Le Michaud d'Arçon, Jean 154, 155, 156
Les Rousses, fort of 213, 214
Leszczinska, Maria 5
Liberté, Egalité, Fraternité 9
Liédot, fort 205
Liefkenshoek, fort 227
Lillo, fort 225
Louis XIV 5, 50, 135
Louis XV 5
Louis XVI 6
Louis XVII 14, 42
Louis XVIII 42, 42, 45
Louis Philippe 45, 189
Louisbourg 103, 104
Louisiana Purchase 24
Lunette 47, 49, 232
Lunette of Arçon 154, 155, 157, 214, 265
Luneville, Treaty of 22
Lycée 23, 202

Malet, Claude François de 39
Malta 256, 257, 258
Mandar, Charles-François 153
Marat, Jean-Paul 13
Marengo, battle of 22
Maresco, Armand Samuel 156, 196, 205, 206
Marie Antoinette 7, 14, 31
Marie Louise of Austria 31, 42
Marie Louises 40, 41
Martello tower 166, 167, 168
Martini, Giorgio di 71
Marxism 16
Mayence 243, 244
Metz 87, 90
Military roads 258, 259, 260

Miner 139
Minou, fort of 197
Mirabeau, Honoré 7
Mobile 105, 106
Modern French System 58, 59
Mont Dauphin, fortress of 214, 215
Montagnards 11, 12
Montalembert, Marc-René 61–77
Montbarrey, fort of 199
Montreal 103
Mortar 121, 122
Moscow 30
Murat, Joachim 29, 40
Muzzle loading 116, 118
Myth Vauban 55

Napoleon I *see* Bonaparte, Napoleon
Napoleon II 31, 42
Napoleon III 45, 189
Napoleon battery 190
Napoleon, fort 229, 231
Napoleonic style 114, 115
Napoleonic warfare 2, 38
National Constituent Assembly 7, 8
National Convention 11, 16
National Goods 9, 25, 43
Naval gun 127
Necker, Jacques 7
Neerwinden, battle of 12
New Holland Water Line 79
New Orleans 106, 107
Ney, Michel 42, 43, 160
Nieuwe Hollandse Waterlinie 79
Nouvelle-Orléans 106, 107

Oberer Kuhberg, fort 264
Oléron Island 211, 212
Optical telegraph 175
Ordre mixte 61
Organisation Todt 187, 198
Orillon 46
Ouiatenon, fort 99, 100

Palma Nova 251, 252
Papal palace in Avignon 182
Paris 183, 184, 264; treaty of 44
Pasqualini, Alessandro 246
Perpendicular fortification 62
Pertuis 202
Peschiera 178
Petit Caporal 38

Philippe of Orleans 5, 107
Pioneer 139
Pitt, fort 108
Pius VII, Pope 23, 30
Plans reliefs 171, 172
Polygonal fortification 67, 264
Pommets, fort of 219, 220
Pompadour, Marquise of 5
Pondichery 112–113
Pontivy 199, 200
Portalet, fort of 216
Postern 48
Pressburg, treaty of 26

Quebec 101, 102
Querqueville, fort of 191

Rade, fort of 203, 204
Rammekens, fort 229
Rampart 72
Randouillet, fort of the 89, 93
Red-hot shot 129
Redoubt 29
Redoute modèle 163, 164
Reign of Terror 13, 14
Relief-map 171, 172
Republic of Virtue 14, 15
Republique Batave 223
Revolutionary Calender 267
Rifled artillery 79, 149, 168
Robespierre, Maximilien 11, 13, 14
Rocca of Anfo 248, 249
Romanov, Anna 31
Rousseau, Jean-Jacques 6, 18
Royaume de Hollande 223
Russia, campaign of 38–40

Saint Charles, fort 111, 112
Saint Helena Island 44
Saint Marcouf, fort 189, 190, 192, 193
Salettes, fort of the 89, 91
Saliceti, Antoine 19
Salient 47
Sans culotte 13
Sappers 136, 139, 140
Saumonards, fort of the 212
Schönbrunn, treaty of 31, 252
Second Polish War 39
Séré de Rivières, Raymond, Adolphe 81
Serment du Jeu de Paume 7
Seven Years' War 6
Siege warfare 2, 82–84, 158–163

Sieyes, Emmanuel-Joseph 7, 17, 21, 22
Simon, Antoine 14
Simplon Pass Road 260
Steam automobile 172, 173
Steamboat 174
Stevin, Simon 185, 186
Strasbourg 215, 216
Submarine 174
Supreme Being 14
Surrender with honor 83

Talleyrand-Périgord, Charles de 16, 17, 42
Tenaille 48
Tenailled fortification 62, 63, 64, 65, 145
Tennis Hall Oath 8
Terreur 13
Tetes, fort of the 89
Texel Island 232, 235
Thermidor 15, 20, 268
Thionville 85
Ticonderoga, fort 109
Tigné, fort 258
Tilsit, treaty of 26, 38
Torenfort 79, 81
Torres Vedras, lines of 28, 29
Toulon 217–223; siege of 158
Tour modèle 117, 162, 163, 164, 165
Toussard, Stephen de 258
Tracé Italien 46
Trafalgar, battle of 26, 163
Traverse 49
Turgot, Robert-Jacques 7

Ulm 80; battle of 26
United States of America 7, 24, 44, 98, 109, 143, 174, 205

Valetta 257
Vallière, Jean-Florent de 119
Valmy, battle of 11
Varennes 9
Vauban, Sébastien Le Prestre, Marquis de 2, 50, 51, 52, 53
Vendemiaire 20
Vente de la Louisiane 24
Vernet, Horace 42
Vienna, Congress of 44, 248
Vigie, fortlet of the 222
Vlissingen 227, 228
Voltigeurs 35

Wagram, battle of 31, 127
Walewska, Marie 31
Waterloo, battle of 18, 44, 142, 158, 184, 253
Wattigny, battle of 14
Wellington, Arthur Wellesley, First Duke of 29
Wesel 242, 243
Whites 14

Yaverland, fort 147

Zara 253